TRENT

Part One, 1905-45

By
David Bean

ATTENBOROUGH,NOTTS

To
Michael and Jenny

Other Transport Titles by the Publisher:

Barton (Part Two, 1950-1961)
Barton (Part Three, 1961-1986)
South Notts
Hulley's

Front Cover Illustration

Albert Street, Derby was a centre of Trent operations from the beginning until 1933. Artist Dave McDonald has captured an impression of activity there in this delightful period scene, featuring three of the Company's Tilling-Stevens buses, in about 1922. In the background is the old Derby Co-op store, later demolished to make way for the present building, whilst to the left is the Corn Exchange which still stands.

Designed and Published by

Attenborough

TRENT

Part One, 1905-45

CONTENTS

ISBN 0 948854 10 3

Foreword

Trent Buses today is a vibrant player in a changing market. Voted UK Best Bus Company in 1997 by its customers it is the largest company in a small local bus group owned entirely by those who work in it or have retired from it. Other companies in that group are Barton, Midland General and Notts and Derby who feature in much of David Bean's story and more recently Kinch who have brought the Loughborough operations back into the fold after an absence of 10 years.

However, it is not difficult to see evidence of the earlier periods of innovation and consolidation described by David Bean. Much of today's service network has its origins in key corridors pioneered by CCHL or Trent not to mention those won from or lost to competitors and subsequently purchased.

On the vehicle front preserved 417- the SON - is a stark reminder of conditions past which it is all too easy to forget in today's double glazed, air suspended, low floor world.

Buildings are another pointer. You have only to go into the Belper or Manvers Street, Nottingham garages to feel the touch of history and, of course, as I write this Derby Bus Station continues in use struggling to cope with l2metre vehicles and the perfectly reasonable demands of customers quite used to air conditioned shopping malls.

It was only in October 1997 that we finally vacated Uttoxeter New Road, Derby in favour of Midland General's main site at Langley Mill. Supermarket car parks have consumed the Loughborough and Melbourne depots in the last decade whilst Shipley, vacated by Trent in 1972 has only been demolished within the last few months. Wirksworth and The Watchorn at Alfreton are still identifiable as former Trent garages despite alternative uses for over 20 years. Reading David's text reminded me about NCT's Parliament Street extension but The Spot in Derby really had me fooled! Just go and look for yourself.

And so to people. I first came to Trent in 1968 as District Traffic Superintendent, Nottingham (a post oft referred to in this book). My office was in Kent Street almost over Dutton's Unity garage (recently lost to an office development housing amongst others the T&GWU) and close to Huntingdon Street Bus Station. Many of the staff employed then had lived through the period described in this book. In fact, if my memory serves me correctly the longest serving had joined in 1924.

It was during this time that I met the then retired Traffic Manager Steve Ferry and MGO's W. Williamson both of whom had large parts to play in this story.

Today our longest serving employee started in 1950 but this still tells us a lot about the Company and its people. It is a good stable employer which attracts loyal staff. 50 years' service were not uncommon in the past and 40 years plus is not uncommon now. Such are the ingredients of longevity.

Trent is successful today because of hard headed business management but that does not prevent us from being the custodians of history and stewards of a company well on course to achieving its century doing what it has always done - serving the transport needs of the East Midlands.

I commend David Bean's first volume to you as a chronicle of the initial 40 years of this great company.

B R King
Managing Director
Trent Buses

Mansfield Road,
Heanor,
Derbyshire.
DE75 7 BG

August, 1998

Introduction

I suppose it might have been expected that a boy with an interest in technical matters, living in a great railway town like Derby, would develop an interest in railways, rather than buses. I did indeed have an early interest in railways, and my slightly later interest in buses came out of this, quite by chance. Some Saturday mornings in my very early years were spent at Breadsall Crossing in Ford Lane Allestree, (removed following the construction of the A38 Abbey Hill dual carriageway which made it redundant) watching Jubilees, Black Fives and other more mundane locomotives passing by, and collecting their numbers in the usual way.

A friend's older brother showed me something slightly different that he was doing, which was collecting Trent bus numbers and writing them in a book, then colouring each number with a crayon to match the background colour of the metal numberplate on the bus. I took up the same thing, and that small, almost trivial occurrence to a boy aged about seven led to a lifelong history in transport, especially buses, and especially Trent. My interest in railways ceased abruptly at that point, although re-kindled in later years as my interest in transport history set road and rail in context.

So far as early vehicles are concerned, I remember a school trip on one of the utility Daimler CWG5s, and in fact can remember all of the utility vehicles. I came along too late to really know the SOSs, or Sosses as they tended to be known, on which so much of the Company's early fortunes were built, although I can just remember those which were rebodied after the war and lasted longer, but I'm fairly sure I never travelled on one. I was much more interested, at the time, in the new Leylands then being delivered, so the vehicles I knew best will feature in the next volume.

In 1959, I moved with my parents to live in Croydon, but we still had friends and relatives in Nottingham and Derby, which meant return visits to Trent's operating area, to keep abreast of Trent developments. I have, therefore, always maintained a special interest in Trent, although my transport interest is a great deal wider, and even impacts on my employment.

Trent was not one of the noted operators in the pre-nationalisation years - it wasn't a Midland Red, or a Southdown, a Ribble, or even a North Western. Unlike these, it served a compact area and its express services mostly served the seaside, never reaching London until 1965, and so it did not have nation-wide recognition. It had its own characteristics, and was greatly relied upon in the part of the East Midlands which it served, but it just quietly got on with the job.

The Company's early development involved extensive use of Tilling-Stevens Petrol Electrics, but later came to be closely associated with Midland Red, which built sometimes strange looking buses under the name SOS for its own use, and supplied some to Trent as well. Later on, AECs and Daimlers were extensively used, and the Company took over very many small operators as part of its development.

After the Second War, it took on the standard appearance of other BET operators, so far as vehicles were concerned, and in 1968 was taken into state ownership as a subsidiary of the National Bus Company. Since the Company returned to the private sector, under the steady and able guidance of Managing Director Brian King, and his colleagues, it has been pleasing to see the steady progress made, with industry leading initiatives, culminating in national recognition and the Company being voted the UK's Best Bus Company. However, the later part of the story really belongs in a subsequent volume.

Little has been written about the Company history in the past, and I would have liked to have written the definitive history. However, the passage of time means that some records have been lost, and some of the details with them. I have immensely enjoyed researching this book, time consuming though it has been, and have also enjoyed meeting many people as a result. I know some have been waiting patiently, and I hope they and all readers feel that this first volume of the story has rewarded their patience.

David Bean.
Buntingford, Hertfordshire.

August, 1998.

The CCHL garage in Hall Street, Alfreton around 1912. The garage provided overnight vehicle accommodation, and also included a small workshop with facilities to carry out repairs, together with offices for administration and traffic functions. Part of the small fleet of Commer WP models is visible in front of the garage, and identifiable from left to right are CH 850, EE 374, LN ??68 and LN 9904, of which probably only the first passed to Trent, along with the garage, in 1913. LN ??68 has identical bodywork to LE 9601, on page 75, which was, therefore, probably also built by Scammell & Nephew. CCHL also had an operation in Grimsby, in association with the Grimsby Tramways Co Ltd, and in view of the Grimsby registration, EE 374 may have seen earlier service there.

Chapter One
Commercial Car Hirers 1905 to 1913

The twenty or so years from 1905 were those in which the motorbus gained public acceptance as a reliable means of transport, and it was during this period that many of Britain's territorial bus companies were formed or originated. Each of these companies have individual aspects to their histories, but the events leading to the formation of the Trent Motor Traction Co Ltd, of Heanor, Derbyshire were very unusual.

Trent was registered on 31st October, 1913 and began business on the following Monday 3rd November, but can trace its origin to events of 1905 when Commercial Cars, Ltd was formed to manufacture commercial vehicles incorporating a novel form of preselector gearbox invented by the Company's Chief Engineer, Mr Charles Linley. Digressing briefly, it is appropriate to record that Commercial Cars Ltd, which sold its products under the abbreviated name Commer Car and later Commer, built its factory at Luton, Bedfordshire. The erstwhile Luton plant of Renault Truck Industries Ltd (a subsidiary of the French company, Renault Vehicules Industriels) was, via the kinds of changes in fortune and ownership which have characterised the motor industry over the years, the direct descendant of the Commercial Cars Ltd operation. In later years, Commer vehicles were built in a newer factory at nearby Dunstable and although nowadays it is this factory which produces the successor Renault trucks, the Luton plant continued in use, making and machining some of the components used at Dunstable, until it was closed in July, 1985.

During the early years from 1905, Commercial Cars Ltd established a good reputation and became a leading manufacturer of commercial vehicles. Initially, a 4 ton lorry was offered, but within two years, this had been joined by two lighter models for loads of 1fi and 2fi tons. In 1908, sales to both home and export markets were brisk, and the range was further expanded by the addition of both lighter and heavier chassis until it consisted of ten distinct models.

Despite the progress made, it was felt necessary to find an additional outlet for the factory production and, to further this requirement, a subsidiary company, Commercial Car Hirers Ltd (CCHL) was registered on 18th June 1909. According to the Memorandum and Articles of Association of the new company, its principal objectives were to carry on business as general carriers, railway and forwarding agents, bonded carmen, warehousemen and to hire all kinds of vehicles for a wide range of purposes. Various individuals held shares, but the largest single shareholding was that of Commer Cars Ltd.

Mr J Coventon Moth was General Manager of CCHL at the beginning and, in 1915, was to become a Director of Trent, a position he held until his death, at the age of 76, in February 1963. In 1948, Mr Coventon Moth recalled for the "Trent Bulletin", the then recently introduced journal for Trent staff, how CCHL hired a 2 ton shooting brake to a party of sportsmen for a shooting trip to Scotland. Among the guests was the late Sir Peter Walker, owner of the now demolished Osmaston Manor, near Ashbourne, Derbyshire, who was said to have been so impressed by the vehicle that he took it on hire for use in transporting his domestic staff between Derby and Ashbourne. As a result of this, and " to avoid the complications of hiring ", it was decided to start a regular service.

There is some ambiguity in this part of the story, for there is no record of any payments to CCHL in the contemporary estate records of Osmaston Manor. Furthermore, on 14th August, 1909, a letter appeared in the Derby Daily Telegraph suggesting that the time was ripe for a motor service to be provided between Ashbourne and Derby. This subject was taken up in the next day's leading article which remarked that the existing railway service was unsuited to the journey. In those days, the leading journals covering the commercial motor trade would report details of motor services for which there was thought to be a demand, and notice of the need for a Derby-Ashbourne service duly appeared in "Commercial Motor". This was shortly after, and perhaps prompted by, the two items in the Derby newspaper. Very quickly, and following an inspection of the route, CCHL began a thrice daily service between Ashbourne and Derby on Tuesday 14th September, 1909.

Precisely how this service began may never be known. Although Mr Coventon Moth's recollections were made some 39 years after the event, they cannot be wholly erroneous but, equally, the items in the local and trade press cannot be without substance. The Ashbourne-Derby service was not CCHL's first effort at running a bus service, for they had been running a service between Buxton and Hulme End since 5th July, 1909 and were also planning services at Dorking in Surrey and Maidstone in Kent. Perhaps an explanation of the ambiguity is that CCHL sent a vehicle to Sir Peter Walker on free trial and, realising it to be well used, saw an opportunity to add to their bus services and were prompted by the Commercial Motor announcement to send their representative to Derbyshire to survey the route. A favourable report having been made, they were not slow to act.

The service was an instant success, for the only means of transport hitherto available between the two towns, apart from the common carrier whose main business was the carriage of goods, had been the service of the North Staffordshire Railway Company. That line, however, went via Uttoxeter, in the opposite direction, and the journey, taking between 1 hour 18 minutes and 2 hours 9 minutes depending on which train was used, was considered rather expensive at around 2/6d (12½p) for a 3rd Class single. In contrast, the new bus service took just under one hour and the fare was 1/6d (7½p) single or 2/6d (12½p) return with appropriate intermediate fares.

The first journey from Ashbourne to Derby ran

about half full, and the vehicle used was a small chain driven Commer with a twenty seat char-a-banc body. Departure times were 9.30am, 12.30pm and 3.30pm from Ashbourne, with return from Derby at 11.00am, 2.00pm and 5.00pm, the service being run on Monday, Tuesday and Thursday to Saturday. On Wednesdays and Sundays, excursions were run to such local attractions as Dovedale, Haddon Hall and Chatsworth House.

Unfortunately, one Friday afternoon, soon after the service was opened, an accident occurred when a bolt sheared on the steering mechanism and the vehicle ran out of control. Luckily, no-one was injured, although four people, including the local police inspector, were thrown from the open sided char-a-banc. The Commer was taken away for repair and the service temporarily suspended, but reinstated the following afternoon using a fresh vehicle sent up from Head Office in London. There seems to have been no repercussion from the incident, but minor accidents of this type were fairly frequent and serve to indicate how fragile the early vehicles were.

Spurred on by the success of the Ashbourne service, CCHL opened a further service, this time between Alfreton and Derby. Once again, the route was competitive with a less than adequate train service, for Alfreton & South Normanton Station, on the Midland Railway was, and remains today, some one mile distance from the first town after which it was named. An additional shortcoming was that the train journey between Alfreton and Derby could not be accomplished on a direct line.

The service began on 27th October, 1909 and, except on Thursdays and Saturdays, a small Commer with saloon body made the one and a quarter hour journey three times, leaving Alfreton at 8.30am, 12.30pm and 4.30pm, returning from Derby at 10.15am, 2.30pm and 6.15pm. Fares of 1/6d (7½p) single and 2/6d (12½p) return were charged for the full journey, or 6d (2½p) for a trip between any of the villages of Ripley, Marehay, Denby, Kilburn, Coxbench and Little Eaton which the route served. On Thursdays the bus ran instead a service between Ripley and Nottingham via Codnor, Aldercar, Eastwood and Bulwell and on Sundays it was initially available for private hire, although before very long a Sunday service was added to the Alfreton-Derby route.

The success of this second service came to the notice of the Heanor Tradesmen's Association. This body was concerned that their town was losing trade to the nearby town of Eastwood, because Langley Mill shoppers had to make the long ascent of Heanor Hill. It was felt that if a motor service could be provided, then Langley Mill residents would be tempted to shop in Heanor which was the larger centre. Local thoughts revolved around the idea that the service might run from Derby to Nottingham via Morley, Smalley, Heanor, Bulwell and Basford or, alternatively, start from Kilburn (connecting with the Derby- Alfreton service) and run via Horsley Woodhouse and Smalley.

The Tradesmen's Association contacted CCHL in London and after some negotiations, during which the motor firm requested a financial guarantee from the local people to cover the first two weeks operation, a service began on 20th

CH 537 was new to CCHL in July, 1911, and passed with the business to Trent in 1913, where it remained until withdrawal in July, 1917. Following withdrawal, it returned to CCHL, but eventually finished its time as a lorry in Southampton. Lettered for the Alfreton service, it seems to have a good load and, with the enclosed front, affords much better protection for the crew than many other vehicles of the period. The driver appears to be wearing a uniform type of tunic and cap, perhaps similar to those worn by contemporary chauffeurs employed by the gentry, whilst the conductor wears a normal cap and greatcoat.

PUBLIC NOTICES.

A Motor Omnibus Service

Will be commenced on

MONDAY NEXT, DEC. 20th,

BETWEEN

RIPLEY & NOTTINGHAM,

Via Codnor, Heanor, Langley Mill, Eastwood, Kimberley, Nuthall, and Basford.

For particulars see bills.

This advertisement is in typical style of the period, and appeared in the Heanor Observer to announce the forthcoming, and short lived, service between Ripley and Nottingham. Note the lack of any reference to the operator!

December, 1909. This ran from Ripley to Nottingham via Codnor, Heanor, Langley Mill, Kimberley, Nuthall and Basford, through country later to be made famous by the works of D H Lawrence who was born at Eastwood. It seems likely that this led to the withdrawal of the previous Thursdays only, Ripley-Nottingham service running via Aldercar.

On the weekend of 18th/19th December, 1909, the whole of the Erewash Valley was covered in a thick blanket of snow. Consequently, the new service had an inauspicious beginning, but by the end of the week a thaw had set in and conditions became easier. This time, CCHL were to find success elusive. There were allegations of high fares and irregular running. Certainly, the fares charged were higher than those charged by the Midland Railway over comparable journeys, but the Heanor Observer was moved to remark that, high though the fares were, the service was only on trial and a fare of some sort had to be fixed. However, success could not be found.

The Company complained of poor running conditions, particularly on the Nottinghamshire side of the border, and this led to extra maintenance requirements on the vehicle, with consequent increased running costs. An offer made to the Tradesmen's Association, to provide them with a car at £25 per week so that they could try to make a go of it themselves, was ignored and early in February, 1910 the unhappy enterprise reached a conclusion when CCHL withdrew the service and transferred the vehicle to a new route.

The new route opened on 6th February, 1910 and a 16 seat Commer vehicle ran between Alfreton and Chesterfield via Shirland, Higham, Clay Cross, North Wingfield, Grassmoor and Hasland. The service had been introduced at the request of Clay Cross Urban District Council for, as in the case of the Ashbourne and Alfreton services, the local train service was considered inadequate. For the first time, CCHL encountered some opposition from another operator, and indeed were beaten off the mark by Mid Derbyshire Motor Services of Kimberley, which succeeded in starting on the Saturday preceding CCHL's start on the Monday. In line with previous services, three journeys ran each day and such was the demand for the service, despite the competition, that the 16 seat vehicle had soon to be augmented by a larger one.

It is interesting at this point to reflect on local reactions to the arrival of these new bus services. The services were almost universally welcomed, but as with any new development there were sceptics. Some people felt that the services would take trade away from the towns that they served and were unable to see that services which took people out could also bring other people in. The most significant factor, in the case of these mid-Derbyshire services, seems to have been that CCHL were able to provide services specifically designed to serve towns which, for one reason or another, were historically poorly placed in relation to the railway network which, by the early 1900s, was complete in this part of Derbyshire. It is notable that the Ripley - Nottingham service was in

THE MOTOR BUS.

Dear sir,—Re your remarks about motor bus which is travelling between Nottingham and Ripley. You say there has not been a rush of patronage. This is hardly likely when the charge is considered, 3s. 6d. return. Compare this with that of the M.R. 2s. 2d. return, also with the M.R. you get comfortable and convenient travelling. I heard of half a dozen factory girls enquiring of the fare from Heanor to Codnor. They were told by the driver that it was 6d. each, 3s. for the half-dozen. But by the M.R. it was 9d. for the half-dozen. A charge of 2d. each from Heanor to Codnor would be reasonable. During Heanor Fair brakes ran from Heanor to Codnor at a charge of 2d. each, also every Saturday brakes run from Ripley to Codnor at the same rate.

I have noticed the motor bus pass my window many times with a solitary passenger in it. While I am writing it passes with two passengers. I am not a prophet but, I guess and dare calculate (as the Yankee says) unless the fare be reduced to compare favourably with the railway fare, the venture will be a failure.

O.T.

Codnor, Dec. 28th, 1909.

THE MOTOR SERVICE.

To the Editor of the *Heanor Observer*

Sir,—I am glad that "O.T." has written regarding the fare charged by the Motor Company between Heanor and Codnor. I am surprised that the charge should be sixpence for two miles while the Railway Company only charges a penny per mile. It the Motor Car Company would reduce their prices to the same rate their enterprise would be a success. About fifty girls travel to Heanor every morning from Codnor and Loscoe, and a good number of children travel daily between Ripley and Heanor. If the motor owners would reduce the fares, and advertise their stopping places it would be an advantage to those who wish to use the bus.—Yours, etc.

Codnor, Jan. 3rd, 1910. A.S.R.

CCHL found success elusive between Ripley and Nottingham. These letters, which appeared in the Heanor Observer, seem to sum up the local feelings.

Disaster seems to have befallen this CCHL Commer, evidently whilst in service judging by the conductor standing by the rear offside corner. Location is not identified, and unfortunately it is not possible to identify the registration number, but the original photograph was captioned "Wallace", thus confirming the vehicle as one of the CCHL Derbyshire Commers. Note the stepped waistline of the body and the rail on the roof for securing goods. Possibly the cause of the breakdown was a broken axle, since the twin rear wheels have the brake drum still fixed, and a section of drive chain lies on the road, close to the rear nearside wheel position.

direct competition with a good railway service between Ripley and Langley Mill and failed to attract sufficient traffic.

A further development, early in 1910, was a request by the Post Office for CCHL to carry the mail on their Derby-Ashbourne service, but apart from this, together with the construction of a garage at Alfreton and the introduction of new vehicles, there appear to have been no further developments until early in 1912. CCHL then considered a new service between Matlock and Derby, prompted by the need for a replacement for the local horse bus service between Cromford and Matlock Bath which had just been abandoned. The Company went so far as to send a vehicle to make a trial run over the route but, although there was said to be much local demand, nothing seems to have come of this proposal.

Early in March, 1912, the precise date being unclear, a new Thursdays only service was introduced, running between Alfreton and Mansfield, and on 23rd of that month there was a further development with the start of a new service running between Derby and Melbourne on Saturday evenings to serve the needs of theatre-goers and the like. This service became an all day service by the following May.

PUBLIC NOTICES.

COMMERCIAL CAR HIRERS LTD.

WHY DEPEND ON TRAINS ?

Well appointed Saloon cars run daily at frequent intervals to Derby, Chesterfield, Tupton, and to Mansfield (on Thursday's only); also Derby to Ashbourne daily.

NOTE.—Extra Car on Ashbourne Service on and after March 19.

On and after March 23rd a Car will run from Derby to Melbourne and back on Saturday evenings.

Private Parties & Excursions catered for

BOOK EARLY TO AVOID THE RUSH.

PARTICULARS FROM:

LOCAL MANAGER, ALFRETON

4300

Competition between bus and train is nothing new! However, this newspaper advertisement, taken from the Alfreton and Belper Journal for Friday 15th March, 1912 has greater significance than at first appears, for the National Union of Mineworkers was holding its first national strike, which had started at Alfreton. Due to haulage by steam locomotives, the railways were adversely affected and bus operators were quick to take advantage.

By August, 1912, there were six vehicles operating out of a garage in Hall Street Alfreton which had been constructed soon after the Company began its mid-Derbyshire operations. There were some seventeen people employed in various capacities and no doubt there were also one or more additional employees at Ashbourne where the vehicle serving that town was out stationed at the Green Man and Blacks Head Hotel.

In September, 1913, another new service began, running between Derby and Uttoxeter, and the Alfreton to Mansfield Thursday service was withdrawn because it did not pay sufficiently well. By October, 1913, only a few weeks before Trent was formed, Commercial Car Hirers were advertising the following list of services:-

Alfreton - Derby
Alfreton - Chesterfield
(Sundays excepted)
Derby - Ashbourne
(Sundays excepted)
Derby - Uttoxeter
(Sundays excepted)
Clay Cross - Chesterfield via Tupton
(Sundays & Wednesdays excepted)
Derby - Melbourne
(Saturdays only).

Already it may be seen that the centre of operations was moving towards Derby, and the position shown by this list was maintained until, on 31st October, 1913, the Trent Motor Traction Co, Ltd was formed, becoming responsible for all these services on the following Monday, 3rd November.

Commercial Car Hirers, Ltd.

Registered and Private Offices
BROAD SANCTUARY CHAMBERS, WESTMINSTER.
Telephone: 1446 City.

General Offices and Works:
CREMORNE WORKS, LOTS ROAD, CHELSEA, S.W.
Telephone: 150 Kensington, 2574 Western.

Local Depôt: HALL STREET, ALFRETON. Telephone: 38.

MOTOR OMNIBUS SERVICES
ASHBOURNE and DERBY
MAY, 1913.

		Mondays only.			Tuesdays, Thursdays and Fridays.					
		a m	p m	p m	a m	a m	p m	p m	p m	p m
ASHBOURNE	dep.	8 45	12 30	4 30	8 45	10 30	12 30	2 30	4 30	6 30
OSMASTON LANE	"	8 57	12 42	4 42	8 57	10 42	12 42	2 42	4 42	6 42
EDNASTON LODGE	"	9 9	12 54	4 54	9 9	10 54	12 54	2 54	4 54	6 54
BRAILSFORD (Rose and Crown)	"	9 21	1 6	5 6	9 21	11 6	1 6	3 6	5 6	7 6
KIRK LANGLEY (Post Office)	"	9 33	1 18	5 18	9 33	11 18	1 18	3 18	5 18	7 18
MACKWORTH	"	9 45	1 30	5 30	9 45	11 30	1 30	3 30	5 30	7 30
DERBY	arr.	10 0	1 45	5 45	10 0	11 45	1 45	3 45	5 45	7 45
		a m	p m	p m	a m	a m	p m	p m	p m	p m
DERBY (Corn Exchange)	dep.	10 30	2 30	6 30	8 45	10 30	12 30	2 30	4 30	6 30
MACKWORTH	"	10 42	2 42	6 42	8 57	10 42	12 42	2 42	4 42	6 42
KIRK LANGLEY	"	10 54	2 54	6 54	9 9	10 54	12 54	2 54	4 54	6 54
BRAILSFORD	"	11 6	3 6	7 6	9 21	11 6	1 6	3 6	5 6	7 6
EDNASTON LODGE	"	11 18	3 18	7 18	9 33	11 18	1 18	3 18	5 18	7 18
OSMASTON LANE	"	11 30	3 30	7 30	9 45	11 30	1 30	3 30	5 30	7 30
ASHBOURNE	arr.	11 45	3 45	7 45	10 0	11 45	1 45	3 45	5 45	7 45

		Wednesdays only.			Saturdays only.					
		a m	p m	p m	a m	a m	p m	p m	p m	p m
ASHBOURNE	dep.	10 30	2 30	6 30	8 45	10 30	12 30	2 30	4 0	7 0
OSMASTON LANE	"	10 42	2 42	6 42	8 57	10 42	12 42	2 42	4 12	7 10
EDNASTON LODGE	"	10 54	2 54	6 54	9 9	10 54	12 54	2 54	4 24	7 20
BRAILSFORD (Rose and Crown)	"	11 6	3 6	7 6	9 21	11 6	1 6	3 6	4 36	7 30
KIRK LANGLEY (Post Office)	"	11 18	3 18	7 18	9 33	11 18	1 18	3 18	4 48	7 40
MACKWORTH	"	11 30	3 30	7 30	9 45	11 30	1 30	3 30	5 0	7 50
DERBY	arr.	11 45	3 45	7 45	10 0	11 45	1 45	3 45	5 15	8 0
		a m	p m	p m	a m	a m	p m	p m	p m	p m
DERBY (Corn Exchange)	dep.	8 45	12 30	4 30	8 45	10 30	12 30	2 30	5 30	11 0
MACKWORTH	"	8 57	12 42	4 42	8 57	10 42	12 42	2 42	5 42	11 10
KIRK LANGLEY	"	9 9	12 54	4 54	9 9	10 54	12 54	2 54	5 54	11 20
BRAILSFORD	"	9 21	1 6	5 6	9 21	11 6	1 6	3 6	6 6	11 30
EDNASTON LODGE	"	9 33	1 18	5 18	9 33	11 18	1 18	3 18	6 18	11 40
OSMASTON LANE	"	9 45	1 30	5 30	9 45	11 30	1 30	3 30	6 30	11 50
ASHBOURNE	arr.	10 0	1 45	5 45	10 0	11 45	1 45	3 45	6 45	12 0 midnight

FARES (please note Reductions).

	ASHBOURNE.		OSMASTON.		EDNASTON		BRAILSFORD.		KIRK LANGLEY		MACKWORTH		GOLF LINKS.		DERBY CORN EXCHANGE	
	s.	d.	s.	d.	s.	d.	s.	d.	s.	d.	s.	d.	s.	d.	s.	d.
Derby (Corn Exchange)	1	4	1	2	1	0	0	9	0	6	0	4	0	3	—	
Derby (Golf Links)	1	2	1	0	0	10	0	7	0	4	0	2	—		—	
Mackworth	1	1	1	0	0	9	0	6	0	3			—		—	
Kirk Langley	1	0	0	11	0	7	0	4								
Brailsford (Rose & Crown)	0	9	0	7	0	3			0	4	0	6	0	7	0	9
Ednaston Lodge	0	6	0	4			0	3	0	7	0	9	0	10	1	0
Osmaston Lane End	0	3			0	4	0	7	0	11	1	0	1	0	1	2
Ashbourne			0	3	0	6	0	9	1	0	1	1	1	2	1	4

Yeldersley to Rock of Stones, 3d. Yeldersley to Brailsford (Burrows Lane), 6d.
Kirk Langley to Brailsford (Burrows Lane), 3d.
Fares from ASHBOURNE to DERBY (and vice-versa), 1 4. Reduced Fares for Intermediate Villages.

THESE CARS may be HIRED for PRIVATE PARTIES and EXCURSIONS.

No Return Tickets issued. This Time Table is subject to alteration.

All complaints should be addressed to- THE MANAGER, COMMERCIAL CAR HIRERS, LTD., CREMORNE WORKS, LOTS ROAD, CHELSEA, S.W.

A Commercial Car Hirers timetable handbill. Original size 10" x 8".

The original caption to this newspaper photograph suggested that it is dated around 1922. However, three Commers are shown, and as almost all of these had all left the Trent fleet by 1915, the picture is clearly somewhat older than stated, and was almost certainly taken in the final months of Commercial Car Hirers, or the early months of Trent operation, that is around 1913/14. The location is in Albert Street, Derby, near the junction with Tenant Street, always an area of Trent departures, until the new Central Bus Station opened in the thirties.

Chapter Two
A New Source
1913-22

At its formation, Trent was owned jointly and in equal proportions by Commercial Car Hirers, Ltd and the British Automobile Traction Co, Ltd (BAT). The latter company was itself a subsidiary of the British Electric Traction Co, Ltd (BET) which had been formed in 1895 as the British Electric Traction (Pioneer) Co, Ltd, to further the use of electric power and traction. In order to promote the use of motor vehicles as feeders to tramways, especially from districts where the lower traffic levels did not justify the heavy investment in permanent way, overhead and rolling stock required for a tramway system, BET formed a Motor Committee, in 1905. This subsequently became the basis for a subsidiary company, the British Automobile Development Co. Ltd, but the combination of initials was rather unfortunate, so the name was changed to the British Automobile Traction Co, Ltd (BAT). By early 1913 a change of policy occurred and it was decided that BAT would exploit motor services in its own right in areas where there were no BET tramway undertakings, either by starting up directly or by buying into existing businesses.

In 1913, BAT wrote to the Nottingham Corporation Watch Committee offering to provide bus services into the city from outlying districts, but this offer was turned down. However, in due course an approach was made to CCHL concerning their nearby services in Derbyshire and it was decided to form a joint company, taking the name Trent from the principal river in the proposed area of operation.

All the services operated in Derbyshire by CCHL passed to Trent, together with the six Commer vehicles then in use, the price paid being £8,381 for the goodwill and all the assets. Day to day management was initially in the hands of CCHL under a management agreement, an arrangement which was to last until 1923 when, following the sale of the Company's shares in Trent in 1922, the agreement was terminated and all formal connection severed.

CCHL, which also had other bus interests, principally in London and Essex, then went into a prolonged receivership, being finally voluntarily wound up in 1931. However, Mr J Coventon Moth, who was Secretary to CCHL and later a Director, fulfilled a similar role for Trent until his elevation to that Company's Board in 1915, and remained with the Company for many years.

Trent's first Directors were, as might be expected, drawn principally from CCHL and BAT, with two others who were locally based in Derbyshire. These latter included the Chairman, Alderman William Hart, JP, of Derby, a notable local politician who had been Mayor of Derby in 1908-9. The Deputy Chairman was Mr R J Howley, a prominent BAT man who was already associated with several other BAT bus undertakings, including the Birmingham and Midland Motor Omnibus Co., Ltd (BMMO), popularly known as Midland Red, of which he was Chairman. It appears that Mr Howley would take the lead in operational matters, whereas Alderman Hart, being a local man of some influence, tended to play a part in negotiations with landowners and local authorities. Mr Howley took the Chairman's seat, following the death of Alderman Hart, in November, 1929.

The Board of the new Company had much to concern themselves with, including the consideration of new services, the purchase of more vehicles and the acquisition of new premises in Derby for a garage. The first service started by Trent began on the 8th November, 1913 and was a daily hourly service from Derby to Stapleford, mid-way between Derby and Nottingham. No doubt the arrangements for this service, which ran via Spondon, Borrowash and Sandiacre had already been made under the auspices of CCHL.

Early consideration was given to the purchase of new vehicles and following the receipt of a few more Commers and a 2-ton Maudslay, probably obtained through CCHL, tenders for further vehicles were received from Commer, Daimler, BAT and Maudslay. The tender of Maudslay Motors, Ltd being the most acceptable, an order

MOTOR OMNIBUS SERVICES.

TRENT MOTOR TRACTION COMPANY, Ltd., beg to give NOTICE that they have acquired from

Messrs. COMMERCIAL CAR HIRERS, Ltd.,

the SERVICES at present running between
Derby and Ashbourne,
Derby and Uttoxeter,
Derby and Alfreton,
Alfreton and Chesterfield,
Derby and Melbourne,
Derby and Borrowash and Stapleford.

Further extensions are under consideration, and additional 'Busses will be run on the present Routes. The Management will be obliged if all enquiries, suggestions, or complaints are addressed to

TRENT MOTOR TRACTION COMPANY, Ltd.,
CAXTON HOUSE, WESTMINSTER.

MOTOR OMNIBUS SERVICES.

Messrs. COMMERCIAL CAR HIRERS, Ltd., desire to give notice that they have, with the co-operation of the BRITISH AUTOMOBILE TRACTION COY., LTD., floated a SUBSIDIARY COMPANY under the title of TRENT MOTOR TRACTION for the purpose of acquiring the Motor Omnibus Services running in the district and further extensions.

Soon after Trent started, the public was informed of the new arrangements by press advertisements. This pair of adverts appeared in the Derbyshire Advertiser for a period from 28th November, 1913.

was placed for six 3-ton chassis at approximately £465 each. Six bodies at £190 each were ordered from the BET associated Brush company at Loughborough, whilst six sets of tyres were ordered from the Continental Tyre Co with a guarantee of 12,000 miles per set. The chassis order was soon amended to 4-ton chassis at approximately £500 each and then all the orders were increased from six units to twelve.

As already mentioned, the focal point of the services was moving away from the original office at Alfreton and this made it essential to find new premises for a garage in the larger town of Derby, which was becoming of greater importance to the Company. A garage in London Road, not far from The Spot and nowadays used by an amusements centre, was inspected and taken on a short term lease. However, a more permanent arrangement was required and in 1914 a site was purchased in Uttoxeter New Road opposite the Company's former Head Office, vacated in 1997. Owing to the cost, the difficulty of obtaining materials and the outbreak of the 1914-18 war, the construction of a building could not be undertaken immediately, but was completed by the middle of 1915 and the Company's presence in Uttoxeter New Road was thus established at an early stage.

The newly opened service was cut back after a few weeks to run only to Spondon, but before 1913 had drawn to a close, attention was being turned to developing services in the Nottingham and Chesterfield districts and here difficulties were to be encountered with the municipal authorities. At Nottingham, a deputation from Trent was allowed to attend the meeting of the Watch Committee on 14th January, 1914 to discuss the Company's proposal to run into the City from outlying districts. The City Tramways Committee were already considering their own proposals to run buses in the city, but a scheme had not yet been prepared and the Tramways Committee requested that the Watch Committee grant no further bus licences until the City's own proposals had been discussed. As a result of this, the Watch Committee resolved that Trent's application should stand over and be referred to the Tramways Committee. At their subsequent meeting on the 25th February, 1914, the Watch Committee resolved that they were not yet prepared to grant licences for buses to run into the City from outlying districts. In order to overcome this set-back, Trent decided to run buses into Nottingham on a bookings system, under which the need for a licence was avoided by not plying for hire (or, at least, claiming not to do so).

The vehicles used for this service were garaged temporarily at Mitchell's Garage in Derby Road, Nottingham and, whilst their use led to allegations by the Chief Constable of plying for hire without a licence, the Watch Committee did eventually grant licences which, owing to problems caused by the war, could not be used.

The first new buses for Trent were six Commer WP 36hp models, registered on 8th January, 1914 as CH 892-7, but no clue has been found as to the make of bodywork fitted. On 23rd February, 1914, the first of the 4 ton Maudslays was registered CH 930 and it received a second hand body purchased from CCHL for £150. The other eleven were delivered between April and July, 1914, and were fitted with Brush bodies from the order for twelve, leaving one spare to begin with.

This 1997 photograph shows the building used as the first Trent Derby depot in London Road, close to The Spot. Built in 1911, the building was used by Trent from early 1914 until the move to Uttoxeter New Road in mid 1915.

Fleetnumbers D101-12 were allocated to the twelve, and it has been suggested that the D prefix may have been to indicate "Derby", to distinguish from vehicles operated elsewhere by either BAT or CCHL. Alternatively, they may have been licence numbers issued by Derby Police. However, no evidence has been found to support either of these meanings, or any other. Subsequently, Thornycroft and Vulcan vehicles entered the fleet, and these received numbers prefixed T and V respectively. The Company appeared to use these numbers, which were painted onto the chassis frame, as fleetnumbers until a new system of numbering was introduced in about 1924.

In early March, 1914, a forward programme was drawn up, under which new services would be developed in the following order:-

1. **Nottingham - Sandiacre.**
2. **Nottingham - Sawley.**
   via Beeston and Long Eaton.
3. **Chesterfield - Dronfield.**
4. **Chesterfield and District.**
5. **Derby - Duffield, Belper and Ambergate.**
6. & 7. **Nottingham - Ilkeston & Heanor.**
8. **Alfreton - Derby.**
   Additional car.
9. **Derby - Hatton.**
   Renewal of service which had originally run to Uttoxeter, and recently been withdrawn.

Even before this forward programme had been prepared, and with the intention of taking possession of the road before Chesterfield Corporation, a service between Chesterfield and Staveley had been opened with considerable success, takings in the first week amounting to 1/1d

(5½p) per mile, a good figure in those days. However, Chesterfield Corporation were actively developing their bus services and began running in opposition to Trent on the Alfreton - Chesterfield service, as far as Clay Cross, and to Brimington on the Chesterfield - Staveley route.

A meeting was arranged between Alderman Hart, Mr Wreathall, Mr Short, the other local Director who was based in Chesterfield, and the Chairman of Chesterfield Tramways Committee. This was to no avail, however, as the Corporation were resolute in their intention to run buses. Consideration was given to buying a garage in Brimington, to service the Chesterfield area, but the property needed considerable work to put it in order, so the matter fell into abeyance. Eventually, the idea was overtaken by other events, and nothing became of it.

About this time, a Unic 12/14hp chassis was purchased from CCHL to help with running the mail service between Derby and Ashbourne. The contract with the Post Office authorities for this work had been renewed in April, 1914, thus continuing the arrangements described earlier, which had been started by CCHL.

At variance with the forward programme was a service started by June, 1914, which ran from Mansfield to Bulwell, via Sutton in Ashfield. The three vehicles used on this service were kept overnight at the Mason's Arms in Mansfield. After early resistance from Nottingham Corporation, a licence was eventually obtained to run through to Nottingham, but was not taken up, although the full service service was advertised. The Ilkeston-Nottingham proposal was pursued with Ilkeston Council, which agreed to grant licences, but this was also not followed up, due to the loss of vehicles to the Army, following the outbreak of war.

On 4th August, 1914, war broke out with Germany and the War Office began to requisition vehicles for use by the Army. Trent sent five of the newly delivered Maudslay chassis to London with a view to selling to the War Office and eventually all twelve were sold in this way, showing the Company a profit over book value. The War Office required that the vehicles be fitted with lorry bodies and, because it proved difficult to find accommodation for the displaced bus bodies in Derby, the first five were placed in store at the Brush works in Loughborough, whilst the remaining seven were taken into store at CCHL's premises in Highgate, North London.

This disposal left the depleted fleet standing at one 2-ton Maudslay and nine Commer W.P.s, which naturally caused an immediate retrenchment of services, the Chesterfield area, Mansfield-Bulwell and Derby-Melbourne services being the first to be withdrawn.

An engineers report on the remaining vehicles showed that all were in need of attention and it was decided that all the Commers would be taken to CCHL's workshops for overhaul prior to sale. As a result of this action, all remaining services were withdrawn except for the original Derby-Ashbourne and Derby - Alfreton services, together with the Derby - Belper and Derby - Burton, which had started in during Summer, 1914. These were to be carried on in the best manner possible until new vehicles could be obtained.

The Manager was asked to resign on account of the reduced business, and CCHL's Engineer was appointed Engineer/Manager on a temporary basis. Advertisements were placed in local newspapers explaining that the Company's services were much reduced because their vehicles had been taken by the War Office.

By October, 1914, six of the Commers had gone and the remaining four vehicles were put to work on the Derby - Alfreton and Derby - Ashbourne services. Eventually, by mid-February, 1915, only two vehicles, a Commer and the 2-ton Maudslay remained, these being used to run just the Derby-Ashbourne service, which survived because of its importance in carrying the mails. In the circumstances, it is remarkable that at the Company's second Annual General Meeting, the Chairman was able to report a modest profit of £500 18s 7d (£500.93p) for the twelve months ending 31st December, 1914, which amount was carried forward to the next year's accounts and no dividend paid.

Although the Ashbourne service was running at a reduced level, the Company was in some difficulty because the two remaining vehicles were in need of overhaul. Early in 1915, a vehicle was obtained on hire at 8d (3.3p) per mile from the Potteries Electric Traction Co.,Ltd., a BET enterprise based at Stoke on Trent and nowadays called First PMT, Ltd., after its later name Potteries Motor Traction, Co., Ltd. This vehicle provided a relief which enabled the remaining Commer to be despatched to CCHL in London for overhaul, but by March it too had to be withdrawn, because it was requisitioned by the War Office. However, the prospect of further relief was now at hand, because in February, 1915, an order was placed for six Tilling-Stevens 40hp petrol electric chassis, with an option to purchase six more, to be exercised within one month of delivery of the first chassis.

The Tilling-Stevens chassis had a 4 cylinder petrol engine, driving a dynamo which was provided in place of the conventional clutch and gearbox. The dynamo supplied electric current to a traction motor which drove the overhead worm type of rear axle. This resulted in a vehicle which was smooth in operation, and the lack of clutch and gearbox made it easy to drive in those days when most gearboxes were unsophisticated and drivers were moving over from horse drawn vehicles.

Although having these advantages, the vehicles were relatively heavy (and therefore slow) and the electrical equipment required specialist skills for maintenance. In view of this, the vehicles were considered by the military authorities to be unsuitable for use in the war and so they escaped impressment. Tilling-Stevens were to become the standard vehicle in the Trent fleet for the next nine or ten years, and during the War years, the main constraints on their supply were the availability of materials to manufacture them, and the lack of petrol to run them..

The first four Tilling-Stevens chassis were delivered in April/May, 1915 and, after being fitted with the Brush bodies from the 1914 Maudslays,

This early line up of three Tilling-Stevens TS3s with Brush bodies transferred from the 1914 Maudslays was probably taken soon after the vehicles entered service. Sadly, the quality of the newspaper print does not allow identification of the individual vehicles, nor has the location been identified. However having regard to the destinations just visible it seems likely the picture was taken somewhere in Derby, possibly in the vicinity of the new premises in Uttoxeter New Road.

put to work on the Ashbourne service and also the Alfreton-Derby service which was restarted. Commencing on Whit Monday, 31st May, 1915, and on Sundays thereafter through the Summer, a special service was run from Derby to Matlock and Bakewell with five journeys each way at fares of 1/5d (7.2p) to Matlock and 2/- (10p) to Bakewell.

A total of seven Tilling-Stevens chassis were received during 1915, six being obtained direct from the manufacturers and a seventh acquired from CCHL. These were given fleet numbers D 100 - 6 and enabled, in addition to those already mentioned, further services to be started or restarted to Belper, Burton, Spondon, Wirksworth and Melbourne, all of which were operating out of Derby by September, 1915. However, judging by contemporary newspaper advertisements, the Wirksworth service at that time lasted only until the following November.

Towards the end of 1915, the question of services to Nottingham was again brought up and it was decided to open routes between Alfreton and Nottingham, via Ilkeston and between Derby and Nottingham via Borrowash and Sandiacre. To further these proposals, and in preparation for others, a request was submitted to the Nottingham Watch Committee for licences to run buses into the City from Derby, Ilkeston and Mansfield. Also to Ilkeston Urban District Council for licences to run between Heanor and Ilkeston, Sandiacre and Ilkeston and Nottingham and Ilkeston.

These licences were all granted, those from Nottingham including a condition that the Company should not pick up within the City any passenger wishing to be set down within the City. However, a few years were to elapse before the Nottingham-Derby licence was taken up.

In March, 1916, the Company made the first of what would become, over a number of years, a long list of takeovers of small independent operators. This was Messrs Dawkins and Ballard of Alfreton who had been operating on the Derby-Alfreton service, in competition with Trent, using a Thornycroft vehicle. Dawkins and Ballard, who, so their advertising said, had formerly worked for the Daimler Motor Company in London, began their service in February, 1915, very soon after Trent had been compelled to give up the route owing to a shortage of vehicles.

After Trent resumed running on the route, there followed a period of strong competition between the two, which was only brought to an end by the takeover. The Thornycroft was purchased by Trent but not used, being immediately sold to the Barnsley & District Traction Co., Ltd., forerunner of Yorkshire Traction. Subsequently, Trent gave up their existing garage in Alfreton and leased the Dawkins & Ballard premises.

Consideration was given to reopening the service between Alfreton and Chesterfield via Clay Cross, but correspondence with Chesterfield Corporation, who claimed to be adequately serving the district, was unfavourable and the matter was dropped. Services around Chesterfield were then left to W T Underwood (later East Midland), and Trent buses from Alfreton and Derby did not reach Chesterfield again until the 1950s.

There was a much concern about fuel consumption of the vehicles and their general standard of maintenance. Attempts were made to obtain the services of Mr L G Wyndham-Shire, Chief Engineer to Midland Red and a gifted engineer, on a regular consultancy basis. This did

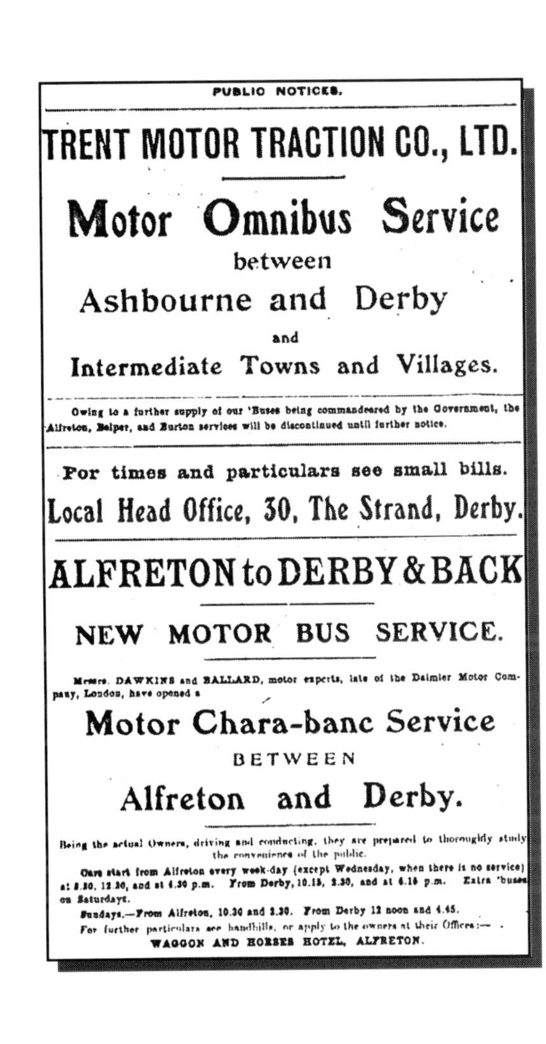

PUBLIC NOTICES.

TRENT MOTOR TRACTION CO., LTD.

Motor Omnibus Service

between

Ashbourne and Derby

and

Intermediate Towns and Villages.

Owing to a further supply of our 'Buses being commandeered by the Government, the Alfreton, Belper, and Burton services will be discontinued until further notice.

For times and particulars see small bills.

Local Head Office, 30, The Strand, Derby.

ALFRETON to DERBY & BACK

NEW MOTOR BUS SERVICE.

Messrs. DAWKINS and BALLARD, motor experts, late of the Daimler Motor Company, London, have opened a

Motor Chara-banc Service

BETWEEN

Alfreton and Derby.

Being the actual Owners, driving and conducting, they are prepared to thoroughly study the convenience of the public.

Cars start from Alfreton every week-day (except Wednesday, when there is no service) at 8.30, 12.30, and at 4.30 p.m. From Derby, 10.15, 2.30, and at 6.15 p.m. Extra 'buses on Saturdays.

Sundays.—From Alfreton, 10.30 and 2.30. From Derby 12 noon and 4.45.

For further particulars see handbills, or apply to the owners at their Offices:—

WAGGON AND HORSES HOTEL, ALFRETON.

The juxtaposition of these two advertisements in the Alfreton and Belper Journal of 5th March, 1915 was, perhaps, a little unfortunate from Trent's viewpoint. Just as they were having to announce a reduction in services, including withdrawal of that between Derby-Alfreton, along came Dawkins and Ballard to replace them. As related in the text, Trent fought back as soon as they had the vehicles to do so, and the interloper soon sold out.

not prove possible, but it was agreed that Mr Shire could visit Derby on special occasions. Following one such visit, various improvements to the methods and equipment used in the garage were made and this was the first event in what was to prove a lengthy association with the Birmingham company.

Mr J Harrison of Ashbourne had been in competition with Trent on the Ashbourne service since the start, and with CCHL before, the intensity of this competition being such that on one occasion a Trent driver was prosecuted for running Harrison's bus off the road. A number of attempts were made to reach agreement and eventually, in February, 1917, Harrison's "Ashbourne and Derby Motor Service" was acquired, together with his Star bus which joined the Trent fleet. Harrison was appointed the Company's agent in Ashbourne, also agreeing to provide washing and garaging facilities in the town. At the end of the year, he also took on the carriage of mails on the route, under sub-contract.

Under the provisions of the Local Government (Emergency Powers) Act, 1916, local authorities were empowered to levy a mileage charge on bus operators to help towards the cost of maintaining the roads. This again brought the Company into conflict with the Nottingham authorities who, on renewal of the Company's licences, sought to impose a charge of ⅝d (0.26p) per car mile. Further, the decision, made on 9th May, 1917, was retrospective to 16th May, 1916, the date on which the buses had started to run.

Following representations by the Company, some retrospective charges were waived, but the Watch Committee stuck to their earlier decision in relation to future charges. As a result of this, the Company threatened to withdraw their Ilkeston-Nottingham service, but the Nottingham Watch Committee refused to back down. It is not clear whether the Company carried out their threat, although it does appear doubtful whether the service was immediately withdrawn.

Throughout the war years, the Company was in continual difficulties over obtaining adequate petrol supplies. By 1917, this problem had become acute and in that year only two new vehicles, both Tilling-Stevens TS3s, were purchased because it was considered inadvisable to buy more owing to the restricted petrol supplies. It is likely that these two vehicles, which received fleetnumbers D107 and D108 may have been fitted with second hand bodies purchased from Midland Red.

Some economy in the use of petrol was achieved by cutting out lesser used journeys, but further efforts in this direction were made by equipping a number of vehicles with gas storage bags fitted on the roof, so that they could use coal gas as fuel. The first bag was supplied, at a cost of £21, by neighbouring Barton Bros of Beeston who were extensive users of gas propulsion in their own fleet. In order to more readily obtain gas supplies, two gas standards in Albert Street, Derby were rented from Derby Corporation, commencing in March, 1918. Further gas bags were purchased, although this time from the North British Rubber Co at £54 each, and it appears that by late 1918, ten bags had been purchased. As the fleet at that time numbered about sixteen vehicles, a significant proportion must have been running on coal gas.

At the end of 1917, a report by the General Manager, Mr H F A Roche, had shown that petrol supplies were available to run some 13,000 miles per month and 6,430 miles could be run on gas. There was, therefore, a shortfall compared with the scheduled service mileage of 21,000 and, in view of the number of bags purchased, it seems there was probably a further squeeze on petrol supplies. Certainly, beyond opening the routes to Nottingham, there was little or no attempt to expand the services.

A notable event during 1917 was the publication of the Company's first printed timetable booklet. Measuring approximately 6" x 3ª" and printed in black on cream paper, this showed the services as follows:-

Derby - Melbourne
Derby - Alfreton
Derby - Ashbourne

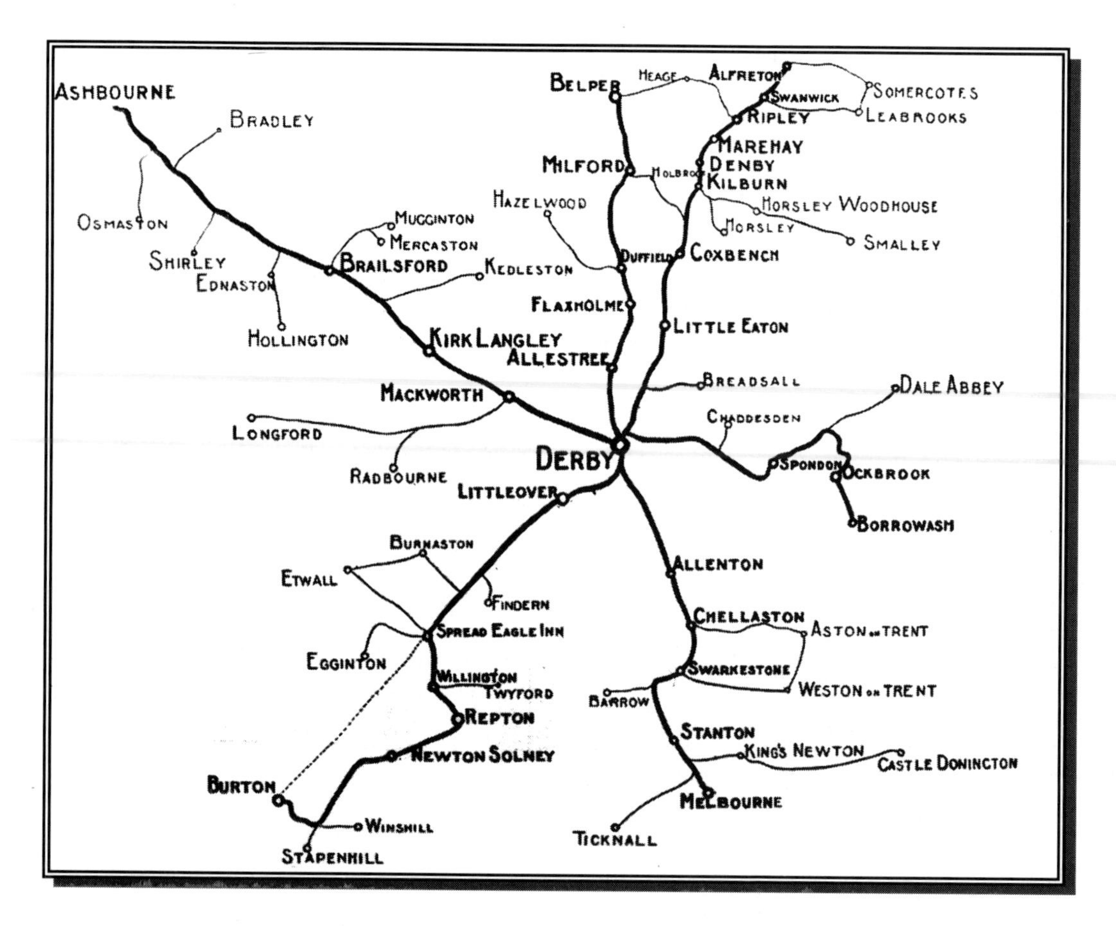

The first official map of the company's services was published in timetable book No 2, which appeared in November, 1918, following No1, published without a map just a year earlier. Note that only the routes shown by the bold lines were served by the Company's buses. Intending passengers had to walk to the nearest route from the villages shown by the lighter lines.

Derby - Duffield and Belper
Derby - Spondon and Borrowash
Derby - Burton
Ilkeston - Nottingham
(not Thursday or Friday)
Alfreton - Ilkeston via Heanor
(not Thursday or Friday)
Nottingham - Mansfield
(not Tuesday or Friday)
Ripley - Alfreton (Saturday only)

One year later, In November, 1918, issue No. 2 was published, in similar format but including additionally an interesting map of the services which were largely the same except that the Ilkeston - Nottingham and Alfreton - Ilkeston services were not shown, suggesting that, initially, these services had only a short life.

At the end of 1917, the wages of the drivers were increased to £2 7s 6d (£2.37½p) per week, they having previously been paid at varying rates of £2 0s 0d, £2 2s 6d (£2.12½p) and £2 5s 0d (£2. 25p).

Petrol supply problems continued through 1918, and all vehicles required a petrol licence. The continuing close relationship with CCHL proved of great benefit in this respect, since the latter company, through its Hadleigh Motor Bus Co subsidiary, was able to provide, on hire at a cost of £10 per week each, two buses with petrol licences for 1,000 gallons per month and this helped considerably. One vehicle was returned quite soon, but the other, a Tilling-Stevens fleet number D115, was bought a few months later for £800.

Late in 1918, attention was turned to the acquisition of further vehicles. A tender was sought from Tilling-Stevens, on whose chassis the fleet was by now standardised following the sale of the last Commer and the small Maudslay, with the following result:-

" Complete Tilling-Stevens TS3 40hp four ton commercial chassis (without tyres) with specification of special details and spares and tools: £975.

Subject to discounts:

1-3 chassis	7½%
4-12 chassis	12½%
13+ chassis	15% "

In the event, further negotiations must have taken place because an order was placed for 4 chassis at £950 each, less 15% discount. The war ended on 11th November,1918 and the Directors doubtless felt renewed confidence in the ability of the company to expand in post war conditions for this order was soon increased to six and then early in 1919 further increased to ten. Two second hand

"British" type bodies were obtained from BMMO, but for the rest new bodies were ordered from Holmes Bros of Derby. This latter small firm of coachbuilders survived in name until quite recently, for in the 1930s it merged with another local firm, Sandersons, to form Sanderson and Holmes, garage proprietors and, initially, coachbuilders, who had premises in London Road, Derby until the early 1980s, although latterly part of the Mann, Egerton empire. The arrival of these Holmes bodies introduced detail changes to the livery, although precisely what these were is not recorded.

By now, the Company's operations were quite well established and centred on Derby, Nottingham and Alfreton, but in February, 1919 a fourth centre was added when the business of the Loughborough Road Car Co., Ltd., based on Loughborough was acquired. This grand sounding company had, like Trent, been formed in 1913, but was undercapitalised, having only local backing, and it had run into financial difficulties,. An approach was made by Trent, in the form of Mr Coventon-Moth, and after much heart searching, the Loughborough Board resolved to sell the business to Trent.

This purchase brought Trent two services, Loughborough-Shepshed and Loughborough-Mountsorrell and one single deck vehicle, a Tilling-Stevens TTA2, the only one owned by that time. There was also a garage which occupied part of a site in Derby Road which was later extended and a modern garage built. The site of the Trent garage is now occupied by the car park of a Sainsbury supermarket, following the later sale of the Loughborough services and subsequent events. The price paid, £1517, appears generous in the light of the sale of the Tilling-Stevens to the Stirling and Bridge of Allan Tramways for £800 and the fact the garage came complete with a mortgage of £400.

With the desire to capitalise on this extension to their operating area, the Company made application to Leicester City Council, in the following April, for licences to operate a service between Loughborough and Leicester.The licences were granted for the service to operate from Old Cross in Leicester's Belgrave Gate, but subject to a payment of 3/8d (0.156p) per mile for wear and tear on the roads traversed in the Borough and a minimum fare of 3d (1.25p) to protect the services of the Corporation Tramways.

AY 2224, one of a pair of a pair of Tilling-Stevens TTA2 models with Brush B29F bodywork used to start the services of the Loughborough Road Car Co in January, 1913, as shown in this view. By the time of the Trent takeover, a different radiator had been fitted of the type fitted to TS3 models, which it then resembled. It had also been fitted with a destination box above the front canopy which incorporated a roller destination blind - a modern innovation which was not fitted to any new Trent vehicles until well into the 1930s!

As previously in Nottingham, these road payments were a source of irritation to the Company and representations were made to their trade association, the London and Provincial Omnibus Owners Association (LPOOA), who were lobbying nationally on behalf of their members. On the advice of the Association, Trent wrote to the Leicester authorities offering to undertake to pay, from the date of commencement of the services, such amount as may be fixed by the Government or other competent authority. The response was a curt edict to the effect that, until the authority of the Watch Committee was superseded, and in the absence of a Government Order, the Company would have to pay the 3/8d per mile, if licensed. Negotiations must have continued on this subject, because some eighteen months were to elapse before Trent buses served Leicester.

Attempts to open other services in 1919 were more successful, however, and a new service, initially during the Summer only, was started to Ashbourne serving the "back" route via Quarndon and Cross o' th' Hands, running daily except Wednesdays. A daily service was started to Hatton, via Mickleover and Etwall, and on Wednesday, 1st October, 1919, the Derby-Nottingham service was at last started, running via Borrowash, Sandiacre and Stapleford. Soon after this, Nottingham was linked to Loughborough by a new service which started on Wednesday 19th November, 1919 and ran via Wymeswold and Ruddington. In addition, some services which had been tried before and abandoned were reinstated, because a number of journeys on the Alfreton-Derby service were extended - some to Clay Cross and some to Mansfield on an experimental basis, starting with the December, 1919 timetable.

In addition to these services, further plans were made, requiring fresh negotiations with the Nottingham authorities, for more services based on the City and serving Ilkeston, Mansfield, Long Eaton, Castle Donnington, Bingham and Newark. As a result of these negotiations, application was made for licences for twenty vehicles, for which it was necessary to obtain an additional £30,000 of

D124, CH 1769 carries a "British" style body, probably built by Holmes Bros of Derby. Compared with the earlier bodies, the appearance is considerably improved, with a rounded front and more evenly spaced, though narrower, window bays. The solid tyres have clearly seen heavy use, to judge from their poor condition.The crew uniforms are now of the military/police style used by bus companies throughout the land and familiar to passengers for many years until changed by the National Bus Company in the seventies. Note the spelling "Wymeswald", on the side destination board. Location is outside the original Loughborough Road Car Company depot, at Loughborough.

extra capital for business development when the licences had been obtained.

In other areas, the Company was mindful of the activities of neighbouring operators and an agreement was reached with Midland Red for a terminus at Burton on Trent. Similarly, consideration was given to running in the Bakewell area and in view of the possibility of the British Automobile Traction Co., Ltd., (BAT), the Company's parent, running in from Macclesfield, it was decided that a service from Derby to Bakewell should be opened before Easter, 1920. BAT's Macclesfield Branch was the precursor to the original, Stockport based North Western Road Car Co Ltd, with which Trent would, in the future, develop a good deal of operational co-operation. (The Company renamed Arriva North West in April, 1998, previously known as North Western and based at Bootle, is a different operation, set up in 1986, and originally formed part of Ribble Motor Services Ltd.)

At the end of 1919, it was decided that more vehicles were required and an order was placed with Tilling-Stevens for a further seven TS3 chassis. Birch Bros of London were asked to supply twelve single deck "British" type bodies for fitting on these chassis and also for replacing old bodies on earlier chassis. Three charabanc bodies were also ordered, probably from Birch, with a view to tapping the private hire market, and fitted to new TS3 chassis. Vehicles taken in during 1919 eventually totalled eleven, which took fleet numbers D116-26.

1920 opened with another order being placed for five more TS3 chassis and an order to Birch Bros for a further six bodies to the standard BAT "British" design. These vehicles were received between January and May, and took fleetnumbers D127-31. Additional deliveries of TS3s during the year took the fleetnumbers to D139 and there were also three other additions for which fleetnumbers have not been identified and which may have been second hand. In August, 1920, Mr S Ferry was appointed assistant to the General Manager. Later, he would become Traffic Manager and thus play a significant part in the Company's development.

As part of the proposals for development in the Nottingham area, serious consideration was given to the formation of a new company to be jointly owned with Balfour Beatty & Co., Ltd, specifically for operations in that area. Balfour Beatty had, in June, 1920 formed the Midland General Omnibus Company, Ltd., for the purpose of running buses in the District of Nottingham and Mansfield, but no capital had been issued and nothing had been done with the Company. Indeed, it was to be 1922 before Midland General became active, but in the early stages, Balfour Beatty had informally indicated a willingness to join interests with Trent.

In addition to this, the Clayton Transport and Motor Bus Co, Ltd, of Nottingham, was commencing small scale operations in the area in opposition to Trent. The Trent proposals were that a separate company be formed in Nottingham, having an authorised capital of not less than £50,000. Trent would take an interest against which they would hand over ten or more buses at cost for cash. Balfour Beatty would be invited to take an interest for cash, whilst Clayton would be invited to take shares against the purchase of their assets for cash or, alternatively, they could be taken over. However, the proposal was not taken up, and in July, 1923, Clayton was taken over by Trent, whilst Midland General went on to develop into a significant territorial bus company in its own right. Ultimately, in 1972, it too was to be taken over by Trent but this was under quite different auspices, to be described later.

Discussions continued with local authorities throughout 1920. In Nottingham, attempts were made to get the Watch Committee to agree that buses running from Loughborough should travel over Trent Bridge and thence via London Road, Fisher Gate, Pennyfoot Street and King Edward Street. However, this route was not deemed desirable - mainly, it seems because the Tramways Committee were keen to protect the Tramways revenue and really wanted Trent's buses to terminate at Trent Bridge, where the trams

Prior to the 1930 Road Traffic Act, which regulated bus services, there was always competition with small operators. Trent made various claims about its activities in this page from the timetable booklet to encourage people to use its services. Having regard to the Company's ownership by BAT, the comment about local shareholders seems to be somewhat stretching the point, especially as share ownership amongst ordinary people was negligible compared with the present day. However, employees did enjoy better wages, although conditions could be hard, and suspensions without pay for fairly minor disciplinary matters were not uncommon. Also, men would be laid off during the winter months when there was less demand for travel.

terminated. Clearly, this was unsatisfactory from the Company's point of view, since it imposed on passengers the need to break their journey.

Other discussions went on at Leicester where the Watch Committee resolved that, for each bus licensed to ply for hire in the City, a charge of not less than £60 per annum would be payable in advance in respect of wear and tear on the roads.

During the course of 1920, various attempts had been made to find garage premises in Nottingham, but there were difficulties and it was decided to use outstations at the various termini. It was not until February, 1921 that it proved possible to find suitable premises, which were at Radford Marsh behind The White Horse, in Ilkeston Road. They were of sufficient size to accommodate twelve buses as well as petrol, stores and a mess room.

New services started during 1920 were from Derby to Belper, via Allestree, to Heanor, via Morley and Smalley, to Loughborough, via Alvaston, Shardlow, and Hathern and, in addition, the Melbourne service was extended on five days a week to the quaintly named Leicestershire town of Ashby-de-la-Zouch.

Interestingly, a couple of journeys on the Belper service were extended on Wednesdays, Saturdays and Sundays via the inland holiday resort of Matlock to Bakewell, the market town of pudding fame. Most shops closed early on Wednesdays in those days, and Saturday was a half day in most other employment, so these journeys enabled people to spend some of their limited leisure time in the Peak District. From Nottingham there was also expansion, with services to Newark, via Lowdham and Southwell, to Heanor, via Stapleford and Ilkeston, and to Bingham, via Radcliffe-on-Trent. Whilst the first two services started conveniently from the Great Northern Bridge, close to the City Centre in Parliament Street, the latter service started from Trent Bridge, a reflection of the conditions imposed on the Company's licence by the City Council.

After the 1914-18 War, many men were demobilised with the benefit of a financial gratuity. In addition, many had also learned skills in the use and maintenance of motor vehicles and were able to put these to use running a bus service with a vehicle bought with their gratuity. Many small operators started in this way and perhaps one such was George Phipps of Horsley Woodhouse, commonly referred to by Trent people of the day as "Phippie".

Phipps ran a service between Alfreton and Derby and sold his business to Trent in 1929 after some development, but in 1921 he was providing competition to Trent. The Company sought to overcome this by negotiating with Phipps that each operator would run to their own times. This proved impossible and in consequence Trent reduced the timetable headway from 60 minutes to 30 minutes (20 on Saturdays), in order to crowd Phipps out, a measure which had only limited success. Indeed, the Company decided to escalate the competition by pirating Phipps on his route to Heanor and reducing their fares from 1/3d (6.25p) to 1/- (5p). It was also decided that the fare to Belper would be similarly reduced and, should Phipps start a service to Belper, as he had indicated in discussions he would, then he would be pirated on that route also.

Pirating, it should be explained, was a common way of competing at that time whereby a rival operator ran a bus on timings immediately before and immediately after those of his competitor. The leading rival bus would leave the terminus just ahead of his competitor to be first at the next stop in order to pick up the waiting passengers. This would have the effect of drawing the competitor ahead of his timetable as he progressed along the route, thus missing passengers who would be picked up by the trailing rival bus.

Behaviour of this kind is generally attributed to the independent operators, rather than the large territorial companies who claimed to always run to a timetable. They did run to a timetable, but Trent were certainly not averse to competitive behaviour as well, in order to attempt to defeat a rival, and in Phipp's case, they would send a few buses down to Kilburn Toll Bar to await the arrival of Phipps' buses from his garage at Horsley Woodhouse. The Trent buses would then each hang on to one of Phipps' buses for the day, following wherever it went.

Doubtless other territorial operators undertook similar activities, from time to time, and there is a tale of one driver who was following a rival around until he eventually turned into a side road. The Trent driver followed, and it was a dead end. The rival stopped his bus, climbed down from his cab, wandered over to the Trent bus and said to the driver " Tha's bin followin' us raarnd all day, tha' might as well come and have a bit o' dinner wimme"!

Competition was a very serious matter for the Company, as the following extract from a private report dated November, 1921 shows:-

"There is hardly one of our services which is free from it (competition). A light car, say a one ton Ford, running on a Friday and Saturday is the usual beginning, but when the owner sees he can make money at it, he runs more often. And we cannot stop him! We have not even one spare bus to increase the service and make it less worth his while. We are tied down to time tables with heavy cars and it is a simple matter for him to "pirate us...."

In order to compete with independent operators, an order was placed for two Vulcan light chassis at a price of £675 less 10% discount, these to be fitted with B22R bodies costing £375 each and built by Birch Bros of London to a design generally resembling the larger bodies fitted to the Tilling-Stevens. These vehicles arrived in October 1921, receiving fleetnumbers V143/4, following on from the previous Tilling-Stevens.

They were immediately put to work, one on the Derby-Alfreton service against Phipps and the other on the Derby-Melbourne service against Higgs & Waller of Melbourne, another small independent operator providing vigorous competition to Trent. Returning a very satisfactory fuel consumption of 12mpg, the vehicles were considered mechanically sound and two more were soon ordered.

During 1921, only three new services were opened, these being Derby-Ilkeston via Chaddesden, Loughborough-Leicester, via Mountsorrell and Loughborough-Leicester via Syston. However, the Loughborough-Derby service which, as will be subsequently seen was to have a rather chequered history, was withdrawn. The Nottingham-Newark service was also withdrawn and the Nottingham-Bingham service was cut back to Radcliffe-on-Trent, but extended to Parliament Street at the Nottingham end, following the agreement of the Watch Committee.

The reason for this setback in the Company's hitherto rapid post-war expansion seems to have been an inadequate supply of vehicles, but it had the effect of allowing competitors in on many routes because they took the excess traffic which Trent was unable to exploit. The reason for this lack of vehicles is not apparent, but it not only caused loss of traffic, it also made the Company vulnerable to overcrowding and breakdowns, with consequent effect on public confidence. Relevant to this, however, is a decision made in November, 1921, when it was decided that the area of the Company's business was sufficiently large and no extension of the area should be made. Instead, the Company would concentrate on stabilising development in its present area.

Much of the management effort during this period was devoted to service adjustments to combat competition. Mention has already been made of the competition from George Phipps and Higgs & Waller, but on the Alfreton-Mansfield route there was competition from Edwards of South Normanton and Burrows and Machin of Hucknall. On the Ashbourne-Derby service there was Bayliss & Sons of Ashbourne and, inevitably, on the Derby- Nottingham corridor there was strong competition from Barton, despite agreements to limit this and the different routes followed then, as now. Clayton of Nottingham had begun a service between Nottingham and Cotmanhay via Wollaton, Trowell and Ilkeston, in response to which the General Manager wrote to say that Trent considered this an unfriendly act.

In October, 1921, Barton Bros as the business of Barton Buses, Ltd was then known, had offered Trent the opportunity to purchase their business for the sum of £25,000, to include a 100' square garage, 2 cottages with two or three acres of land and 25 vehicles of assorted manufacture. After consideration, a price of £13,000 was offered which Barton did not take up and the competition between the two operators continued. A counter offer by Barton to sell for £22,000 was equally not taken up by Trent, and nothing came also of a letter in July,1922 to Midland Red which offered

The Trent bus station in Albert Street, Derby opened in 1922, and this rather poor view was taken ten years later. On the left, 1931 SOS IM6 No 122 with Short B34F body awaits a journey to Buxton, for which longer distance service the 6 cylinder engine offered a significant advantage. On the right is newly delivered 239, an SOS IM4 with Brush B34F bodywork. Note the shallower radiator than on the IM6, reflecting the lesser cooling requirement of the 4-cylinder engine. The two batches of vehicles represent the last use of the CH prefix for new deliveries to the fleet, and the first use of the RC prefix respectively. Both marks were issued by Derby Corporation, which was the local vehicle registration authority in the manner of the day, when registration marks were allocated to individual Councils, rather than the Driver and Vehicle Licensing Agency, as today. Visible against the wall of the indoor Market Hall in the background is at least one SOS ODD type rebuilt from an SOS Standard.

the business complete for £30,000 which was passed to Trent.

The United Automobile Services subsidiary company, W T Underwood Ltd, forerunner of East Midland and then based at Clowne, near Chesterfield was fast developing and by late 1921, following a start in 1920, had built up a fleet of 29 vehicles. It was felt by Trent to be desirable to set a boundary between the two companies with a view to coming to a territorial agreement with Underwoods. In this context, it should be noted that United (renamed Arriva North East in April, 1998) was then a substantial independent operator, having an operating area extending from East Anglia to the North East.

A boundary line was set and a draft agreement prepared, but Underwoods were reluctant to sign. An invitation to Mr E B Hutchinson, Chairman of United, to attend a meeting with a Committee of Trent Board Members to discuss the matter was not accepted, but Mr Underwood attended a subsequent Committee meeting in March, 1922 and a line was agreed. It is not clear whether an agreement was ever actually signed, but south of the Whatstandwell to Alfreton road, north of the Alfreton to Sutton-in Ashfield road to Eight Men's Intake, north of the road between Mansfield, Rainworth, Kirklington and Newark was the line agreed. Matlock to Whatstandwell, and Stretton to Clay Cross were agreed as common roads, and the road from Alfreton to Clay Cross and Stretton was agreed as a Trent road. It was agreed that Trent would not operate north of the line, and Underwood south of it, also they would not compete with Trent between Stretton and Alfreton. The line seems to have been adhered to over the years, and it will be recalled that Trent in their early days had been active in the Chesterfield area. Now it was left to Underwood.

On the south side of the company's operating area, an informal agreement was reached with Midland Red as to a suitable boundary line between the two companies.

Towards the end of 1921, the Company ran into some temporary difficulties over the question of bus stands in Derby. At that time, their services terminated in Albert Street in the vicinity of the Corn Exchange. However, the Corporation had become concerned at the number of operators running into the town and the resulting congestion and began to think about the idea of allocating separate stands for the various routes. The stands proposed were Albert Street, Cheapside and The Spot, each of which are about half a mile apart. Having concentrated their services in Albert Street and provided some facilities there, with obvious benefits to Company and passengers alike, Trent were so concerned about this proposal that a deputation of three directors attended a meeting of the Watch Committee Sub-Committee on 6th December to make representations that they wished to keep the Albert Street stand themselves. This would, they said, enable better supervision and, in addition, they offered to put up additional accommodation for the public.

The Committee decided, however, that the proposed division of stands should go ahead, the arrangement of stands from 1st April, 1922 being:-

Albert Street - 8 stands for Nottingham, Heanor, Ilkeston, Alfreton and Mansfield.

Cheapside and Bold Lane - 5 and 9 stands respectively, to be operated as one stand for Ashbourne, Hatton, Burton and Belper.

The Spot - 2 stands for Melbourne.

These stands were to be shared amongst all the operators running to each destination, but the Company already had better arrangements in hand, for it was negotiating with the Corporation to lease land in Albert Street on which to build a bus station. Agreement being reached in April, a contract was let to J H Fryer, the Derby builders, for erection of the bus station and concreting the

One of the double deck Thornycroft Js was involved in a fatal accident in September, 1922, plunging over the edge of Swarkestone Bridge in an incident involving an overtaking car. The vehicle was photographed being recovered and, regrettably, no other photograph of these vehicles has been found. The bus had Birch bodywork.

land, which had previously been used as a small fairground known locally as "The Muck Heap". The works were rapidly completed and the new bus station was in use from the 21st July, 1922 being one of the earliest bus stations, if not the first, in the country. Ideally situated, close to the town centre, the bus station boasted a covered platform, waiting room, parcels office and toilets and was much acclaimed locally. It enabled all Trent services in the town to be centralised once again.

From the first new timetable in 1922, all services were given route numbers according to the list contained in the Appendix.

The through services from Derby to Mansfield and Derby to Clay Cross, both via Alfreton, which had begun experimentally in December, 1919, were split at Alfreton from June, 1921 into three separate services. However, this was felt to give an advantage to competitors and so the through services were once again reinstated, but by November, 1922 feelings had again changed somewhat, for the service to Clay Cross was once more run separately, from Alfreton only, in order to build up the service and combat competition.

With the continued increase in traffic, it was decided that larger buses would be required. At the time, many surplus wartime vehicles were being sold off from the Army Mechanical Transport Depot at Slough, Buckinghamshire. In consequence of these two factors, thirteen Thornycroft J type chassis were purchased from Slough for around £200 each.

One of these chassis was broken up to provide spare parts, but each of the others was reconditioned and lengthened at an average cost of £55 each. Four double deck bodies were ordered from Birch Bros, a further four chassis were fitted with charabanc bodies purchased sometime previously, and a fourth with a new Birch Bros charabanc body. The remaining chassis received 28 seat single deck bodies. The Thornycrofts, which took fleetnumbers T146-54/7-9 following on from the Tilling-Stevens and Vulcans, were found to be satisfactory in service, returning a fuel consumption of 5.95mpg. However, the gearing was found to be rather low for charabanc work and at least one was fitted with a higher ratio differential which improved consumption substantially.

The first double decker arrived in Derby during the week ending 6th May, 1922 and there was great concern within the Company about the safety of passengers travelling on the upper deck which, of course, was open top. It was suggested that the fitting of posts, (the maximum height of a person standing on the vehicle) should be considered. Also, notices to drivers were posted for special care to be taken in the running of these vehicles with regard to trees and bridges. As a final precaution, the General Manager and the Engineer personally tested every route on which the vehicles were to run to ensure that there were no obstructions from bridges or overhanging trees.

As in the previous year, there were few service developments during 1922, the policy being to consolidate the Company's position on existing services as already described. Nevertheless, the developments which did take place were not without interest.

On 1st June, 1922, the Belper service, 4, was extended to Matlock, via Ambergate and Cromford, to connect with the new BAT (Macclesfield Branch) service to Buxton. The BAT times were shown in the Trent timetable and this was not only the first example of co-ordination with a neighbouring operator's service, but established Matlock as a border town between the two operator's territories. Similarly, on 3rd August, 1922, BAT started a service between Buxton and Ashbourne which connected with Trent's service four times daily in the latter town.

At about the same time, some journeys on service 15, Nottingham-Heanor via Stapleford, were diverted to run via Radford, Wollaton Square and Balloon Houses as service 22. It will be recalled that Claytons had earlier started a similar service and thus these diversions may be seen as a response to that in order to recover lost traffic.

In July, 1922, a further takeover occurred. No formal payment or agreement appear to have been made, but the person concerned, G J Hawksworth of The Castle Inn Tutbury, was taken on as a driver and it is likely that a small sum was paid as compensation for his goodwill. No vehicles were involved, but Hawksworth had run a daily service between Tutbury and Burton on Trent, via Rolleston Station and Stretton, which was withdrawn following the takeover. He also ran a Wednesdays only service between Tutbury and Uttoxeter, via Hatton, Sudbury and Doveridge, with the last journey from Uttoxeter running through to Burton on Trent.

By November, 1922 the service pattern had been changed, so that Trent's existing Derby-Hatton service was extended to Uttoxeter on Wednesdays and Fridays, whilst the former Hawksworth Burton-Tutbury service was extended to Hatton, except on Tuesdays and Wednesdays. Further adjustments to the days of operation followed in 1923.

The Company's first longer distance service began on 4th June, 1922 when a new charabanc service was introduced to cover the 76 miles journey from Nottingham to Skegness at a fare of 16/- (80p) return or 9/- single. Leaving Nottingham at 9.00am and returning from Skegness at 4.30pm, the venture proved a great success and continued throughout the summer taking a total of £500. This was the Company's first effort to cater for the seasonal "bucket and spade" traffic which, hitherto, had been largely in the hands of the small operator and the railways, and other similar services followed in due course. Other efforts were also made to tap what we would nowadays term the leisure market, both from Derby and from the newly opened office at 90, Parliament Street, Nottingham where Mr S Ferry had taken up office as temporary manager to develop business in the Nottingham area.

During 1922, a new garage housing six double deck buses was brought into use at Alfreton and, in the same area, the business of George Edwards of South Normanton, a competitor, was offered, but it was decided not to buy.

This view shows what might be described as a typical cross section of the Trent fleet of the early 1920s, when it numbered around 40 or so vehicles. Nearest the camera is TS 2566, a Tilling-Stevens TS3, possibly fleet number D141, new in 1920 and carrying a 32-seat charabanc body, probably built by Birch. The chara was later rebuilt to forward control and rebodied Brush B32R in 1925, being renumbered 401 and remaining in the fleet until 1929. Centre is CH 1209, D109, possibly with Holmes Bros bodywork, fitted in 1920 to a chassis which had been new in 1914. Furthest away is V143, CH 2786, one of four small Vulcan VSDs bought in 1921 to compete with the lightweight vehicles used by independent competitors. Note that style of the bodywork is identical to that on the Tilling-Stevens, despite the difference in size and manufacturer. Bodywork of similar design was supplied to other BAT subsidiaries, including Midland Red and Ribble.

Chapter Three
SOS - No Danger
1923-30

With effect from 24th January, 1923, the management agreement with Commercial Car Hirers Ltd. ended. It will be recalled that CCHL was a subsidiary of Commercial Cars Ltd, but this company was, by the early 1920s, finding itself in financial difficulty, probably as a result of the surplus of vehicles which had come onto the second hand market following the end of the war, and the reduction in new vehicle sales which this caused. The subsidiary CCHL went into a prolonged receivership from August, 1923, finally being voluntarily liquidated in 1931.

Also in January,1923, Mr O C Power, the noted Traffic Manager of Midland Red, was appointed to the Trent Board and this marked the start of an association with the latter company which would last until 1943 when Mr Power died. The appointment brought immediate effect, for on Wednesday, 28th February, 1923 service 18A, Loughborough-Mountsorrell, was extended to Leicester and operated jointly with Midland Red. It will be recalled that a service to Leicester had previously been started in September, 1921. This lasted only until the end of that year, but even at that time, an attempt was made at a form of joint operation whereby Trent had asked Parr's Garage of Leicester to run between Leicester and Mountsorrell in conjunction with Trent's running of the Leicester-Mountsorrell portion. Nothing came of that proposal, but Trent had cut back the service to Mountsorrell anyway. Thus, the association with Midland Red, who were building up their activities in Leicester and elsewhere, in parallel with Trent's similar activities in the Derby/Nottingham area, allowed reinstatement of the through facility.

An early attempt at pre-sales of tickets off the bus began on 23rd March, 1923, when books of pre-paid tickets went on sale at the following discounted rates:-

No of Tickets	Value	Sold For
20 x 2d (0.83p)	8/4d (41.7p)	7/- (35p)
25 x 3d (1.25p)	6/3d (31.25p)	5/4d (26.7p)
12 x 6d (2.5p)	6/- (30p)	5/- (25p)
10 x 1/- (5p)	10/- (50p)	8/6d (42.5p)

The discounts on these tickets varied between 15% and 17%, and so offered quite good value to those who could afford to buy in advance. The arrangement lasted for several years until it was discontinued in 1929 when it was necessary to increase revenue to alleviate the effects of a tax on petrol which was imposed at that time, costing the Company some £8,000 per annum. An `Anywhere' ticket, costing 3/- (15p) and available on Mondays to Thursdays was also introduced, from 1st July, 1923, but withdrawn in 1929 for the same reason.

Mr G C Campbell-Taylor, General Manager, 1923-46.

On 1st April, 1923, Mr G C Campbell-Taylor took control of the Company as General Manager. The Company had a succession of General Managers in the early years; G A Wearham, for a short time in 1914, a Mr Holtom in 1914/15, H F A Roche, 1915-18, T G Clabburn, 1919-22 and L Annesley-Hunt, 1922/23. Mr Campbell-Taylor, however, was to remain in post until 1946, when he took early retirement due to ill health. He was thus to lead the Company through its expansion and the difficult years of the Second World War.

Competition continued to be a most serious problem and various kinds of competitive responses had to be made to combat this, involving some substantial fare reductions. For example, on the Loughborough-Nottingham service, when a competitor appeared between Bunny and Nottingham, the Company cut their fare from 1/- (5p) to 6d (2½p), but within two or three months the competitor withdrew and the fares returned to their old levels. Between Derby and Ashbourne, along the original Commercial Car Hirers route, Mr H D Bayliss, a grocer by trade, had begun business in the classic small way using a Ford Model T van which was fitted with windows and in which he put wooden benches at weekends so that it could be used as a bus for excursions. This was in 1921 and his business developed, becoming a serious competitor to Trent over several years. In retaliation, Trent put one of the light Vulcans on as a chaser and were able to maintain a satisfactory level of receipts. However, the competition increased and in May, 1923, Bayliss altered his timetable to run just ahead of Trent's times, so the Company cut their fares between the two towns from 1/- (5p) return to 6d (2½p) return.

During the year, four second hand vehicles were purchased from Thames Valley of Reading. These

Some idea of the level of competition between Bayliss and Trent can be gauged from the text of this Bayliss handbill, published at the height of the competitive activity between the two companies. Note the allegation of unfair competition and compare with the similar allegation made by Trent in their own notice, shown on page 21. Such competition was commonplace at the time and, actually, those involved on both sides quite enjoyed it, so perhaps it was inevitable that, sooner or later, legislation would bring it to an end!

were Thornycroft J models, three dating from 1919 with Brush bodywork and the remaining one a Tilling bodied example of 1920, which received Trent fleetnumbers T160-63. They were joined, later in the year by the last Tilling-Stevens TS3.

The Clayton Transport and Motor Bus Co, Ltd, of Trinity Square, Nottingham was taken over in July, 1923 and, as previously mentioned, this company had begun operations in 1921. Various services had been operated, including Nottingham-Cotmanhay, Nottingham-Newark and several Sunday excursions. At the time of the takeover, Clayton were operating a service between Nottingham and Burton Joyce via Gedling and the four Tilling-Stevens TS3 single deckers also acquired had Brush bodies of the "Birmingham" type , like Trent's, and so fitted nicely into the Trent fleet. They took fleetnumbers D164-7.

The services were renumbered in June, 1923, as listed in the Appendix. This renumbering came very soon after service numbers had been introduced, but suffixes were eliminated and services to different destinations were given separate numbers, even if they were merely extensions of another service. Also, the series of numbers was expanded, to allow gaps for new services.

More new services were introduced for 1923, these being:-

12 Derby - Castle Donnington,
via Aston-on-Trent and Shardlow.

16 Derby - Heanor,
via Breadsall and Morley, alternating with existing service 7 which was changed to run only via Smalley.

17 Derby - Ilkeston,
via Breadsall, Morley and Stanley, alternating with existing service 10 via Chaddesden and Stanley.

35 Nottingham - Gedling,
introduced in April and extended to Burton Joyce in July following the takeover of Clayton, when it was renumbered 36.

Every trip on the Castle Donnington service was pirated by a competitor, but it was decided that, rather than give the service up, which would be a victory for the competition in general and would considerably harm the prestige of the Company, the fares would be reduced. This resulted in the fare of 1/9d (8.75p) being reduced to 1/- (5p) and the single fare of 1/1d (5.4p) falling to 8d (3.3p). However, the service was withdrawn by April, 1924, despite the loss of prestige. So far as services 16 and 17 are concerned, these seem to have lasted for only about two months, at that time.

For 1924, it was decided that twenty new vehicles would be ordered. These were to be Tilling-Stevens TS6 models of which ten would be single deck and ten double deck, all with Brush bodywork. The TS6 model was a larger, heavier and more powerful development of its TS3 predecessor. Still featuring the petrol-electric driveline, the vehicles were built to a forward control layout allowing a larger saloon and hence increasing the passenger carrying capacity. The single deck models were longer, being known as TS6 Long Saloons. In addition to these new vehicles, it was decided to obtain greater capacity from the existing fleet by converting a number of TS3 and Thornycroft J models to forward control and fitting new longer bodies, or bodies acquired secondhand from Midland Red.

Some services were renumbered yet again, in January, 1924, as shown once more in the Appendix. New services were opened during the year, as shown below:-

36 Nottingham-Alfreton,
via Watnall, Underwood and Selston. This was later varied to run via Watnall, Eastwood, Jacksdale and Ironville.

12 Derby - Loughborough,
via Shardlow, Castle Donnington, Kegworth and Hathern.

This last service was started around October, 1924, and was the second time a Derby-Loughborough service had been run. This time, however, Castle Donnington was also served, thus replacing the service to that town which had been started in 1923 and withdrawn earlier in 1924.

Also, in March or April, services 32 and 32A from Nottingham were reduced to run only to

Twenty Tilling-Stevens TS6s were received in 1924, of which of which ten were double deck, and ten single deck. These were somewhat longer than the 'deckers, giving rise to the name "TS6 Long Saloons". This unidentified example, taking up duty on a Boy's Brigade outing illustrates the full drop side windows and the curious hand signal, which could be turned to a right angle to the body, to indicate a turn was about to be made. The batch led uneventful lives, being withdrawn in 1931-32.

Ilkeston, instead of Heanor.

In April, 1924, it was decided to change the Company's livery from green to red. The shade adopted was BET light red, as used by Midland Red, and various newspapers reported that this change was to bring the Company into line with its larger sister. No doubt Mr Power's influence was at work in this regard, although it is also true that the majority of BET owned bus companies used a red or maroon livery. Indeed, Trent later introduced BET dark red, a maroon shade, into their livery as relief, together with varying amounts of white or cream, depending on the type of vehicle. In making the change to red, the Board may also have had in mind the joint operations with Midland Red in the Loughborough area.

The Tilling-Stevens TS6s were the first vehicles to be delivered in the new red livery and, internally, they were considered quite well appointed at the time, helping to boost the Company's revenue in the face of keen competition.

Numbered 200-9, for the double deckers and 300-9 for the saloons, these vehicles introduced a completely new series of fleetnumbers, based on the allocation of blocks of numbers to different types of vehicles, the system which remains in use today. The numbers were embossed on a metal plate, the background of which was painted a particular colour to indicate the depot to which the vehicle was allocated, a system which remained in use until a major fleet renumbering exercise took place in 1962.

With the increasing size of the fleet, further garage accommodation was required in Derby and with this in mind another plot of land was purchased on the opposite side of the road from the then existing premises, in Uttoxeter New Road, and this was the building which, in the sixties, became a new Central Works, until vacated in 1997. A new, modern garage was erected, some 210 feet in length and with an uninterrupted span of 90 feet. It was formally opened on 2nd July, 1924 by the Mayor of Derby and the old garage on the west side of Uttoxeter New Road was then converted into a Central Works, in which form it survived until the mid 1960s. Soon afterwards, a piece of land was leased in Manvers Street, Nottingham on which to provide a garage to serve the Company's needs in that City.

In July, 1924, the Company was accepted as an associate member of the British Electrical Federation Limited (BEF) at a fee of 100 guineas (£105) per annum. This was a company set up by BET as a central servicing organisation for its subsidiaries. It provided various services and also a purchasing facility which aimed to provide benefit from economies of scale in purchasing. Initially, it was decided that the Federation would undertake all of Trent's secretarial and accounting work. Later, central petrol supply contracts were negotiated at advantageous terms and other services were also used.

On 9th January,1925, the Company experienced its first strike when a large proportion of the drivers and conductors came out in sympathy for a man who had been dismissed. It was reported that after twenty minutes the buses were all manned by others and running to timetable all day. The men returned after about six hours, following an agreement, and about 100 miles were lost out of a total of 8,131 scheduled for the day.

Once again, in 1925, Barton offered their

business to Trent, Mr Barton stating in a meeting that he had received an offer from the Spanish Government for all of his 15 Lancia buses and offering Trent the goodwill of his business for £5,000. The asking price was considered too high, but the General Manager, Mr Campbell-Taylor, together with Mr Power entered into negotiations with a view to purchase and, indeed, indicated that they would be prepared to purchase six of the Lancias for £500 each. In the event, Bartons refused an offer of £5,000 for the good will and £5,000 for certain vehicles, which suggests that they may not have been serious about selling!

Both Mansfield Corporation and Nottingham Corporation were promoting Parliamentary Bills which were felt to be detrimental to the Company's interests. Opposition to the Nottingham Bill was undertaken by the London and Provincial Omnibus Owners Association and Mr Power gave evidence on the Company's behalf before the House of Lords Committee, whilst Parliamentary agents were appointed to oppose the Mansfield Bill. In the event, the most contentious clause in the Nottingham Bill, dealing with the regulation of bus routes, was withdrawn and the other contested clauses suitably amended. Similarly, Mansfield Corporation met the Company's objections, either by the withdrawal or amendment of clauses.

New vehicles ordered for 1925 were of interest as they marked a change of supplier, an order being placed for 15 Daimler CM chassis equipped with pneumatic tyres and carrying 31 seat Ransomes bodies to BEF Type X design. Here was a turning point in vehicle design, for hitherto, the Tilling-Stevens vehicles used had been extremely heavy and their progress along the road very slow. Indeed, this was true of the vehicles used by other territorial companies as well. There was, theoretically, a 12mph speed limit in force at the time, but when fully laden the TS3s could sometimes barely make even that low speed.

The independent operators, on the other hand, used small lightweight vehicles such as Fords, Lancias and Fiats which could give a good turn of speed and were therefore ideal in a pirating operation. This was the reason why larger operators, such as Trent and others, had bought Vulcans with which to retaliate.

The new Daimlers, numbered 801-14, brought about a change in all this with their unladen weight of only 3 tons 15cwts (3814kg), compared with about 5 tons 10cwts (5593kg) of the Tilling-Stevens. This weight reduction had come about in two ways. Firstly, Daimler, who had been quick to understand the properties of materials and the need for attention to detail in design, had produced their CL chassis which was quite light in weight and reliable by the standards of the day. At the instigation of BEF, the weight of the derived CM model was reduced still further by the inclusion of more aluminium in place of other materials, and this in a chassis on which the wheelbase was increased from 15' 6" to what BEF considered a more suitable 16' 0".

Secondly, the construction of bus bodywork had hitherto been largely based on carpentry methods derived from stage coach and horse bus practice. With the new X type body, BEF introduced engineering principles to their design and as it was also entirely without "frills", the weight of the body was kept down to a mere 18cwts (915kg). The interior of the body was spartan in the extreme, but served its purpose well at the time. Unfortunately, the bodies as constructed proved to be defective in some small way and, after about

One of the Ransomes bodied Daimler CMs, 802, CH 4860 stands in Ilkeston Market Place alongside NU 1991, a Talbot of District Bus Co, and a Thornycroft of Dawson's Enterprise. Dawson eventually sold to Midland General, whilst District sold to Trent in 1929. However, Trent service 32 to Nottingham, on which the Daimler is pictured operating, was eventually sold to Midland General in 1944.

twelve months in service, Ransomes rebated £15 per vehicle on the original body purchase price of £512 10s 2d (£512.51p). Chassis price was £555 10s 0d (£555.50p) each and these were the first larger vehicles (ie other than the 1922/23 Vulcans) to be fitted with pneumatic tyres from new, these costing £52 18s 4d (£52.92p) per set.

In addition to the Daimlers, two SOS vehicles were ordered from Midland Red and as these, and subsequent vehicles from the same manufacturer were to play a significant part in the development of Trent, some digression is necessary to explain their development.

In parallel with the joint development by Daimler and BEF, Midland Red had been pioneering vehicle developments under the able guidance of their Chief Engineer, Mr L G Wyndham Shire who had joined BAT in 1907 and started originally by helping to set up services in Deal, Kent, before joining Midland Red in 1912.

The early development of Midland Red largely paralleled that of Trent in standardisation mainly on Tilling-Stevens vehicles, but by the early 20s, Mr Wyndham-Shire, being a particular man and unable to obtain his exact requirements from Tilling-Stevens, had decided to construct his own vehicles. The early SOS chassis were derived from the Tilling-Stevens chassis and, indeed, this was evident from the style of radiator used, but the engine and close-coupled gearbox were of Shire design.

The engine, at 4.3 litres, was of rather smaller capacity than usual for the day, but this belied its powerful performance, brought about by the high compression ratio and application of the principles of Harry Ricardo, the well known tuning engineer. These resulted in a crisp exhaust note, and the vehicles had a distinctive and easily recognisable sound, especially with the high pitched note of the gearbox, where a low pitched moan had previously been the norm. It was designed for ease of operation and driving, and the body was pared to the minimum to save weight which, with the well tuned engine, gave a high power to weight ratio, and they were very fast by the standards of the day.

Internally, they were very spartan, with hard seats cushioned in a limited way, and although the driver was in the body of the vehicle, he had his own separate cab and partition. He drove with an absolutely horizontal steering wheel on a vertical column, and the gearchange was on the left - commonplace now, but unusual in those days. Despite the spartan finish, they gave a comfortable ride. The new vehicles were named SOS "Standards". The precise meaning of "SOS" has never been revealed, but the most popular theory and certainly the most appealing, is that it stood for "Shire's Own Specification"! Some credence to this theory is given by the fact that Mr Wyndham-Shire retired in 1940. Few vehicles were built by Midland Red during the war, but when full scale production was resumed afterwards, the vehicles were known by the initials BMMO, after the Company's full title of Birmingham and Midland Motor Omnibus Co., Ltd, rather than SOS.

Reverting to Trent, the two SOS Standards were ordered at a price of £1,300 each and Mr Howley who, it will be recalled, was the Chairman of Midland Red as well as Deputy Chairman of Trent, promised to try to obtain early delivery. This was achieved and two vehicles with Ransomes B31F bodies to Shire design which had originally ordered by Midland Red, were delivered to Derby in May, 1925 and put to work on the Derby-Ashbourne service to compete with Bayliss from the following 1st June. They received fleet numbers 900/1 and were registered CH 4946/7.

A further competitor was acquired in July,1925 when Clarke's Bus Service of Nottingham was purchased, operating between Nottingham and Ilkeston with three elderly Daimler Y types which were reconditioned and taken into the fleet for a few months before being resold.

There were frequent adjustments to the services, often just to combat the competition, but sometimes as well to optimise the service with a view to increasing revenue or better to serve the passengers. In August, 1925, the Loughborough-Derby service was severed since it had been found that through passengers were few and the local traffic at each end was better. Thus, service 12 was cut back once again to Castle Donnington and a new service, 42, introduced between Loughborough and Kegworth via Hathern and Sutton Bonnington. However, the through service was soon reinstated, once again, retaining the number 12.

A more permanent change was made to the Nottingham - Ilkeston service from August, 1925, for the direct route via Wollaton had acquired greater importance. Consequently, the 32A service, running via Stapleford, which had shown poor results and was duplicated between Nottingham and Stapleford by the Company's own Nottingham-Derby service, was altered to run between Ilkeston and Sandiacre via Stapleford, an arrangement which lasted only until the end of the year, when the service was withdrawn completely. A number of small operators were active on the Stapleford-Ilkeston corridor and this may have contributed to Trent's decision to make these changes. Meanwhile, the direct service was extended to Cotmanhay, but this too lasted for only a few months before the terminus reverted to Ilkeston.

The question arose of Midland Red taking over the Leicester-Loughborough service entirely. However, it was decided that Trent participation would continue, but Midland Red would control the fares and timetable and maintain the proportion of buses which they operated. This question would, in fact, arise again repeatedly and there was much discussion of the Loughborough- Leicester corridor between the two companies over the years, the question never being satisfactorily resolved until the mid 1960s. Other service developments during 1925 were:-

6B **Derby - Hatton,** extended to Tutbury.

36 **Alfreton - Nottingham.** Renumbered 3 and reduced to run between Alfreton and Eastwood only.

The crew and an inspector stand alongside SOS Standard 926, CH 5446 at Ripley whilst operating the Derby-Alfreton service. Note the pneumatic tyres, single rear wheels and the steep angle of the handrail in the entrance. Also the company name on the radiator top tank and the light brown dustcoats with red trim worn by the crew as summer uniform.

34B **Nottingham-Lowdham,** via Gedling, Burton Joyce and Bulcote. New service which initially ran on Wednesdays, Saturdays and Sundays, but later, daily.

34C **Nottingham - Newark,** via Gedling, Burton Joyce, Lowdham,Halloughton and Southwell. New service,running on Saturdays, Sundays, Mondays and Wednesdays.

37 **Nottingham - Mansfield.** New service, direct via Daybrook, Redhill and Harlow Wood.

41 **Loughborough - Coalville.** Reduced to run Loughborough - Shepshed.

In addition, for a brief period commencing on Friday, 18th September, a Newark-Lincoln service was run on Tuesdays and Fridays, two journeys each day. However, the Deputy Chairman, Mr Howley, was seen by Mr W P Allen, Chairman of Silver Queen, the forerunner of Lincolnshire Road Car Co over this. Mr Allen was active in BET circles and Trent's action was really an incursion into his territory, which does not seem to have lasted very long after the discussion between the two men.

The initial SOS vehicles, with their light weight, sprightly performance and excellent reliability were deemed a success and a bulk order was therefore placed with Midland Red for no less than thirty chassis. Twenty five of these would be supplied as complete vehicles with Ransome B32F bodies to the standard Shire design, at a cost of £1,300 each, as before. The remaining five were to be chassis only costing £800 and would be fitted with Ransome B31F bodies removed from five of the Daimler CM chassis delivered in 1924. A further order was placed, with Davidson, Ltd of Trafford Park, Manchester, for five charabanc bodies at £417 10s (£417.50) each, to be fitted to the 1924 Daimler CM chassis, which were to give up their bodies and receive new numbers 851-5 as a result.

Other steps were being taken to modernise the fleet and during 1925 and 1926 many of the TS3s were converted to gear drive and pneumatic tyres using SOS components supplied by Midland Red. These vehicles were those with saloon type bodies and were known as B types. Those with charabanc bodies were also converted to pneumatics but retained the petrol electric transmission. The four Thornycroft J types which had been converted to forward control were also converted to pneumatics at this time, but the remainder, together with the four Vulcans, were sold over a period between the end of 1925 and June, 1927, apart from odd ones that were converted to lorries for the service fleet.

One of the Thornys sold was also converted to a lorry, but for use carrying coal, and retaining the whole of the front of the bus body as a cab. There is a story that one particular inspector took many years to live down the fact that he jumped out and stopped not a bus, but a load of coal!

The new garage in Nottingham was completed early in 1926 and officially opened on Tuesday, 30th March at 4pm. Built on similar principles to the one at Derby opened two years previously, the garage had a capacity of 45 vehicles and still stands today, forming part of the annex to Nottingham City Transport Ltd's Parliament Street Depot.

The Nottingham services had for some time all started from Parliament Street in the vicinity of the Great Northern railway bridge (the Great Northern Railway was by now part of the LNER under the 1923 railway grouping resulting from the 1921

Railways Act, but the name persisted) but sometime during 1926, the Corporation re-allocated the bus stands in the City so that services running west, north west and north started from Trinity Square, or Wollaton Street, rather than Parliament Street.

The General Strike took place during May,1926 and all the Company's services were suspended for ten days. The collieries remained closed until November, which significantly reduced the spending power of the public in the mining areas, particularly in relation to private hire work. Taken together, these two factors adversely affected the Company's revenue for the year, but it was still possible to show, at around £9,000, an increase of over £2,000 above the previous year due to an expansion of the business overall.

A new garage was purchased in January, in King Street, Alfreton to increase capacity in the town and this replaced the previous garage in Limes Avenue which was later converted into a booking office. Also, in July, a garage with a capacity for six vehicles was bought in Mansfield, the roof of which had to be raised before it could be brought into use, as it had previously been used only for cars.

Much of 1927 was occupied in fighting further Parliamentary Bills which were being promoted by the various local authorities within the Company's operating area. These Bills were promoted by Matlock Urban District Council, West Bridgford Urban District Council and Derby Corporation. In the first two cases, it was just a matter of bus clauses which gave cause for concern, but Matlock agreed to withdraw these, whilst in the case of West Bridgford (which, of course, had a transport undertaking of its own) a suitable agreement was reached which enabled the Company to withdraw its objection.

The Derby Corporation Bill was a much more serious matter. In addition to the outward expansion of the Borough boundary (a not unreasonable proposal, having regard to the spread of the urban area beyond the existing boundary due to building development) the Bill also sought powers to run buses well outside the limits of the Borough. Indeed, there were local suggestions that the Corporation buses would serve the districts of Alvaston, Littleover, Breadsall, Allestree and Quarndon, all of which were then well outside the boundary, although now, with the exception of Quarndon, they are within the City curtilage. Negotiations, however, took place at high level with the result that the Corporation agreed that the powers to run buses outside the Borough would be confined to the enlarged limits of the Borough. In consequence of this, the Company withdrew its petition against the Derby Corporation Bill.

Serious competition arose in the south of the Company's operating area and consideration was given to running through services between Leicester and Nottingham and between Leicester and Derby, jointly with Midland Red. These through journeys were arranged, but it was decided that they should be run solely by Trent so that it would not be necessary for Midland Red to run through to either Nottingham or Derby. These new services began in April, 1927, being:-

12A	**Derby-Leicester,** via Shardlow, Kegworth, Hathern, Loughborough, Mountsorrell and Rothley.
31	**Nottingham-Loughborough.** Extended to Leicester via Mountsorrell and Rothley.
36	**Nottingham-Loughborough,** via Edwalton, Plumtree, Keyworth, Willoughby and Wymeswold.

The services were operated as express journeys, some of which were timetabled to run short to Loughborough only, and all the existing services were retained as before, although the Nottingham - Leicester service took the number 31 from the existing Nottingham - Loughborough service. The nature of the competition is not recorded, but throughout the country generally intense competition was breaking out between road transport and the railways, and as these services covered journeys which could also be made by rail, perhaps this was the motivation for the changes, although Barton also operated between Nottingham and Leicester. Whatever the reason, within two or three months the express services had been withdrawn and the other services reverted to their former pattern

There were other service developments during 1927, as shown below.

3B	**Derby - Swadlincote,** via Melbourne, Ticknall and Woodville.
5A	**Derby - Burton,** direct.
7	**Derby - Heanor.** Some journeys extended to Mansfield, via Langley Mill and Selston.
32	**Nottingham - Ilkeston.** Extended once again to Cotmanhay.
33A	**Nottingham - Nottingham (circular),** via Lowdham, Gunthorpe, East Bridgford and Radcliffe-on-Trent.
39	**Nottingham - Sutton-in-Ashfield.** Withdrawn, reinstated and then withdrawn again.
23	**Alfreton - Eastwood.** Withdrawn.

In addition, certain Friday only market day services to take shoppers to Derby from Heage, Dale Abbey and, later, Stanton-by-Dale, were introduced.

During November, 1927, agreement was reached with Nottingham Corporation that the Company's buses could pick up passengers within the city limits. However, the penalty for this was that the Company was to charge, in the main, twice the tram fare and hand over the difference to the Corporation, thereby maintaining protection for the Tramways. Interestingly, a similar type of arrangement, offered by Derby Corporation a few months later, was considered unacceptable and there Trent was unable to pick up within the Council's boundary until a co-ordination agreement was entered into under the auspices of Derbyshire County Council in 1979!

Once again, there were problems with Nottingham Corporation over services, this time in

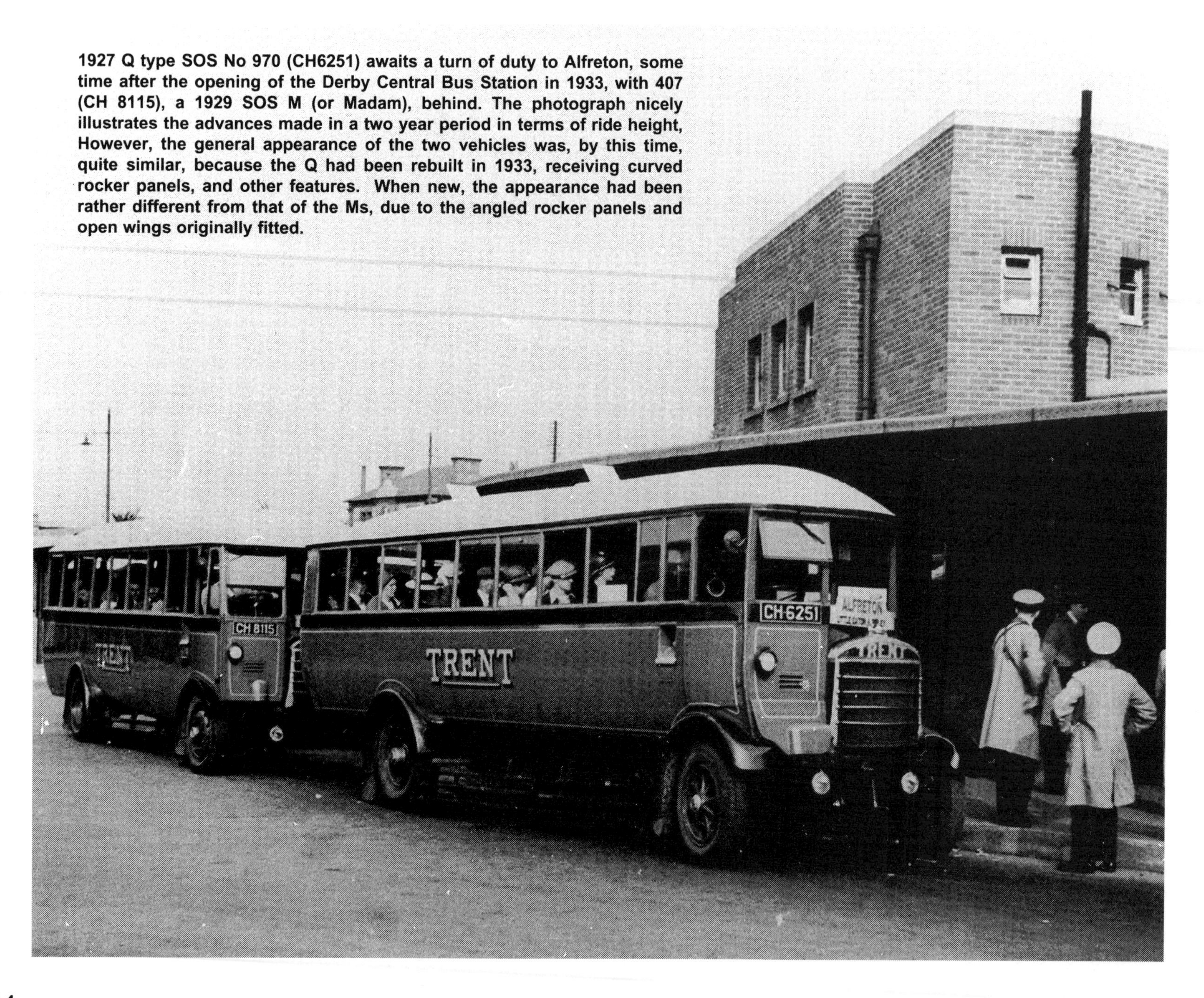

1927 Q type SOS No 970 (CH6251) awaits a turn of duty to Alfreton, some time after the opening of the Derby Central Bus Station in 1933, with 407 (CH 8115), a 1929 SOS M (or Madam), behind. The photograph nicely illustrates the advances made in a two year period in terms of ride height, However, the general appearance of the two vehicles was, by this time, quite similar, because the Q had been rebuilt in 1933, receiving curved rocker panels, and other features. When new, the appearance had been rather different from that of the Ms, due to the angled rocker panels and open wings originally fitted.

connection with their proposals to run services to Arnold, Wollaton and Wilford Hill which the Company felt itself to be adequately serving already. Trent lodged an objection with the Ministry of Transport, to which applications to run the new services had been made under the terms of the Nottingham Corporation Act, 1920, and won a refusal in the case of the Wilford Hill route and agreed conditions in the case of the other two, which enabled the Company to withdraw its objections.

During 1927, the existing fleet was again modernised, by equipping the ten TS6 Long Saloons with pneumatic tyres, which also necessitated fitting split propeller shafts. New vehicles were added to the fleet in the form of twenty SOS Q models with Ransomes B37F bodies to characteristic Shire design. The Q model was the third stage development of the Standard model (the second stage, of which Trent did not acquire any new models, had been a forward control version, the FS, with otherwise identical specification to the original model) having forward control and a longer wheelbase giving greater passenger carrying capacity. They retained much of the high build of the Standards and earned the nickname `Q Boats' in the Trent fleet, perhaps because of the sharp inward taper to their plywood rocker panels. They required careful driving on wet or loose surfaces, since only the rear wheels had brakes and these were prone to locking up under poor driving conditions. In order to make the best use of available space in a compact design, the petrol tank was fitted beneath the driver's seat, and this required a cab door at the extreme front, hinged from the windscreen pillar and front panel.

Five QC coaches with Carlyle C30F bodywork, built in the Midland Red workshops at Carlyle Road, Edgbaston, were also received. These coach versions of the Q had a similar mechanical specification but with the normal control layout which remained popular for such vehicles at the time, because of its affinity to the private car. However, the bodywork showed much improvement over the earlier charabancs in the fleet, for gone were the full width rows of seats, each requiring its own door in the side of the vehicle. Instead, there was a door at the front, alongside the driver, with a central aisle the length of the vehicle. With a hood which could be rolled back to a fixed rear dome, this kind of vehicle was generally known as an `all-weather saloon.' The arrival of the Qs and QCs ousted the four Thornycrofts on pneumatic tyres, eight of the TS6 forward control saloons and the first two of the TS6 deckers. Three of the old TS3 charabancs also left.

Throughout 1928, negotiations took place with the Balfour Beatty associated Midland General, Notts & Derby and Mansfield District companies over various matters. Nottinghamshire and Derbyshire Tramways Company (services later being operated by the subsidiary Nottinghamshire and Derbyshire Traction Company Ltd, following the abandonment of trams and thus retaining the initials NDT) were promoting a Parliamentary Bill which would allow buses and trolleybuses to be operated in lieu of trams. An objection was lodged with the promoters, to whom amendments to the proposals were submitted on behalf of Trent by the London and Provincial Omnibus Owners Association. The Act received the Royal Assent on 3rd August, 1928, but in the meantime negotiations had been in hand for a territorial agreement with the three Balfour Beatty Companies. It appears that a draft agreement was drawn up but it is questionable whether it was ever actually signed. However, there was a subsequent development as the Mansfield District Traction Bill was promoted and Trent lodged an objection to that also.

Early in 1930, there was an interesting development when Trent offered to purchase the bus operations of Mansfield District for £6,000 to include the vehicles and garage. This offer was refused, but a further offer was made of £10,000 for the services and garage, or £7,000 for the goodwill alone. This offer apparently lapsed, but it is likely that, had it been taken up, the business would have been divided between Trent and East Midland.

Reverting to 1928, 500 £1 shares were obtained in Omnibus Stations, Ltd., a jointly owned company holding ownership of Manchester's Lower Moseley Street Bus Station. The site had been acquired by North Western of Stockport and transferred to Omnibus Stations which constructed full terminal facilities. Principal shareholders were North Western and Ribble, but several other Tilling or BAT companies running into Manchester held minority shareholdings of which some, like Trent's, were quite small. Trent was looking towards the future development of long distance services and a deed of licence for the use of the station was sealed on 24th January, 1930.

The British Celanese (nowadays Courtaulds) artificial silk factory at Spondon, some three miles east of Derby, provided a vast source of employment over a wide area and was, therefore, an attractive source of revenue for all the local bus operators, Trent having begun workmen's services to this factory in 1925. As a result of this popularity, there were continual problems with overcrowding, both of vehicles and of the stands in the large parking area facing Derby Road. For Trent, the problems became acute in the Summer of 1928 and every available spare vehicle, including charabancs, was diverted to handle this traffic.

Serious consideration was given to buying six double deckers specifically to handle the Celanese traffic, but this was not proceeded with, and whether sufficiently early delivery could not be obtained, or whether a suitable model was not available is not recorded. However, in the event, orders for twenty-eight QL types from Midland Red were increased to thirty-eight, all of which were received promptly in the Autumn as 500-7/9-15, CH 7129-43, and 508/16-37, CH 7700-12/ 48-57, although the fleetnumbers and registrations did not run in order. The QL was an improved, lower version of the Q, also featuring twin rear wheels and much improved seating and interior lighting. The body order was split between Ransomes and Brush.

Attempts were made to obtain exclusive use of

Few, if any, Trent vehicles are identifiable in this newspaper photograph, taken outside the Celanese Works in the late 1920s, but it effectively illustrates what a valuable traffic objective the works was, and the congestion that occurred at shift changeover time. On Mondays to Fridays, up to 130 vehicles could be parked outside the works waiting to take the workforce home, but on Saturdays, there were nearly twice that number, because two shifts left together. Many of the small operators evident were eventually taken over by either Trent, Midland General or Barton, and the traffic has long since gone, but until the 1960s, vehicles of the three operators could be seen in significant numbers at shift changeover time.

part of the parking area at Celanese, with Trent Inspectors supervising the departures, a concession for which the Company offered fifty guineas (£52-50) per annum, but the Celanese management would not entertain the idea and nothing could be done.

A further takeover, made jointly with East Midland and Lincolnshire in October, 1928, was that of Retford Motor Services, Ltd., operating between Nottingham and Doncaster via Ollerton, which passed to Trent and East Midland jointly, and several other services, which passed to East Midland and Lincolnshire. It was decided to pool the service with East Midland, pro rata to the mileage run by each Company's vehicles. Unfortunately, there were problems with this acquisition, because Doncaster Corporation refused Trent's application for licences for the vehicles taken over. An appeal was lodged with the Ministry of Transport and as a temporary measure, pending its determination, two East Midland buses were garaged at and operated from Trent's Nottingham depot at a charge of 6½d (2.8p) per mile in order to operate the Doncaster route.

The seven AECs acquired were found to be in poor shape mechanically and two were disposed of immediately, but the remaining five were overhauled at a cost of £500 and remained in the fleet until 1930. In due course, the Ministry of Transport held an inquiry into Doncaster's refusal to grant licences to Trent and, following this, the Minister advised that he was unable to support the Council's refusal and suggested that six licences should be granted. As a result, the Council granted the licences, subject to the Company confirming that it was not their intention to apply for licences for other routes in the Borough and undertaking to observe the conditions of the licences.

Problems with the local authority were also encountered at Sheffield where, as part of a plan to develop long distance services, Trent and East Midland had jointly applied to operate a service between Nottingham and Sheffield. The application was refused and it was decided, pending the result of an appeal to the Ministry of Transport, to run the service on a system of through bookings. The appeal took place on 2nd May, 1929 and, during the hearing, the Corporation undertook to approve the service, subject to certain conditions, following which the appeal was withdrawn. However, there is some doubt as to whether the service was ever run, and subsequently a licence was granted by Sheffield in July, 1929, jointly with the LMS and LNER for a service between Sheffield and Nottingham. This was operated only as far as Mansfield by the Sheffield Joint Omnibus Committee, the municipal undertaking in which the two railway companies had a direct interest.

There were plans during 1928 and 1929 to start long distance services to other towns and cities, including London, and licences were applied for in over twenty towns. Five XL coaches were ordered from Midland Red with a view to starting the services in Spring, 1929 but, regrettably, few of the

The takeover of Retford Motor Services in 1928 brought seven 1926 AECs into the fleet. The Retford fleet had included a batch of three AEC 413s with Taylor B30F bodies registered HD 2712-4, as illustrated by this photograph of HD 2713, taken at Trinity Square, Nottingham. The takeover was joint with Lincolnshire and East Midland, to which this particular member of the batch passed, but the other two were taken into the Trent fleet, HD 2712 becoming 1003, and HD 2714 becoming 1004. They were withdrawn in 1930.

proposed services ever ran and, for example, it was not until the 1960s that Trent ran into London on a regular express service and even this was on a restricted basis. It is strange that, despite its position in the heart of the country, Trent never developed into a major express operator. Little clue has been found as to the reason for this and although many express services have been operated over the years, most have been of a seasonal nature. The order for XL coaches was changed to five M type buses to join the other twenty three of this type already on order, although the fact that Midland Red were having problems with the XL due to the heavy coach body on the lightweight SOS chassis may also have been a contributory factor in this decision.

Mention has already been made of the Company's associate membership of the British Electrical Federation, Ltd., and in 1928 a contract was entered into for the Company's petrol supplies to be obtained through BEF. This followed a similar agreement in April, 1927 for the supply of tyres by the Dunlop and Goodyear companies on a mileage basis. Whilst the type of contract used, under which the tyre supplier retains ownership of the casing and 'rents' it to the operator is commonplace now, it was a new development at the time.

There were changes in the holding company's financial arrangements during 1928 when BAT was renamed the Tilling and British Automobile Traction Co., Ltd., (TBAT) following an agreement between BET and Thomas Tilling, Ltd for the pooling of their bus interests. This was something of a tidying up operation in a situation in which, over the years, Tillings had acquired shares in a number of BAT subsidiaries as well as in BAT itself. To remove this anomaly, the share capital of TBAT was increased and most (but not all) subsidiaries directly owned by Thomas Tilling, Ltd and British Electric Traction Co, Ltd were brought into the pool. Both Tillings and BET nominated Directors to the Board of the new enlarged company but, beyond this change in the nature of the parent Company, there was no visible effect on Trent since it was not one of the BAT subsidiaries in which Tillings had held any shares.

In the Budget in April, the Government imposed a new tax on petrol which added about £8,000 a year to the Company's costs over a full year. The Chairman complained that, together with the licence duty, the total taxation amounted to about £20,000, which was more than the annual dividend paid to shareholders. In order to help meet the increased cost of fuel, some cheap ticket facilities, such as bulk discount tickets and "Anywhere" tickets, which had been available for some years, were withdrawn.

Apart from the Retford Motor Services acquisition, there were few service developments in 1928, although the Nottingham-Ilkeston service was again extended to Cotmanhay for a few months. Also, the business of H H Farrer & Sons of Kegworth was offered, but Trent decided not to buy, and the business passed to Barton, in June, 1932.

Negotiations with Higgs & Waller (Melbourne) Ltd., operating between Melbourne and Derby via Chellaston had been in progress, off and on depending on the state of the competition between the two operators, throughout 1928 and the early part of 1929. These were brought to fruition on 30th April, 1929 when Higgs & Waller were taken over, the four elderly AECs joining the fleet as numbers 1005-8 for a while, and Messrs T E Higgs and D G Waller joined the Company's staff, the latter at Nottingham as Road Foreman, and the former at Melbourne as Inspector.

Interestingly, Higgs & Waller's vehicles were equipped with doors and heaters, long before Trent's vehicles boasted such luxury. Some small operators enjoyed local support among the populace and in this instance it is evidenced by the following rhyme which the local children would sing:-

"Travel by Higgs & Waller,
Travel by Higgs & Waller,
The poor old Trent,
Can't pay the rent,
So travel by Higgs & Waller."

There were ten small firms taken over during 1929, plus the purchase from Barton of a Nottingham-Derby via Risley service which they had, rather cheekily, acquired under Trent's nose from Eagle Motor Services, at that time owned by J Turner. The ten included Chapman & Sons, of Belper, and this purchase also bought a small bus station in Belper, which would later be developed into a much larger facility.

During 1928, the four mainline railway companies had obtained bus operating powers by Act of Parliament. Each had small scale bus operations but began to expand their road transport interests by buying into bus operating companies. At first, this action took the form of buying up territorial companies which remained outside the Combines, and both Crosville and the National Omnibus & Transport Company, forerunner of Eastern, Western and Southern National, changed hands in this way, the latter to to all four mainline railway companies jointly, and the former to the LMS. This led to an increase in the share prices of unacquired independent companies and, in order to avoid escalation of these prices by counter-bidding, one against the other, agreement was reached between TBAT and the railway companies whereby the railway companies acquired shares in the bus companies owned by TBAT.

Generally, the shares in the territorial bus companies were acquired by the railway company in whose area the bus company operated, but as Trent's area was served by both the LMS and the LNER, each acquired a share in the company which together equalled that of TBAT. As a result, the railways had equal representation on the Trent board with TBAT, there being two railway officers from the LMS, and one from the LNER, which was roughly in proportion to the two railway shareholdings.

Reference has already been made to the Company's stillborn plans for a network of express services to various towns and cities, and it may have been the railway influence arising from their share in ownership which led to these being abandoned. The railways always jealously guarded their long distance services against road competition, right up until the de-regulation of express coach services under the 1980 Transport Act, when they lost their right of objection and greater competition followed.

There were, however, a number of positive results arising from the railway involvement. As part of the new arrangements, a working agreement was made between the three companies and this provided for the setting up of a Standing Joint Committee of two representatives of Trent and one each from the LMS and the LNER. The Trent representatives were Mr G C Campbell-Taylor, General Manager, and Mr S Ferry, Traffic Manager, and the purpose of this Committee was to determine matters concerning bus services, fares and competition between rail and road services.

The working agreement also provided that the railways would not start to operate any road passenger services within Trent's operating area. Subsequently, the Companies advertised each other's services in their timetables and there were

This map, the original of which was annexed to the working agreement, dated 29th December, 1929, made with the LMS and LNE Railways, is not without interest. Reaching the border towns of Newark, Melton Mowbray, Loughborough, Ashby, Burton on Trent, Uttoxeter, Alfreton and Mansfield, with the isolated fingers reaching to Matlock, Clay Cross and Ollerton, the area within the heavy black line was the operating area agreed for Trent. It was a realistic reflection of the Company's working relationship with the other combine companies, but other substantial operators, outside the main combines, were also present within it. The area south, south west and eastwards from Nottingham was largely occupied by independent Barton, who also had fingers extending from Nottingham to Oxton, and from their base at Chilwell to Ilkeston and to Derby. Trent made little attempt to develop other than the Nottingham-Loughborough corridor in this district, since the area was rather thin, in traffic terms.The centre area, to the north west of Nottingham was occupied by the Balfour Beatty owned Midland General and Notts. & Derbys. Traction companies, in which the railways had no shareholding, and penetration of this area by Trent was also fairly limited, although it has always been good bus country. Thus, it was not until the acquisition of the Barton and Midland General businesses, many years into the future, that the agreed operating area could be fully realised! Even then, there were other developments to vary the area of Trent operations from the boundary shown.

The map was based on the Ordnance Survey map of 1929, which is hereby acknowledged.

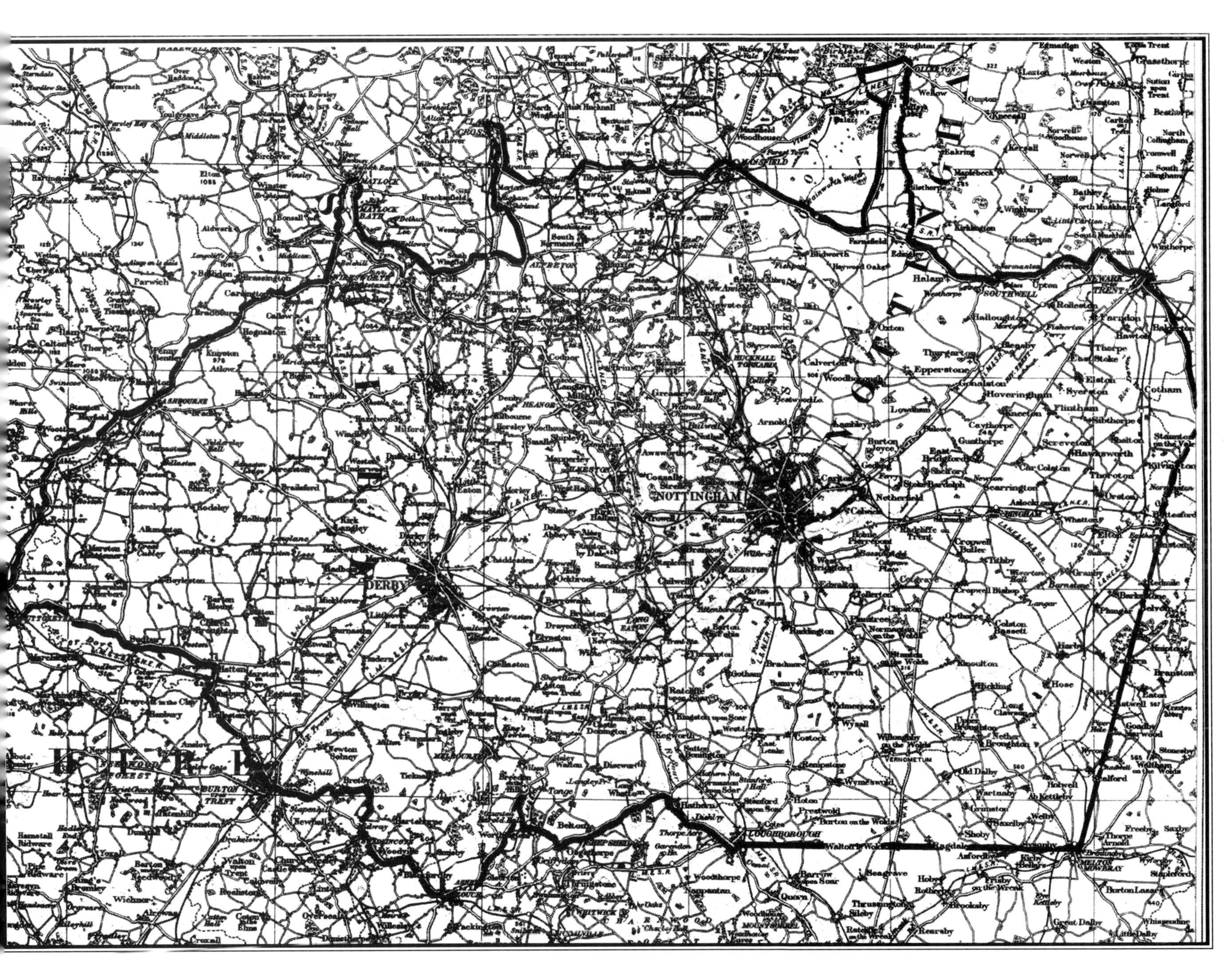
NOTTINGHAM
DERBY
MANSFIELD
MATLOCK
LOUGHBOROUGH
MELTON MOWBRAY
NEWARK
SOUTHWELL
BURTON TRENT
ASHBOURNE
ALFRETON
ILKESTON
HEANOR
BELPER
BEESTON
Long Eaton
Arnold
Hucknall Torkard
Bingham
Kegworth
Castle Donington
Melbourne
Ashby
Shepshed
Coalville
Ollerton
Wirksworth
Brassington
Parwich
Youlgreave
Winster
Calverton
Woodborough
Radcliffe on Trent
Keyworth
Ruddington
Barrow upon Soar
Quorn
Sileby
Rearsby
Asfordby
Scalford
Harby
Long Clawson
Hickling
Old Dalby
Wymeswold
Costock
Sutton Bonington
Breedon
Tonge
Belton
Repton
Willington
Etwall
Church Broughton
Sudbury
Egmanton
Grassthorpe
Collingham
Cromwell
Farndon
Balderton
Cotham
Flintham
Elston
Thurgarton
Epperstone
Oxton
Papplewick
Bleasby
Hoveringham
Gunthorpe
Lowdham
Carlton
Colwick
West Bridgford
Edwalton
Tollerton
Plumtree
Cropwell Bishop
Cropwell Butler
Tithby
Granby
Whatton
Aslockton
Scarrington
Car Colston
Screveton
Hawksworth
Thoroton
Orston
Kilvington
Staunton on the Vale
Bottesford
Redmile
Barkestone
Plungar
Knipton
Croxton
Branston
Eaton
Goadby Marwood
Stonesby
Waltham on the Wolds
Wycomb
Holwell
Ab Kettleby
Wartnaby
Grimston
Saxelby
Welby
Shoby
Rotherby
Frisby on the Wreak
Hoby
Brooksby
Thrussington
Ratcliffe on the Wreak
Seagrave
Walton le Wolds
Prestwold
Hoton
Burton on the Wolds
Cotes
Stanford upon Soar
Normanton upon Soar
Hathern
Dishley
Thorpe Acre
Garendon
Whitwick
Thringstone
Griffydam
Osgathorpe
Worthington
Newbold
Staunton Harold
Ticknall
Hartshorne
Bretby
Stanton
Newhall
Swadlincote
Woodville
Blackfordby
Smisby
Packington
Measham
Donisthorpe
Overseal
Netherseal
Lullington
Walton upon Trent
Rosliston
Coton
Croxall
Alrewas
Wichnor
Yoxall
Barton
Tatenhill
Branston
Rolleston
Anslow
Tutbury
Hanbury
Marchington
Doveridge
Uttoxeter
Sudbury
Foston
Scropton
Hatton
Marston
Egginton
Stretton
Findern
Mickleover
Littleover
Normanton
Chellaston
Swarkestone
Barrow
Stanton by Bridge
Ingleby
Foremark
Newton Solney
Winshill
Stapenhill
Drakelow
Chaddesden
Spondon
Borrowash
Ockbrook
Risley
Breaston
Draycott
Elvaston
Thulston
Shardlow
Aston upon Trent
Weston
Sawley
Thrumpton
Barton in Fabis
Gotham
Bradmore
Bunny
Rempstone
Wysall
Widmerpool
Willoughby on the Wolds
Kinoulton
Colston Bassett
Owthorpe
Normanton on the Wolds
Stanton on the Wolds
Clipston
Tollerton
Stapleford
Sandiacre
Stanton by Dale
Dale Abbey
Stanley
West Hallam
Morley
Breadsall
Little Eaton
Duffield
Kirk Langley
Mackworth
Quarndon
Kedleston
Weston Underwood
Brailsford
Longford
Shirley
Yeaveley
Snelston
Norbury
Mayfield
Clifton
Kniveton
Atlow
Hognaston
Bradbourne
Tissington
Fenny Bentley
Thorpe
Ilam
Calton
Okeover
Mapleton
Turnditch
Shottle
Hazelwood
Milford
Windley
Denby
Codnor
Ripley
Swanwick
Pentrich
Crich
Wingfield
South Wingfield
South Normanton
Pinxton
Selston
Kirkby
Sutton in Ashfield
Tibshelf
Blackwell
Huthwaite
Teversal
Pleasley
Shirebrook
Warsop
Mansfield Woodhouse
Edwinstowe
Clipstone
Rufford
Eakring
Kersall
Kneesall
Ompton
Wellow
Boughton
Laxton
Weston
Sutton on Trent
Carlton on Trent
Norwell
Caunton
Maplebeck
Bilsthorpe
Farnsfield
Edingley
Halam
Kirklington
Winkburn
Hockerton
Bathley
North Muskham
South Muskham
Holme
Langford
Winthorpe
Kelham
Averham
Upton
Rolleston
Fiskerton
Morton
Halloughton
Bleasby
Hawton
Thorpe
East Stoke
Syerston
Sibthorpe
Shelton
Blidworth
Ravenshead
Newstead
Linby
Annesley
Bestwood
Bulwell
Basford
Nuthall
Kimberley
Eastwood
Greasley
Brinsley
Awsworth
Cossall
Strelley
Trowell
Bramcote
Wollaton
Chilwell
Attenborough
Clifton
Wilford
Lenton
Sneinton
Gedling
Burton Joyce
Stoke Bardolph
Netherfield
Shelford
East Bridgford
Newton
Kneeton
Caythorpe
Elton
Langar
Barnstone
Hose
Nether Broughton
Upper Broughton
Melton Mowbray
Thorpe Arnold
Freeby
Saxby
Wyfordby
Stapleford
Burton Lazars
Kirby Bellars
Great Dalby
Little Dalby
Whissendine
Eye Kettleby
Woodhouse Eaves
Mountsorrel
Rothley
Woodthorpe
Nanpantan
Charnwood Forest
Swannington
Heather
Ibstock
Bardon Hill
Leicester
Nottingham
Derby
Stafford
Vernometum
Needwood Forest
Matlock Bath
Matlock Bank
Darley
Rowsley
Bakewell
Hartington
Monyash
Over Haddon
Elton
Aldwark
Bonsall
Cromford
Lea
Holloway
Dethick
Ashover
Brackenfield
Wessington
Higham
Shirland
Morton
Stretton
Clay Cross
Tupton
North Wingfield
Hardwick
Heath
Ault Hucknall
Glapwell
Scarcliffe
Bolsover
Palterton
Langwith
Sookholme
Warsop
Budby
Thoresby
Carburton
Perlethorpe
Ollerton
Kirton
Walesby
Egmanton
L.M.S.R.
L.N.E.R.
R. Trent
R. Dove
R. Derwent
R. Soar
Fosse Way
Sherwood Forest

This view, taken in July, 1930, shows SOS vehicles at The George Refreshment Rooms and Garage at Langworth, near Lincoln. This was the half way halt on the Skegness service, and year old SOS M, 405, is pausing on the return to Derby, with an unidentified Q, heading for Nottingham, waiting behind. The vehicle with the emergency exit open is 410, another M. Note the period styles of dress - the man in plus fours, the man with a bowler hat, and the white dustcoat of one of the bus drivers.

limited attempts at co-ordination by arranging for some buses to call at railway stations at times suitable to connect with trains. The general nature of these arrangements was comparable with those put in place in the other territorial companies where the railways had acquired substantial shareholdings. Arrangements were also made for certain railway passenger services to be replaced by buses where the low level of traffic could be served more economically.

Development of vehicles was rapid during this period, and the 30 SOS M type vehicles added to the fleet during 1929 were a great improvement on the previous year's QL types. They took the fleet numbers 400 - 429, with registrations in the block CH 81xx, although not in order. Most had Brush bodies, except the last five, which had Ransomes, and they retained much of the characteristic SOS appearance but had a much lower build and twin wheels on the rear axle. They were known as "Madams", because they were reputedly intended to encourage more women to travel and shop more, and they incorporated pairs of thick bucket seats which were very comfortable. Their arrival enabled a number of the old Tilling-Stevens and Thornycrofts to be withdrawn from service, together with an assortment of vehicles acquired with small operators' businesses.

The West Bridgford municipal transport undertaking, with its characteristic maroon and deep cream vehicles, was notable as one of the few operated by an Urban District Council, rather than a City or Borough Council. During 1929, thoughts turned briefly to its take over by Trent, but this came to nothing and the undertaking survived independently until take over by neighbouring Nottingham in 1968, following boundary changes.

These were still the formative years of the bus industry and there were many negotiations and agreements reached intended to aid orderly operation and examples of this were two made with Lincolnshire (nowadays operating as Road Car), firstly for joint operation of services between Nottingham and Grantham, and between Nottingham and Lincoln. Secondly, as Lincolnshire had paid £500 to a small operator, Albert Warburton, to leave their routes, it was decided that Trent would pay £150 towards this. Quite how Warburton came to be operating in this area is unknown, since he had been based in Leeds and sold to West Yorkshire in July, 1927. Possibly he moved to Lincolnshire after this.

Joint operations of this kind developed in many places throughout the country where services crossed inter-Company boundaries, because they were a convenient way of getting the first and last journeys of the day covered without large amounts of dead mileage on positioning journeys to the remote end of the route. They also helped to share out the traffic equitably amongst those operators having a legitimate interest. Trent has run joint operations with most of its larger neighbours over the years, as well as with the municipal operators at Derby and Nottingham.

In the Autumn, the Chairman, Mr (formerly Alderman) William Hart died and his place was taken by Mr R J Howley, the Deputy Chairman. Although Mr Hart, a prominent local business man and politician, rendered services to the Company, these were, it would seem, mainly to do with local negotiations, such as with land owning neighbours and local authorities.

No doubt the fact that he was well known locally was helpful in getting the right decision or in breaking log jams in negotiations. His accountancy practice also provided the Company's accountancy services in the early days. However, the main figures from the operational stand-point were R J Howley and J C Moth, with O C Power also playing a part after his appointment in the early twenties. Mr Howley, as a BET man, seems to have been especially influential on the Company's early development.

Barton Transport Ltd once again featured in the deliberations of the Board, but a decision was deferred pending publication of Barton's balance sheet and an examination of their books and accounts. A conference of representatives of Trent, the LMS and LNE railways took place over this matter, but nothing further came of it.

Of special interest on the services front was the inauguration, on 15th May, 1929 of express services between Derby and Manchester and between Nottingham and Manchester. Both operated jointly with North Western of Stockport, the Derby service ran via Ashbourne, Leek, Macclesfield and Stockport, terminating at Manchester's Lower Moseley Street Bus Station, in the south of the city centre. The Nottingham service ran via Ilkeston, Heanor, Ripley, Matlock, Buxton, New Mills and Stockport, also terminating at Lower Moseley Street.

In April, 1930, following protracted negotiations over the allocation of revenue, a joint service numbered 2B was instigated between Derby and Buxton via Belper and Matlock, combining into one the separate services previously run between Derby and Matlock by Trent and between Buxton and Matlock by North Western. It was decided to operate the service on a "pool" basis, with each Company taking revenue in proportion to the mileage operated.

Other service developments were less significant, being fairly minor revisions, although there was a new Saturday service, 36, between Nottingham and Ollerton. This was soon withdrawn, although later reinstated as part of the service to Doncaster operated jointly with East Midland, following resolution of the licensing problems with Doncaster Corporation, described earlier.

In addition, the Derby-Hatton-Uttoxeter service,

TRENT Holiday Tours, 1929.

Before arranging your Summer Holidays this year enquire at the TRENT Offices for our Holiday Programme.

10-DAY TOURS IN SCOTLAND.

10-DAY TOURS IN DEVON AND CORNWALL.

5-DAY TOURS IN NORTH WALES.

5-DAY TOURS IN LAKE DISTRICT.

5-DAY TOURS TO BOURNEMOUTH AND NEW FOREST.

Send a Post Card for full particulars.

TAKE A TRENT HOLIDAY THIS YEAR.

For many years, a regular programme of holiday tours was run, and a fleet of suitable coaches was kept for the purpose. The QC and QLC charabancs, of 1927 and 1928 respectively would have been used to operate the programme for 1929, as advertised on this page from a contemporary timetable booklet. The invitation to send a post card for full particulars is a reminder of the slower pace of life in those times!

which had run on Wednesdays and Fridays was withdrawn, sometime around May, 1930. The section of route between Derby and Hatton was covered by other services, and the section between Hatton and Uttoxeter, which was in any event rather thin, was left to PMT, with their Derby-Hanley service.

1930 was a landmark year in the industry, for Parliament passed the 1930 Road Traffic Act, which introduced road service licensing for bus services. This set the background for the industry for over 50 years until all was swept away, initially by the 1980 Transport Act for express services over 30 miles and, later, by the 1985 Transport Act for other services.

Prior to the 1930 Act, licensing had been in the hands of local authorities with varying degrees of efficacy and consistency. Initially, they licensed crews, and many (including Nottingham and Derby) licensed routes operated as well. Subsequently, some Councils also licensed timetables, but often with little control over the services operated, compared with those actually licensed. Licences could often be obtained fairly easily and services were, to a considerable extent run as a free for all.

Another reason for implementing the Act was the differing requirements which neighbouring authorities had in relation to vehicle size and the positions of doors and emergency exits and other matters. This led to difficulties for operators running in the area of more than one Council.

The larger companies, such as Trent, claimed to run always to timetables and by and large did so, although, as already described, Trent were not averse to a bit of "swinging and chasing" against their smaller competitors when they were proving particularly troublesome in "pirating" their services.

The effect was often chaotic and unpredictable, but the new Act changed everything. Licensing was taken out of the hands of local authorities and passed to the Ministry of Transport. The Ministry divided the country into some ten Traffic Areas, plus one for Scotland, each of which was presided over by a Chairman of the Traffic Commissioners. Trent was at that time covered by the East Midland Traffic Area, with offices in Nottingham and the first Chairman of the Traffic Commissioners was Mr J H Stirk.

The Traffic Commissioners were responsible for licensing all services in their area. In the event that a service crossed the boundary between two or more Traffic Areas, it was necessary to obtain further licences (known as backing licences) in each Traffic Area.

The effects of the new system were two fold. Firstly, it granted a virtual monopoly on any route where an operator could show itself to be well established. Secondly, it controlled timetables and fares and by this means it brought stability to operations. If licences to operate any new services were applied for, then existing operators could object, as could the railways and local authorities. Essentially, once the new system was in place and fully operational, it was for any new applicant to demonstrate that their proposed service would be in the public interest.

In parallel with the changes to service licensing, there were changes to vehicle licensing resulting in much higher standards of vehicle condition as buses and coaches were required to have regular inspections and have a valid Certificate of Fitness.

The new rules proved too much for many of the small operators. For example, several sold out to Trent in 1929 and no doubt some of these were anticipating the effect of the 1930 Act. However, this trend accelerated and in the period between 1930 and 1935, no less than 39 operators sold out to Trent. This reflected the situation in many other areas of the country, as services were gradually

TRENT MOTOR TRACTION CO., LTD.

On Tuesday, August 12th, 1930

THE SERVICES OPERATED ON THE

DERBY, MELBOURNE and SWADLINCOTE

ROUTE, by

Wagg's Super-Service 'Buses

will be taken over by The TRENT MOTOR TRACTION COMPANY, LTD., who will run INCREASED SERVICES from the 'Bus Station.

Messrs. WAGG'S Return Tickets will be accepted on any 'bus on the above routes, up to and including Saturday, Aug. 23rd.

For TRENT Motor Traction Co., Ltd.,
G. C. CAMPBELL-TAYLOR, General Manager.

The year 1930 saw a small flurry of takeover activity, doubtless at least partly in anticipation of the effects of the 1930 Road Traffic Act causing some small operators to consider offering their businesses for sale. Each time a takeover took place, notices were posted in vehicles to give advance warning to the travelling public. Three vehicles were acquired with the Wagg's business, taken over as advertised by this notice.

concentrated into the hands of the large, territorial operators.

It must also be remembered, however, that once the new licensing system came into operation, there was more incentive for the large companies to take over their competitors. This was because, although the licences could not be bought and sold, the large company could purchase the goodwill of the business from a competitor and was normally able to have the right to a licence transferred, and a replacement licence issued in its own name, thus acquiring the right to oppose a further licence being granted to a new competitor.

During 1930 there were many negotiations between Trent and the small independents. Those brought to a successful conclusion were:

E Bramley, "Prince of Wales Service", Cotmanhay
Cox & Pollard " TPS Omnibus Service" and "Cox's Service", Derby
Turner & Wagg, "Wagg's Super Service", Derby
Bayliss and Sons, Ashbourne

Some of these were of particular interest. The Bramley takeover was joint with the Midland General subsidiaries Williamson's Garage and Dawson's Enterprise. These had been taken over by Midland General in 1928 and were run as subsidiaries until 1931. Two of the Williamsons were taken on by Midland General and one, W Williamson, eventually became its General Manager which post he held for a considerable number of years. Bramley's route was Ilkeston - Nottingham on which both Trent and Williamson were active, along with others, and hence the joint takeover for the sum of £2,500 each.

Dawson's Enterprise Omnibus Company, Limited was also a joint operator, since this was a Midland General subsidiary which had, like Williamson's, been taken over but not wound up for a period of time. This was a measure aimed at avoiding the possibility of the local authorities granting licences to a new operator. Within two years, the 1930 Act, described above, was in operation and this was no longer relevant, so the two Companies could be wound up.

Cox and Pollard had been quite unusual amongst the small independents in running a Leyland TD1 double decker, although this had gone by the time of the Trent takeover. Cox had run at fares considerably lower fares than Trent, which had caused the Company some loss of traffic.

Bayliss had really led Trent quite a merry dance on the Ashbourne road over the years from 1921 and by 1930 he had a respectable fleet of eleven vehicles. Competition had been intense and there was a high level of animosity between the two, with tales of running each other off the road and at least one prosecution being reported against a Bayliss driver for precisely that.

Fares had been cut to quite extraordinary levels, and the animosity was such that negotiations for purchase were undertaken by intermediaries. Initially, this had been by Mr Rogerson of W & G Rogerson Ltd, of Burslem, Staffs, which Company had been taken over by BET, and operational

The Bayliss fleet became quite substantial, and eleven vehicles passed to Trent, including four Leylands, three Albions, two Dennis, a Commer and a Bristol. This typical snapshot shows some of the Bayliss crews with RA 5365, a 1928 Leyland Lion PLSC3 with Leyland B32F bodywork. The vehicle took fleet number 1306 on take-over by Trent in 1930, and lasted there until withdrawal in 1934, the Leylands being kept longer than the other models.

As the Company's network of seaside express services developed, vehicles were frequently spot hired at busy times to cope with the crowds. This unusual Crossley, owned by Norfolk Motor Services, of Great Yarmouth, loads for the return journey to its home town, whilst operating on hire to Trent. Note the luggage being loaded onto the roof rack, the outward opening door, after the style of a car, and the large nearside front windscreen, on which has been placed the "On hire to Trent" sticker.

control passed to Potteries Electric Traction Co, Ltd, in July, 1928. The Rogerson company was then used by BET for a variety of purposes (including the construction of a garage at Newcastle Under Lyme for PET!) and in this instance was used as an intermediary. Later, negotiations were by the LMS Railway, Trent being brought in only at the end, taking over the business on 7th December, 1930. The service via Brailsford was extended to Uttoxeter as 4B, whilst the service via Cross o' th' Hands became 18.

Other negotiations in progress at the time were with Barton but, as usual in those days, these came to nought, although the railways had also been involved and had gone to the trouble of carrying out an extensive valuation. In another case, the Mansfield District Tramways, Ltd, an offer of £16 000 for the company had been turned down by Sir Joseph Nall, Chairman, but a further offer was made of £10 000 for the services and garage, but not the vehicles. It was suggested that the purchase price and services should be apportioned with East Midland but, although further meetings were held, it was decided not to pursue the matter.

New services started in 1930 were:

38, Nottingham-Granby, via Gamston, Tollerton, Cotgrave, Cropwell Bishop and Langar.

12A Nottingham-Chesterfield, via Hucknall Road, East Kirkby, Sutton in Ashfield and Mansfield. Joint with East Midland.

New vehicle deliveries in 1930 were of some interest because, in addition to a solitary SOS M, number 409, purchased to replace one of the 1929 batch destroyed by fire, they comprised 17 SOS CODs with Carlyle bodies. Taking fleetnumbers 450-466 and registrations CH 8900-16, these were nominally designed by Mr P G Stone-Clarke, Trent's Chief Engineer and the designation probably indicated Clarke's Own Design.

Based on the SOS XL chassis design, these vehicles had a sleeker and more modern appearance than the Madams, brought about partially by the elimination of the rather idiosyncratic porch type entrance of the earlier design and thus having a continuous roof line. The appearance was made sleeker by the use of longer window bays and the use of a more rounded rear dome with a radiussed side window at the back. When compared with what had gone before, they looked quite attractive. Internally, they were equipped with full length overhead luggage racks, in place of the nets used previously, and had bucket seats similar to those on the Madams, except that they were moquette covered, rather than leather. They were intended initially for long distance services, such as Manchester and the coastal expresses, but were used on other routes as well. Their arrival enabled a number of second hand vehicles to be disposed off, as well as some of the Tilling-Stevens deckers.

Following on from the acquisition of an interest in the Company by the railways, certain railway services were withdrawn, and arrangements made for Trent to provide alternative facilities by bus. From 1st June, 1930, the LMS withdrew their Ripley-Derby service and Trent extended some journeys on their Alfreton-Ripley-Derby service to terminate at the LMS station in Midland Road. From the same date, some journeys on the Derby-Ashbourne main road service were similarly extended to the LMS Station. Further changes followed, and from 23rd September 1930, Trent altered their Melbourne service to pick up at Midland Road station. The LMS stated that these changes were due to the low number of passengers carried, claiming that trains had run with as few as half a dozen passengers. As Castle Donington Station was also affected by these changes, it seems likely that services to that town were altered to pick up at the LMS Station at the same date.

The weather does not look promising for Nottingham holidaymakers heading for Skegness on this Brush bodied SOS COD in August, 1931! Nominally designed by the Company's Chief Engineer, and initially numbered 465, CH 8915 was re-numbered 215 in 1932, and remained with Trent until 1940, when it passed to Midland Red, in the early days of the war.

This photograph conveys very well the layout and architecture of Aslin's new Central Bus Station in The Moreledge, Derby, when it was new in 1933, as referred to on page 49. It was evidently taken around the time the station opened, as the signboard of Derby contractor Gee, Walker & Slater is still in position. One of Barton's Leyland Lions occupies pole position for Nottingham, on platform 4, whilst Trent has a similar position on platform 2 for the same destination with a Madam. One can almost imagine them racing away to steal the lead at the appointed time of departure. Note the London & North Eastern Railway parcel van, pulling away in the fore ground. Visible in the centre background is the original Derby Cattle Market, often used as a parking area by Trent, in post war years, but obliterated beneath the Inner Ring Road in the late sixties and early seventies.

Chapter Four
Restricted Competition 1931-39

A total of twenty eight new vehicles were delivered in 1931, these being sixteen SOS IM6s, which became the main vehicles used for the Manchester and other long distance services, alongside the CODs, and twelve IM4s, all with Short 34 seat bodywork of a style similar to the earlier CODs. Numbered 120-35, CH 9900-15 the IM6 models, with six cylinder engine were, naturally, more powerful and they featured a new "silent third" gearbox. The IM4s took fleetnumbers 470-481, CH 9916-27, and all were a development of the previous M models, the new designation meaning "Improved Madam".

Other vehicles to join the fleet were five Leylands following the takeover of Reynolds Bros of Bulwell in February, 1931. One of these, a Lion LT2, had been delivered new, but not used by the time of takeover, and was first registered by Trent as CH 9750. It took fleet number 1310 and remained with Trent until 1936. Reynolds had provided opposition on the Nottingham-Hucknall via Bulwell service and the Trent District Traffic Superintendent of the day reported that they repeatedly ran more buses from Huntingdon Street than they were licensed to do, citing one Saturday afternoon and evening on which Reynolds ran 63 departures compared with a licensed timetable indicating 33! The takeover of this operator was joint with Nottingham Corporation, each paying £7625.

Reynolds had been something of a thorn in the side of the Corporation as well, since they had persisted in picking up along the tram route, thus taking the Corporation's traffic. As already described, Trent had previously reached agreement with the Corporation that they would add the tram fare onto theirs and pay the extra to the Corporation. The result of this was that passengers ignored Trent buses and waited for Reynolds instead. Following the takeover, additional journeys were incorporated into the timetable for service 30, and there was inter-availability of return tickets between Trent and the Corporation.

The 1930 Road Traffic Act has already been mentioned and, as well as affecting the licensing of services, there was also a requirement to make vehicles comply with certain standards. Against this background, most of Trent's vehicles required new windscreen wipers, additional grab handles, together with first aid boxes. Some also needed alterations to the petrol filler and a few also required attention to their exhaust systems.

In November, 1931, Arthur Farnsworth's Blue Bird Service of Huthwaite, operating between Mansfield and Hucknall, via Sutton in Ashfield was taken over. The purchase, for £3500, included five vehicles which were immediately resold for £700, and not used by Trent. The timetable for this service, which had previously been run by R Johnson & Sons, of Annesley Woodhouse, was designed largely to run in front of Trent, so that the takeover enabled a significant improvement in takings to be achieved, and the timetable for service 30, Nottingham-Mansfield, via Hucknall was modified to suit. A Farnsworth & Co were a firm of local coachbuilders, and they had acquired the Blue Bird business on a short term basis, reputedly in settlement of unpaid bills.

The Road Traffic Act 1930 had been effective from 1st April, 1931 and by the end of the year, the new licensing regime was having an impact in compelling operators to run in a more ordered

CH 9750, the Leyland Lion LT2 that Trent acquired with the business of Reynolds Bros of Bulwell, was involved in an accident, in icy conditions, one wintry morning on Nottingham Road in Spondon. Photographed under recovery for the local newspaper, it is just possible to see the vehicle's fleetnumber plate, 1310, on the damaged side panel, beneath the driver's window. Note how the destination box has been converted to take the standard Trent route number stencil box, and doubtless the destination itself was shown on an angled slip board above the bonnet, similar to the practice on the SOSs.

fashion and to co-ordinate with each other more effectively. This effect, together with the purchase of various small operators led one District Traffic Superintendent to report that instances of so called swinging and chasing had become few and far between.

During the year, the Company made application for licences for 211 services, most of which were granted, and made representations or objected in the case of over 400 applications by other operators. As a result of the representations, they had been able to arrange for fare agreements and timetable co-ordination affecting some fifty operators and 21 Trent routes. This had caused an enormous volume of work for the Company's officials, and the General Manager, Mr Campbell-Taylor had learned many of the skills of advocacy in presenting the Company' case in the Traffic Court.

Despite the close association between Trent and the railway companies, (it will be recalled that both the LMS and LNER together held 50% of the company's shares) there was an argument in the Traffic Court with the LMS when Trent and East Midland applied jointly to run six journeys a day between Derby and Chesterfield. Mr Campbell-Taylor put the case for the joint operators and stated that they received many inquiries for through running because the bus journey could only be accomplished with two changes on the direct route and one change on the indirect route. The two bus companies lost the argument and it was not until the mid fifties that through running was achieved, as will be described later.

The Company found themselves in trouble with the Traffic Commissioner when, with the April 1931 timetable, a new service, 1A, was started between Derby and Alfreton via Coxbench, Horsley and Kilburn Toll Bar. Subsequently, they were instructed to apply for a licence and the service was temporarily suspended whilst this was done. However, the licence was refused, and the service could not be resumed!

Service 34D, Nottingham-Southwell was modified in the May, 1932 timetable, so that 34D ran via Lowdham, Hoveringham and Halloughton on Wednesdays and Sundays, 34G ran via Lowdham, Bleasby and Fiskerton on Wednesdays, Fridays and Saturdays, with 34H running via Lowdham, Epperstone and Gonalstone on Tuesday, Thursday and Saturday. However, 34G and 34H were not shown in the September timetable, and only the Wednesday and Sunday journeys on the most direct route, 34D ran after that, because it was deemed a "policy" route.

The term policy route is taken to mean that, despite a poor financial return, the service was kept running to prevent any other operator from taking up the licence. However, it was reduced to Sundays only in 1934, and renumbered 74 in 1935, being withdrawn altogether in 1939, when services were greatly curtailed following the outbreak of war.

New deliveries for 1932 consisted of a further 24 IM4s, 232-56, RC 407-26, 537-41, with Brush bodies, and 10 IM6s, 136-45, RC 901-10, all with Short bodywork, both types of similar style to the previous year's deliveries, but they introduced plum coloured leather for the internal upholstery, in place of the brown which had been used before. They also introduced the Derby Borough registration mark RC to the fleet for the first time, the previous CH marks having reached 9999.

From September, 1932, through bookings to Liverpool became available, using the Trent/North Western Manchester services and changing at that

The first vehicles to introduce the RC series of registrations to the fleet were the 1932 SOS IM4s and IM6s. Here, 246, RC 421, one of the IM4s of that year with four cylinder engine and Brush B34F body awaits service to Mansfield on the indirect route via Hucknall and Sutton in Ashfield. The brackets above the side windows were intended to carry large advertisement boards, although these do not always seem to have been used.

city onto the Liverpool services operated jointly by North Western and Lancashire United.

The pace of takeover activity accelerated in 1932, with no less than thirteen operators selling out in one way or another, as listed below:

January 1932	P & J W Poundall, Belper.
March 1932	J W Longdon, Mason's Bus Service, Derby.
March 1932	Mrs L Green's Blue Glider Motor Service, Wymeswold.
April 1932	E Barlow, Belper.
April 1932	J Clewes, Spondon Ex-Servicemen's, Spondon.
April 1932	W Liewsley, Liewsley's Bus Service Spondon.
May 1932	E G Buxton, Vincent's Reliance, Ockbrook.
May 1932	F H Rolstone, Vincent's Devonian, Borrowash.
May 1932	H O Oxenham, Orange Coaches, Borrowash.
July 1932	J W Harwood, Costock
August 1932	Alfreton Bus Association, various operators.
August 1932	S P Radford, Mayfield
October 1932	City Coaches, Ltd, Derby.

Mrs Green ran between Nottingham and Loughborough and Harwood ran between Loughborough and Costock, the takeover of his service being joint with R E Horspool, of Loughborough, who was also operating between Loughborough and Nottingham. Most of Mrs Green's Blue Glider timings were incorporated into Trent's existing service 31, and although the Traffic Commissioner did not allow the Company to run all of the journeys, the position following the takeover was reported as "very satisfactory".

Clewes and Liewsly operated a joint service serving Spondon from Derby, and their takeovers coincided. The same applied in the case of Buxton, Rolstone and Oxenham, although this time the service involved was Derby-Ockbrook, via Borrowash. No vehicles were involved in any of these takeovers.

The Alfreton Bus Association was a group of small operators working in co-operative fashion and they retained a number of other services after this takeover. However, the remaining services were subsequently taken over by Midland General.

The Poundall service, became 14 in the Trent timetable for February, 1932, and the Radford service, Ashbourne-Leek became 19 in the September timetable, following that takeover. The City Coaches transaction was simply a covenant to withdraw an application for excursions and tours licences from Derby, and to close their business.

Only three small operators succumbed to takeover in 1933. C W Rhodes' Rhodeland Motor Services of Derby, whose Derby-Wirksworth service was taken over in March and became service 20 in the Trent timetable, operated five vehicles and sold out for £6 000. This service had been run for ten years and except for market days, was one of the few in the county with no competition.

Later, on 3rd April, J Henshaw and F Upton, of Jacksdale sold their "White Lion Service" running between Alfreton and Spondon via Jacksdale and Ripley to serve the Celanese factory. Finally, on 12th December, J W Taylor's Maroon Service of Whatstandwell, operating between Whatstandwell and Ripley via Crich and Bull Bridge was taken over, becoming Trent service 15A, changing to 21 soon afterwards. The remaining part of Taylor's business was sold to Alfreton Motor Transport Co, which was later sold to North Western and Midland General, in parts on separate occasions.

Two major infrastructure events occurred in 1933, for a new modern garage was opened in Nottingham, and the new municipal bus station came into use in Derby. There was much discussion amongst operators about the new Derby bus station which required them to move from the established street locations at The Spot, Bold Lane and Cheapside, whilst Trent, of course, had their

Trent 243, one of the 1932 IM4s, inaugurates Derby's new bus station after the Mayor, Ald A E Moult, JP, just visible on the left of the picture, had cut the ceremonial tape. Note the large crowd present to witness the event.

existing off street facility in Albert Street. Some operators were concerned that their revised route into the town centre would be congested by trams, but Trent were happy to move and rented platforms 2 and 3, together with the offices located thereon.

The new bus station, which was considered a model of its type at the time, was owned by the Council and had been designed by C H Aslin, the Borough Architect of the day, who later became an architect of some note, being a one time President of the Royal Institute of British Architects, and later becoming the first County Architect at Hertfordshire County Council. He had undertaken the Derby scheme as part of a major redevelopment of the Morledge area, to incorporate the new Council House, the Bus Station and also a new outdoor market, although latterly the market has been relocated to the Eagle Centre and the Crown Court now stands on its former site, next to the Bus Station.

Although subjected to some modifications over the years, particularly when the Inner Ring Road was constructed, the essential character of the bus station remained unchanged at the time of writing in early 1998. Badly in need of refurbishment and locally listed as being of architectural and historic merit, it was about to be re-developed - a sad move for historians, but potentially offering better facilities for Trent passengers.

The new station opened on Monday 3rd October, 1933, and one of Trent's vehicles, 243 (RC 418), an IM4 of 1932, was the first to use the new facility. The lease on the Albert Street premises was then handed back to the Corporation which, for many years, used the old bus station for storing its own surplus buses during off peak periods of the day. However, this use had long ceased when the building was demolished in the late 1980s to make way for some shops.

At the Company's invitation, the new depot at Manvers Street, Nottingham was opened on 26th May, 1933 by Mr J H Stirk, Chairman of the East Midland Traffic Commissioners. The new depot replaced smaller adjoining premises which were sold to Nottingham Corporation and remain in use by Nottingham City Transport, Ltd as an annex to their Parliament Street Depot, although much modified and unrecognisable.

With increased urban development around the outskirts of Derby, the Corporation sought to expand the Borough boundary to include these areas. This could have adversely affected Trent's interests, since the Council would then have powers to run buses within the additional areas already served by the Company, and this caused great concern. However, agreement was eventually reached with the Corporation, giving Trent protection in the disputed areas.

Negotiations took place with Sir Joseph Nall, Chairman of the Balfour Beatty bus companies regarding the possible takeover of the Ebor Bus Co, Ltd of Mansfield by Trent, East Midland, Midland General and Mansfield District. However, little progress was made and Ebor was eventually taken over by the British Transport Commission and handed over to Mansfield District alone in 1950.

The service between Nottingham and Cotmanhay, taken over jointly with Williamson's Garage and Dawson's Enterprise in 1930, has already been mentioned. Although retained as subsidiaries of Midland General, the two companies were wound up in 1931 and the joint operation was thereafter with Midland General. However, there was concern that Notts and Derby Traction (a sister company to Midland General) would lose traffic on the section of its Hallam Fields-Cotmanhay trolleybus route between the junction of Brook Street, on Nottingham Road, just inside the Ilkeston boundary, and Cotmanhay.

In order to overcome this there had been an arrangement under which protective fares were charged over the section of Nottingham Road from Brook Street junction into Ilkeston town centre, and the buses did not run at all between Ilkeston and Cotmanhay. However, in 1933 this was changed and it was agreed to hand over to Notts and Derby two thirds of the receipts derived from purely local traffic and the agreement not to operate buses to Cotmanhay was terminated.

There were no major service initiatives during 1933, although a minor new service from Loughborough to Markfield Sanatorium was started on 26th February and ran on Sundays and special visiting days. At first, this was un-numbered, but acquired the route number 42 in Spring 1934.

"The only thing it doesn't do is speak" claimed the newspaper report accompanying this photograph showing a smartly attired Trent conductor with the new Setright Insert ticket machine. Journalistic licence, perhaps, but the new machine was certainly a major advance on the old Bell Punch machine which it gradually replaced.

Vehicle developments in 1933 were the delivery of a further 25 IM4s, 257-81, RC 1276-1300 these having Short bodywork. However, in addition, the 25 Qs numbered 950-74 delivered in 1927 were rebuilt with a considerable effect on their appearance.

Early in 1934, two Setright ticket machines were purchased. These were "Insert" model machines, in which a pre-printed ticket with a blank space at each end was inserted into a slot in the front of the machine, and validated by the conductor turning a handle on the side which printed the date, value and stage detail on a blank portion of the ticket, having first set these values using a set of rotatable rings, also on the side of the machine.

More of these machines were, over a period of several years, to supersede the previous Bell Punch machines and offered considerable accounting and waybilling advantages, since a record of tickets issued and pence taken appeared in two small transparent panels on the machine. This was a great

One of the stylish and elegant SOS ONs delivered in 1934, the only new vehicle intake that year, referred to on page 52. Note the four bay construction, the tapered window pillars, and the outswept skirt panels of the Duple DP32R bodywork . The vehicles were used on longer distance and express services, as here, where 683, RC 1803 was caught on layover at the parking area opposite Manchester's Lower Mosley Street bus station in September 1934, having run in on the X1 or X2 service from Derby or Nottingham.

the punchings had to be extracted from the Bell Punch machine and counted individually by clerical staff to check the takings against the tickets issued. However, the disadvantage was that statistics of the individual fares issued were no longer available.

Only twelve new vehicles were purchased for 1934, but what vehicles they were! Midland Red had newly introduced its SOS ON type chassis to take advantage of the then maximum permitted length for single deckers of 27ft 6ins (8.38m) and it featured a six cylinder petrol engine with the silent third gearbox used on the earlier IM6s. However, instead of the usual Midland Red style body, these had stylish 32 seat dual purpose bodies of the "Rodney" type by Duple.

Numbered 680-91 and fitted with heaters, these were quite sumptuous vehicles for the day and generated some good spreads for the Company in several of the local newspapers. They were put to work on seaside services, the two Manchester services, the Doncaster service and also on the Nottingham-Derby service against Barton's Leylands.

During the Summer of 1934, Trent's first oil engined vehicle took to the road when 265, one of the IM4s delivered the previous year, was fitted with a Gardner engine. This was, of course, longer than the SOS engine, and so the bonnet and radiator protruded several inches beyond the cab. The drawback for drivers was that when changing gear, the engine revs were slow to die, and this made the crash change, which required double de-clutching, very slow. However, it was a very good, reliable starter, and for this reason was stationed at Wirksworth for a good many years. It saw use as a tree cutting vehicle when its service days were over.

During July, 1934, half a dozen buses were taken on loan from PMT for a period. These were SOS Standards from the original batch constructed by Midland Red on Tilling-Stevens frames before their own production was fully under way.

Two concurrent takeovers effective from 1st July, 1934 were those of Boxall's, owned by W Haywood, of Cotmanhay, and his brother J H Haywood of Shepshed, Leicestershire, who had acquired the business from Boxall's around 1930. Also, Blue Bus Services (Derby), Ltd., which was owned by Messrs Whitehall & Brannan, and is not to be confused with the similarly named service owned by Tailby & George, of Willington, which ran between Derby and Burton until takeover by Derby Corporation in 1973. Although the two agreements were dated differently, the effective dates, 1st July, were the same, so there may have been a link of some kind.

W Haywood ran a Derby-Cotmanhay service via Ilkeston, and Blue Bus ran Derby-Ilkeston, both using the same route via Morley and Smalley Common. Trent already ran service 10, Derby-Ilkeston via Chaddesden, Stanley and West Hallam and, following the takeover, these two services were merged and given the number 10B, or 10C in case of certain journeys extended to Cotmanhay. The earlier revisions to the agreement with Notts and Derby, made in 1933 and permitting Trent to run to Cotmanhay, became of relevance in the case of this takeover, and perhaps the agreement was altered in anticipation.

More minor takeovers during the year were of a service run by J H Wood between Alfreton and Ripley, via Leabrooks and Somercotes, and the purchase from Midland General of excursions from Alfreton which they had acquired with the business of J H Booth of Westhouses. The ex Wood service received the route number 101.

An interesting statistic is that departure charges from Derby bus station were fixed for the year at £385 for 220,000 departures.

Several minor new services started during 1934. 9D ran on Sunday, Tuesday Wednesday and Friday from Derby to the tiny village of Dale Abbey, near Ilkeston, via Spondon Village and Ockbrook Lane End, although it will be recalled that Dale Abbey was already served by a Fridays only service. 3C was a circular from Derby serving Cavendish, Twyford, Swarkestone and Chellaston. 22 was Derby-Horsley, via Breadsall Moor, Morley Moor and Smalley Mill taken over in July from Whitehall & Brannan with their Derby-Ilkeston service, and running on Fridays and Saturdays. Service 20A ran Derby, Allestree, Duffield, Hazel Green to Blackbrook. Interestingly, when the application to transfer the licence came before the Traffic Commissioners, a licence condition imposed required the use of a vehicle of 30cwt or under, during the winter months. We can but speculate what vehicle Trent used for the purpose!

Finally, on 31st December, 1934, the Eagle Services of S O Stevenson were purchased, bringing a daily service from Derby to Cavendish via Sunnyhill which took the number 49 and a Friday and Saturday service from Derby to Stenson, which was numbered 50.

Samuel Oscar Stevenson was an unusual person to be running buses, as he was the General Manager of Kennings Garage in Derby. Kennings were dealers for Morris Commercial and it seems that local operators H S North and J Turner of Findern bought buses from Kennings but were unable to meet all the hire purchase payments. As a result, Stevenson took them over and ran the services.

Stevenson ran this business as a sideline, but with the knowledge of Sir George Kenning and, indeed, the purchase by Trent included a covenant by Kennings not to operate on the routes for a period of ten years. The name Stevenson will occur again in the future, and the Eagle name has already been mentioned in connection with the takeover of J Turner in 1929.

With the publication of the January, 1935 timetable, the services had been extensively renumbered in accordance with the list in the Appendix. The services operated jointly with East Midland are noteworthy since, both operators having previously used the same number, 12A in the case of Nottingham-Mansfield, and 36 in the case of Nottingham-Chesterfield, Trent changed to 63 and 64 respectively, but East Midland retained the old numbers! Similarly, the Nottingham-Grantham service joint with Lincolnshire had been numbered 33C by both, but Trent changed to 79 and Lincolnshire kept the old number.

improvement on the earlier system, under which During 1935 there was, once again a resurgence in takeover activity with no less than twelve operators selling out, leading to further expansion and consolidation. In January, A Slater & Sons, of Mayfield sold their Ashbourne-Uttoxeter service, together with Excursions from Ashbourne and Mayfield. The small fleet included two Gilfords, one normal control, and a half cab forward control version, together with a Morris Commercial Dictator, a Tilling and three others. Trent took the vehicles away, but did not use them. Slaters continues today as undertakers and garage proprietors.

Next, in March, was Kingfisher Services Ltd, of Derby, with their Derby-Quarndon and Derby-Allestree services, and excursions from Derby. The Allestree services took the numbers 56 (via Kedleston Road) and 57 (via Darley Abbey), although before long these were connected to run as circular routes running in opposite directions, straight through to Derby instead of laying over in Allestree. The Quarndon route was numbered 58 and combined into the existing Trent service 150, which was diverted to run to Ashbourne via Quarndon and Cross o' th' Hands.

The A Slater & Sons fleet included this normal control Gilford. Note the fleet number, 3, and the spare wheel carrier. Possibly, Wycombe Motor Bodies built the body, as they did on many Gilfords, but that is not confirmed in this case, and Duple is another possibility.

Also taken over in March was H S North, Ltd of Derby, who sold their Derby-Heanor and Belper-Heanor services. The latter service had been taken over from P & J W Poundall in June, 1932, soon after they sold their Belper-Ripley service to Trent in January the same year. S O Stevenson of Eagle had some involvement in this business at one time, because, so it is said, North was unable to meet his hire purchase payments.

Stevenson took the business over and had the licences transferred to his name. He than brought the business round and was able to return to North his garage together with a sum of money. However, by the time of the takeover by Trent, he seems to have had no involvement, since the principal shareholder was E J Knight, a local businessman who owned the Friary Hotel and was also the principal shareholder in Kingfisher Motor Services.

H S North's shareholding was, by this time, a minority one, but he restarted his own business again in April, 1936 by taking over Poundall's Belper-Shottle service. He also undertook private hire work, including troop movements during the war, and will feature again later.

S O Stevenson appears once again, because in April, 1935, he sold his Eagle Services works services which served the LMS works at Siddalls Road, Derby from Littleover via two different routes.

Two operators were taken over in June. A small one was F, T and Mrs R Butler, running between Sutton in Ashfield and Annesley Woodhouse, which took route number 81, but receipts from this service were found after the takeover to be rather poor. The other was the joint takeover with East Midland and Lincolnshire of Retford Coachways under an agreement between East Midland and Retford dated 4th December 1934, but not coming into effect until 9th June, 1935. This company had

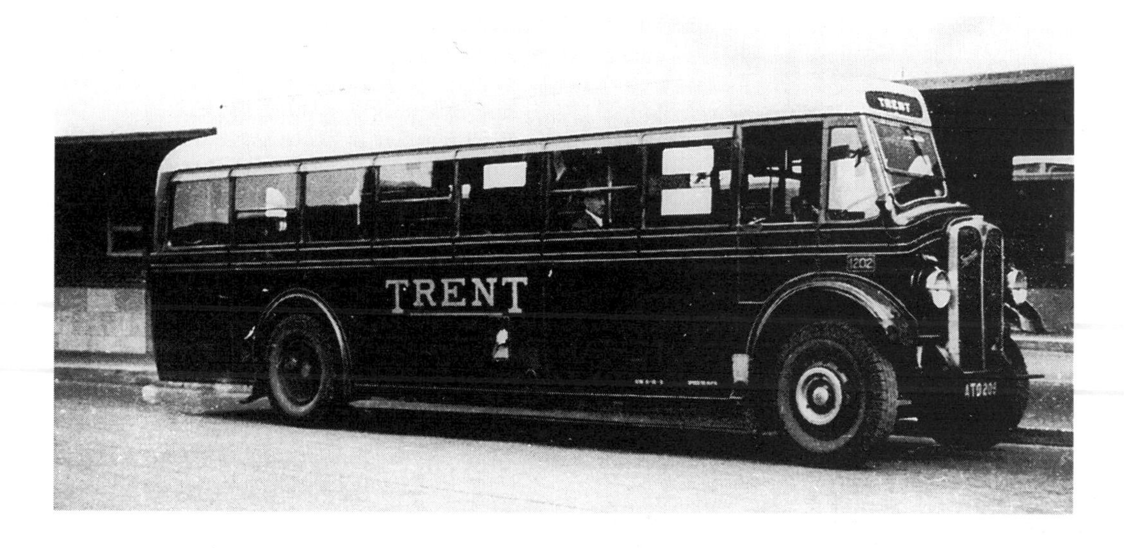

This 1934 AEC Regal with Willowbrook DP32F body joined the Trent fleet with fifteen other vehicles from Dutton's Unity Service of Nottingham, when that concern sold out in 1935. Initially numbered 1213, it was renumbered 1202 in February, 1936, which number it carries in this photograph. The lack of a canopy over the bonnet was commonplace on coaches, since it was reminiscent of the normal control form similar to the private car, but it was unusual on this type of vehicle.

eight vehicles and ran between Retford and Nottingham, some direct and some via Ordsall, and between Retford and Dunham. It also had Excursions and Tours licences based on Retford.

The service via Ordsall was abandoned, but Trent and East Midland operated the direct Nottingham service jointly, with Lincolnshire taking the Dunham service. East Midland and Lincolnshire shared the Excursions and Tours. East Midland paid 50.64% of the purchase price, with Trent contributing 36.21% and Lincolnshire 13.15%. Whilst awaiting the necessary transfer of licences, the business was operated as a sub depot of East Midland. Trent took two of the vehicles, an Albion and an AEC, and the joint service with East Midland was numbered 80 by Trent, and 37 by East Midland.

A major takeover in August was Dutton's Unity Service Ltd., a substantial operator with fifteen vehicles running three routes on a co-ordinated timetable between Nottingham and Sutton in Ashfield, either the direct route, or via Annesley Woodhouse, or via Summit Pit. These took Trent route numbers 84, 85 and 86 respectively. Formerly known as Dutton Bros., before incorporation as a limited company, Dutton's were reported to be issuing free passes on their Sutton-Nottingham service for passengers who had booked on their Nottingham-Skegness service. Also, they, and Direct, another small operator, were carrying more passengers between East Kirkby and Nottingham, because their fare was 1/3d (6.25p), compared with 1/6d (7.5p) on Trent.

A J Daley, of Ripley, who ran 8 vehicles on services based on Ripley and Belper under the name Pippin Services was the next to sell in mid October, and S O Stevenson sold the last of his Eagle Services to Trent at the end of October, 1935. These were a complicated group of services which Stevenson had either acquired, or was in the process of acquiring. They are listed below:-

Belper-Ripley,	
via Holbrook and Kilburn,	ex H E Bell
Heage-Spondon,	ex A Eaton
Derby-Spondon,	ex Cox
Derby-Sutton on the Hill,	ex Turner
Derby-Longford,	ex Yeomans
Derby-Hollington,	ex Yeomans
Derby-Trusley,	ex Yeomans

The Spondon services were works services serving the Celanese factory. There was also a service between Rodsley and Ashbourne which Stevenson acquired from Yeomans, but had agreed with Mrs Frost of Yeaveley not to operate, and the ex Yeomans service to Longford had originally run to Rodsley, but Stevenson had agreed with Mrs Frost not to operate the section of that route between Longford and Rodsley. Frost's of Yeaveley were an operator at one time, although no longer in business as such.

A further takeover in October 1935, provided some consolidation of the Company's position in Loughborough, for it was the takeover of R E Horspool, operating four vehicles on Loughborough and Coalville works services, Loughborough town services, and country services from Loughborough to Nottingham, Willoughby, Nanpantan, Coalville, together with Excursions and Tours From Loughborough. The service to Nanpantan was operated jointly with Allen's Blue Buses, who also ran other services on a sole basis. In October, 1937, it was arranged that the bus used on the Coalville service would out-station there overnight to eliminate unremunerative mileage.

The final takeover in a very active year took place on 30th December, 1935 and involved Partlow and Tarlton, Ltd, who ran between Heanor and Kilburn Toll Bar, via Loscoe Chapel, Bulls Head and Denby Church. The service took the number 159, and was the subject of an agreement with Notts and Derby Traction to provide protection over the section, between Heanor and Loscoe, common with the latter's trolleybus route. The whole business was purchased for £2850, but the three small Guy buses, numbered by Trent 1242-4 and varying in age between 3 and 6 years, were soon sold for a mere £27!

Unsurprisingly, these takeovers resulted in the addition of a variety of second hand vehicles to the fleet which took fleetnumbers in the series 12XX and which were mainly of AEC, Dennis or TSM manufacture. Other second hand additions were ten SOS FS types with Brush bodywork which were acquired from Midland Red following a few months extended hire, and these took fleetnumbers 800-9. The FS was a forward control version of the original S or standard model, being the first stage of development of the original Wyndham-Shire design.

In addition to these takeovers, negotiations took place early in 1935, jointly with Barton, to purchase the businesses of E W Campion, of Nottingham, and H Squires, of Ruddington, operating between Nottingham and Ruddington. However, owing to the high price, Trent withdrew and Barton was the sole purchaser.

Consideration was also given to the purchase of Brewin and Hudson, of Heanor, operating between Hucknall and Heanor. However, it was decided not to proceed with this, possibly because the Heanor end of the route ran over the Notts and Derby A1 trolleybus route which would have had to have been given protection. This may may have been felt in this instance not to have been worthwhile, and the Brewin and Hudson business passed to Midland General in August, 1935.

Negotiations also took place for the purchase of the Alfreton Motor Transport Co, Ltd, operating routes based on its home town, having previously also had a garage at Matlock that had been sold to North Western in October, 1933. £30,000 was offered, but the business passed to Midland General in April, 1935 for £35 000. Subsequently, Midland General sold on to Trent the goodwill of the Excursions and Tours which Alfreton Motor Transport had licensed from Alfreton.

New vehicles were a further six SOS ONs with Duple bodywork which, although to full coach specification and having bodywork with a stepped window arrangement and sloping roof line, lacked the subtlety in design which distinguished the previous year's bodies from the same builder. They were not particularly successful vehicles, being prone to boiling when used on the seven day tours of Scotland, mainly due to the coach bodies being rather heavier than the bus bodies on similar chassis.

A further vehicle 1208, however, was not without interest, for it was a Daimler COG5SD with 32 seat front entrance bodywork of modern appearance by Brush. The vehicle had been exhibited at the previous year's Commercial Motor Show at Olympia and subsequently bought by Trent. It was to prove a trend setter for the Company, not just because of its manufacturer, who would supply more chassis in the future, but also because it was fitted with a Gardner 5 cylinder diesel engine.

This was by way of an experimental vehicle and, with the development of the diesel engine as an everyday power unit, the Company were considering what make of diesel engine should be

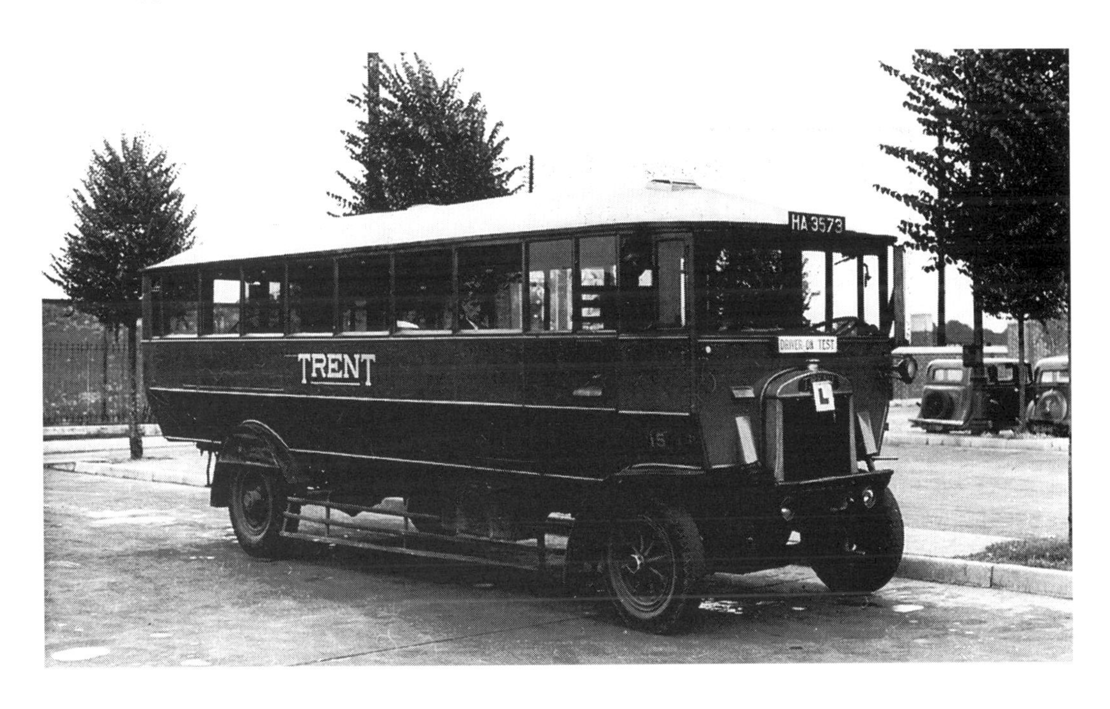

Trent never bought new any of the second stage development of the SOS, designated FS, which was a normal control version of the S. However, ten were taken on long-term hire from Midland Red and eventually bought. By the time this photograph was taken, in September, 1949, this one, 802, HA 3573, had been converted to full front, with dual controls, for use as a driving instruction vehicle and renumbered 15, in the service vehicle numbering series of the time. It was nick named "The Chocolate Box" in this form.

fitted to their future vehicles. In the meantime, the first bulk deliveries of diesel SOSs were received, in the form of thirty DON type with Brush body work, numbered 300-29.

The DON chassis was fitted with a 7.7 litre AEC diesel engine and was, essentially, the ON chassis with a diesel engine and hence the revised designation. The first fifteen bodies seated 36, and the remainder 34. Whilst the appearance was more modern than before, it still seemed somewhat crude when compared with the sleeker products by then being produced by manufacturers to their own designs, as exemplified by the Brush body on 1208.

From 1st October, 1935, Trent took over the journeys run by Nottingham Corporation on service 61, Nottingham-Hucknall and thus became the sole operator. As a result, and having regard also to the takeover of Dutton's Unity service mentioned earlier, it became possible to reduce the number of journeys and improve the level of takings, although the profits in excess of a specified sum were paid to the Corporation. At the same time, the Corporation opened a new trolleybus service, by extending their former tram service from Bulwell Market to Bulwell Hall Estate, probably receiving protection of revenue.

During the year, the seasonal, seaside express services which, with the exception of 35 to Skegness, had been unnumbered, received numbers with an X prefix, as listed below:-

X3 Derby-Nottingham-Skegness
X4 Derby-Nottingham-Mablethorpe-Sutton on Sea
X5 Derby-Nottingham-Cleethorpes
X6 Nottingham-Derby-Blackpool
X7 Nottingham-Great Yarmouth

It will be recalled that the numbers X1 and X2 had earlier been allocated to the Manchester services. New expresses, introduced for summer 1935 were X8 Belper-Alfreton-Mansfield-Skegness and X9 Alfreton-Ripley-Heage-Belper-Ashbourne-Blackpool, both of which ran from 29th June until 28th September.

An interesting episode in the Traffic Court took place on 11th December, 1935, when the Commissioners heard an application by Trent for a service between Derby and the proposed new municipal airport at Burnaston, to the south west of Derby. Mr Campbell-Taylor explained that the Company simply wanted to operate services to the airport on the occasion of special events. The Chairman, Mr Stirk, reminded Mr Campbell-Taylor that the aerodrome was not even built, whereupon he replied: "I know you appreciate enterprise. Immediately the proposals for an aerodrome were published in the press, we wished to be in the field, and we are only asking to run to special events." "In other words," reflected Mr Stirk, "this is a very clever application." Mr Campbell-Taylor went on to contend that as the leading bus company running out of Derby, they were the right and proper people to run the service. After debate and discussion, Mr Campbell-Taylor agreed to withdraw the application, for the time being. Such was the Company's enterprise, however!

After a break of a few years, double deckers appeared in the fleet once again in January, 1936 these being fifteen SOS FEDDs with 56 seat front entrance bodies by Metro Cammell, numbered 1000-14. Of quite appealing appearance, the bodies were metal framed and featured a sliding entrance door which, if left open, was liable to slam shut with a startling bang as the vehicle came to a halt. The vehicles had long lives, lasting until 1950-51, apart from one destroyed by fire in 1948. One, 1011, RC 3333 survived into preservation following use as a shed but, sadly, had to be scrapped before restoration could be carried out.

These vehicles were an immediate success and

The first double deckers in the fleet after a gap of some years were fourteen SOS FEDDs with well proportioned Metro-Cammell bodywork, as exemplified by 1004, RC 3326, seen in Derby Bus Station on 8th August, 1936, soon after delivery. Although the destination was now shown by a roller blind, the use of stencils for the route number still persisted.

enabled much duplicate mileage to be eliminated. For example, at Nottingham depot, six were put to work on the 61, Nottingham-Mansfield, via Hucknall route and 700 duplicate miles per week were discontinued as a result. They were also used on the 62, Nottingham-Mansfield direct, whenever they could be spared.

Other new vehicles were a further forty SOS DONs, 330-69, with 36 seat Brush bodywork of more modern appearance than those delivered in 1935, featuring a curved rear dome with correspondingly radiussed rear side windows and a more conventional windscreen and cab design. This latter improvement was brought about by the relocation of the fuel tank to the lower offside, instead of beneath the driver's seat, which had necessitated a cab door hinged from the front offside corner pillar on the previous year's deliveries. The general appearance bore considerable resemblance to the Brush body on the Daimler COG5SD delivered the previous year.

Six SOS ON coaches, numbered 631-6, with petrol engines for their quieter running were also delivered. These had Duple bodies similar to the previous year's, but attempts were made to lighten the construction of these to minimise the overheating problems experienced on the previous year's deliveries. It had been intended to order seven, but this was reduced by one due to the nearly new Dennis Lancet coaches acquired with the Duttons business, one of which, ATV 4, 1212, later 1230, with Willowbrook 32 seat body was referred to by the Company as a Dennis Lancet deluxe and considered to be of high standard.

Takeover activity slowed during 1936 but, in January, C E Salt's Red Star Bus Service with two services and three vehicles was acquired. This operator, whose operating name was chosen because his first vehicle was of Star manufacture, and painted red, ran his main service between Derby and Belper via Allestree and Duffield. He also had a Sunday service which served Duffield Church. This service had never paid, and was not taken up by Trent, but had been started in 1930 because Duffield Church was situated well outside

341, RC 3712, one of the forty SOS DONs delivered in 1936, photographed on an excursion duty some years later, by which time the original large fleetname had given way to a smaller version. These were quite appealing vehicles and were the first bulk order for the style of bodywork which was to be the Tent single deck standard for the next few years. Many of the batch were rebodied after the war, in which form this vehicle remained in the fleet until 1958.

the Town. Over the years, there had been a long running battle with Trent who would run buses before and after the Red Star timings, in the days before the 1930 Road Traffic Act.

In May 1936, Midland General gave an undertaking to Trent not to pick up passengers at Derby on the Ilkeston-Blackpool service which they had acquired the previous month from Straw and Fletcher of Ilkeston, for which Trent paid £260.

Interestingly, Trent acquired 60,000 shares in Barton Transport from a new issue which Barton floated at that time. These were added to 20,000 which had been purchased the previous year. The 6d (2½p) shares were later consolidated into 20,000 2/- (10p) shares and remained in Trent's ownership until they were transferred to the National Bus Company, when it acquired Trent in 1968.

In July 1936, the goodwill of Heanor-Ilkeston, via Rose & Crown and Stanley Common service of the Heanor & District Omnibus Co, Ltd was acquired. however, the licence for the service had expired in June, and had not been renewed, so it was never run by Trent, and the event was only a prelude to a further takeover the following year. It had originally been started by Mrs Lydia Saxton, after the family business had been sold by her husband to Williamson's, with an agreement that he would not operate buses for a period of some years.

A further works service acquired was that bought from A J Walters & Son, of Derby, running from Allenton to the Celanese plant at Spondon. No vehicles changed hands, but the service must have earned good money, judging by the price of £1,750 that Trent paid for it.

Other service developments during the year related to minor adjustments or renumberings. The regular changing of services was now more difficult and less necessary, following the 1930 Road Traffic Act and the purchase of many of the Company's competitors.

There was extensive development of the Company's depot facilities during 1936, covering existing or newly proposed premises at Belper, Derby, Hucknall, Loughborough, Shipley and Wirksworth. Most of these related to the purchase of land, but at Wirksworth there was investment in the garage acquired with the Rhodeland business by concreting the floor, and at Derby a contract was let to local builders Gee, Walker and Slater Ltd for the construction of a garage on land newly acquired from the LMS in Meadow Road. In the meantime, arrangements were made for temporary accommodation at a foundry in the Stores Road area of Derby.

At Belper, Hucknall and Loughborough, land was bought next to the existing premises, and at Shipley land was bought to build a new garage to replace a dilapidated garage at Horsley Woodhouse, which had been taken over from the District Bus Co and was needed to serve the Company's developing needs in the Heanor, Ripley and Ilkeston areas. The Company was steadily consolidating its position within its whole operating area.

Six new coaches were delivered for 1935, and although new single deck buses delivered to the Company at the same time had AEC 7.7 litre diesel engines, the coaches continued to be specified with the SOS petrol engine for quieter running. Duple bodywork was specified. An Inspector supervises loading for this pre-war excursion to Alton Towers, where the attractive gardens would have provided rather more sedate entertainment than today!

This rear view shows 704, RC 4605, one of the ten AEC Regals with Duple bodies at Derby on 7th September, 1938. The small oval plate on the nearside of the rear panel carried the psv licence number, and was a requirement at the time. Note the similarity of the moulding design to that of the vehicle in front, which is a Brush bodied SOS DON delivered in 1936.

For 1937, there was a complete change of policy, so far as new vehicle deliveries were concerned, because the fifty new vehicles were all of AEC manufacture, consisting of thirty Regent double deckers with Weymann composite framed front entrance bodywork numbered 1015-44, RC 4623-50, and twenty Regal single deckers with front entrance bodywork, ten by Duple, 700-9, RC 4601-10 and ten by Willowbrook, 710-9, RC 4611-20. Significantly, all had AEC diesel engines.

The reasons for the change are not recorded, but it seems likely that Midland Red had insufficient capacity to build chassis for associated companies whilst also meeting its own requirements. Trent already had considerable experience with AEC diesels in the earlier batches of SOS DONs, which may have led to the choice of this manufacturer for complete chassis, and a two week visit by AEC demonstrator AML 774, at the end of August, 1936 may also have played a part in the decision.

The delivery of the AECs enabled the withdrawal of the SOS QLs of 1927, and a start was made on withdrawing the first of the 1928 Madams. Consideration was given to reconditioning and rebodying ten of the Madams, but this was not proceeded with.

With the consolidation of activity which had taken place, there were no takeovers during 1937 and, indeed, in terms of developments the year was fairly uneventful. This paralleled developments elsewhere in the area, and at the 500th sitting of the Traffic Court for the East Midlands Traffic Area, which took place in Nottingham on 23rd June, 1937, the Chairman, Mr Stirk, reviewed the activities of his Court since its first meeting in 1931. He remarked that whereas there had then been 928 separate operators in his area, there were now only 494.

The Corporations of Stoke on Trent and Newcastle under Lyme promoted a Parliamentary Bill intended to allow a joint board to be established representing local authorities in Cheshire, Shropshire and Staffordshire, and having both compulsory purchase powers and powers to operate buses.

This was of some concern to Trent, because the area of the proposed board included Uttoxeter on the western fringe of their operating area. The Omnibus Owners Association, on behalf of Companies potentially affected, petitioned against the Bill and it was rejected for a second reading in the House of Commons. Various other local authorities promoted bills during this period aimed at increasing their abilities to operate buses and these were all opposed unless clauses could be negotiated to protect the Company's interests.

The property developments continued, and the new Shipley Garage, built by F Sissons and Sons, Ltd, opened to traffic from the 30th May, 1937. Proposals were drawn up for a new garage at Hucknall, which involved demolition of the existing property and the construction of a new garage on an enlarged site, a contract for the new building being let to Gee, Walker and Slater who were just completing the new garage at Meadow Road, Derby, which opened to traffic from 4th July, 1937.

At Loughborough, the old garage in The Rushes, acquired from the Loughborough Road Car Co, was demolished and a new one formally opened on an extended site on 26th November, 1937. The Loughborough allocation had meanwhile been housed in a disused engine shed, temporarily rented from the LMS, whilst the work was in progress.

At Belper, consideration was given to extending the Company's premises there, but this was

RC 4634, fleet number 1028 from the batch of thirty AEC Regent double deckers with Weymann body work delivered for 1937. The forward entrance seemed particularly popular with local operators during the immediate pre-war period, since both Barton and Midland General took vehicles to similar layout. 1028 awaits return to Nottingham from Gedling, soon after delivery.

deferred for the time being.

In 1938, takeover activity once again resumed, although there were only four. The first, which took place on 2nd January, was not without interest. During 1935, Midland Red, who had been very active in taking over the many small businesses operating out of Leicester had acquired the business of J Squires of Barrow on Soar, which included a service between Leicester and Sileby. This was considered to be largely within Trent's area and discussions took place with Midland Red about acquiring it. These were successful, an agreement being concluded on 13th December, 1937 coming into effect on 2nd January, 1938.

In March, the short workmen's service operated between Stanley Common and Mapperley Colliery by Robert Vallance of Stanley Common was purchased, and this was followed in May, 1938 by the Heanor and District Omnibus Co, Ltd which was taken over jointly with Midland General and Barton.

Trent paid 24.6% of the price for Heanor and District, with Midland General paying 55.74% and Barton 19.66%. No vehicles were intended to be taken over and it was left to Trent to sell them all for the best price, with the proceeds going to the three companies in the same proportions as their share of the purchase price. However, Midland General had an urgent need of vehicles and they had to use four of the Heanor and District vehicles for a short period, pending the delivery of new ones.

Heanor & District was mostly owned by members of bus operating families who had operated in their own right at various times, these being Thomas Brough, Joseph Aldred, Lydia Saxton, Ethel Buxton, together with Aaron Hartshorne, the local coachbuilder mentioned previously, whose bus bodies were used by some of the local bus proprietors.

Two days later, on 14th May, 1938 the services of Mr John Harris Haywood were acquired. Originally based at Shepshed, then Quorn, Haywood was based at Sileby by the time of the Trent takeover, but it will be recalled that he was also involved with his brother Wilfred, and the Boxall business at Cotmanhay, which they had sold to Trent in 1934. Wilfred, however, had no connection with the Sileby business, but J H Haywood ran two services, these being Loughborough-Sileby, via Walton and Seagrave, and Loughborough-Walton, via Cotes and Burton on the Wolds. Haywood had originally acquired the business from Burnham of Seagrave, who had run Loughborough-Sileby via Walton and Seagrave on Monday, Thursday and Saturday, and Loughborough-Seagrave, via Cotes and Sileby, on Monday, Tuesday, Wednesday and Friday.

By July, 1938, Trent had revised the service to run on two separate licences, these being for Loughborough-Seagrave via Quorn, Barrow and Sileby, as service 127, and Loughborough-Walton, via Cotes and Burton, as service 128. The services ran on Thursdays and Saturdays only, and the licence included a provision that no double deckers be used, although it seems questionable whether the amount of traffic would have justified such a provision. Excursions from Seagrave were also acquired with this business. Together with the ex Squires service acquired from Midland Red, this helped consolidate Loughborough Depot business, although they did not make a major contribution towards receipts, due to the thin territory through which they operated.

Until the takeovers of Midland General, Barton and part of North Western, which took place under different circumstances in future years, the development of the Company's network was now largely completed. There would be other isolated takeovers in the future, and routes would be opened to serve new traffic objectives such as housing estates but, essentially the job was now done and Trent had assumed the shape which was to remain familiar for many years.

The new vehicles delivered in 1938 marked a further change in policy, for they were Daimlers with Gardner engines, as foreshadowed by bus no 1208, delivered in 1936. There were fifteen COG5 double deckers with Weymann forward entrance bodywork numbered 1045-59, RC 5994-6008, and eight COG5/40 single deckers with Willowbrook 35 seat front entrance bodywork, numbered 500-8, RC 5724, 5980-93. The first of the single deckers arrived in 1937 and was exhibited at the Commercial Motor Transport Exhibition at Earls Court that year, originally being numbered 600, but renumbered 500, before entering service.

There were also six COG5/40 coaches numbered 637-42, RC 5998-93, with Duple 32 seat bodywork of similar appearance to that supplied previously on SOS chassis. As with the AECs delivered in 1937, the reasons for this change are not recorded, but as the vehicles featured the Gardner 5LW engine, noted for its frugality, they doubtless appealed to the management, and this was coupled to the Daimler version of the Wilson pre-selector gearbox, which doubtless appealed to drivers, so long as they avoided the kick back which the gear selector pedal could sometimes deliver if not operated quite correctly. These vehicles enabled the 1927 Qs and the rest of 1929 Madams to go.

This superb portrait shot of 1056, RC 6005, taken soon after delivery at Wilford Hill, Nottingham, shows to good effect the Trent livery of the day. Based on the standard BET light red, the livery featured BET dark red (maroon) as relief, with white roof and all accompanied by simple lining out. Note the raked back radiator.

1064, RC 7075 attracts a good load for the journey from Derby to Belper under the supervision of an Inspector. Overcrowding was a continual problem during the war years. This vehicle, a Daimler COG5 with Weymann H54F bodywork of 1939, has wartime head-lamp masks, as well as white markings on the front wings. Note the lack of tread on the front tyres - definitely a case of getting the most mileage possible, since supplies of rubber were short.

Chapter Five
Frugality
1939-45

On 28th January, 1939, two workmen's services were purchased from Mrs Hilda Swinn of Bulwell. These operated between Cinderhill and Gedling Colliery and between Bulwell and Gedling Colliery. No vehicles were involved. Soon afterwards, in March, 1938, an express service run between Barrow on Soar and Leicester Football Ground on match days, together with excursions from Barrow on Soar, were acquired from Mr F Harris.

War broke out in September, 1939, but preparations had been in hand for this eventuality since the beginning of the year, and possibly even before that. An advisory committee, consisting of representatives of various transport undertakings was set up and the Company was represented by Mr Campbell-Taylor. The purpose of the advisory committee was to assist the Chairman of the Traffic Commissioners (who had a new, wartime role as Regional Transport Commissioner) in considering the allocation of vehicles in the event of an emergency.

The committee met for the first time early in 1939, well before the war started, and in addition to the Company's co-operation with the authorities in this effort, 550 Trent staff attended courses on air raid precautions. Contingency plans were made for schedules assuming cuts of 25%, 50% and 75% in the Company's fuel supply.

Despite the preparations for war, new vehicles were received, which consisted of another twelve Daimler COG5 double deckers with Weymann bodywork, numbered 1060-71, RC 7081-82, which were similar to those received the previous year. In the case of single deckers and coaches, however, there was a return to SOS, for there were twelve SONs with Willowbrook 34 seat bus bodywork, numbered 400-11, RC 7089-100, and six with 31 seat coachwork, also by Willowbrook, numbered 643-48, RC 7083-88.

The SOS SON was a further development of the ON type and featured a new, almost silent gearbox by ZF of Germany, together with a new 8 litre diesel engine of SOS manufacture and designated as its' K type. The Willowbrook bodies were of modern design, similar to those fitted to the earlier Daimler COG5/40s and, in the author's view, having a more pleasing appearance than the contemporary SONs entering Midland Red's own fleet with bodywork to their own design.

The chassis introduced a new more modern design of SOS radiator which was deeper and featured space on the top tank for a large triangular badge having the initials TMT. The style was not unlike that of AEC, but the general outline was rather heavier, and the shell tapered inwards quite sharply towards the bottom. They were a pleasing, modern vehicle.

Interestingly, the vehicles withdrawn as a result of these new arrivals, were probably stored in anticipation of the need for ambulances, and the transfer of vehicles to the War Department. Perhaps also with potential shortages in mind, it was decided to spend up to £3,000 on buying between one and two years supply of spare parts and units for chassis which it was intended would remain in service for three to four years.

On 17th September, 1939 Mr W S Wreathall died - he had been a notable personality in BET circles, and had been a Director of Trent since the beginning, in 1913. Mr B G White was appointed

This post-war view shows 644, RC 7084, one of the batch of six SOS ONC coaches delivered with Willowbrook bodies for the 1939 season just before war broke out, leaving Manchester for Derby. They had the later style of SOS radiator, as fitted to the ONC buses delivered the same year, which gave a more modern appearance, although the Willowbrook bodywork was perhaps less stylish than contemporary offerings from the then more mainstream coachbuilders, such as Duple and Burlingham. The batch lasted until 1954.

to replace him.

When war eventually broke out on 3rd September, the effects on the Company were immediate. Blackout regulations required that the lights in buses had to be screened and dimmed so that no light was visible outside. During the first week, all bus and train excursions from Derby to the coast and the country were cancelled.

Notices appeared in newspapers advising that "Owing to the closing of places of entertainment, Trent Services have been curtailed at night time....". The effect of this was that very few last buses ran later than 9.30pm. However, this was found to be too severe and, a couple of weeks later, further advertisements appeared for late buses for cinema patrons, after the cinemas had reopened.

Similarly, Sunday services were curtailed, but then reinstated on a limited basis, because people wanted to visit children who had been evacuated. In addition to the various curtailments, a large number of services were suspended indefinitely, as efforts were made to run along the main routes and cut out little used country services, or those which were within a short distance of a main service.

The timetable book issued for the month of November was subtitled "National Emergency Services", with a footnote "The timetables shown in this book are subject to alteration at short notice." There were quite a number of adjustments to the level of services before the wartime pattern of services was settled. The contingency plan for a 50% cut in fuel supply, drawn up earlier was brought into operation and the main priority was in getting people to works and other places of employment. Efforts were made to obtain a little more fuel, and by July, 1940, the Company was running 64% of the mileage that had been run twelve months earlier.

Not that it was all bad news, for the Nottingham District Traffic Superintendent was able to report that, as a result of the curtailments, he had been able to turn certain services into profit, whereas

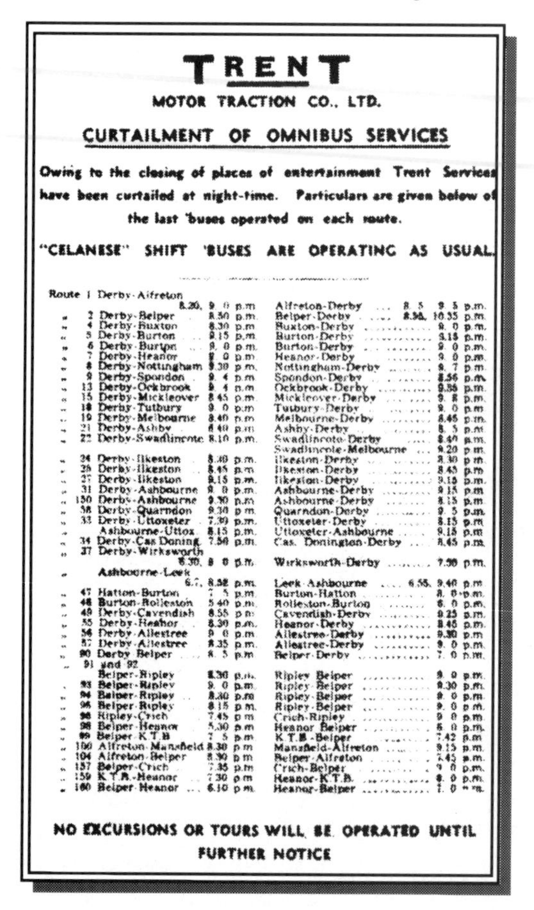

TRENT

MOTOR TRACTION CO., LTD.

CURTAILMENT OF OMNIBUS SERVICES

Owing to the closing of places of entertainment Trent Services have been curtailed at night-time. Particulars are given below of the last 'buses operated on each route.

"CELANESE" SHIFT 'BUSES ARE OPERATING AS USUAL.

Route				
Route 1	Derby-Alfreton	8.20, 9. 0 p.m.	Alfreton-Derby ...	8. 5 9. 5 p.m.
" 2	Derby-Belper	8.30 p.m.	Belper-Derby ...	8.35, 10.35 p.m.
" 4	Derby-Buxton	8.30 p.m.	Buxton-Derby	9. 0 p.m.
" 5	Derby-Burton	9.15 p.m.	Burton-Derby	9.15 p.m.
" 6	Derby-Burton	9. 0 p.m.	Burton-Derby	9. 0 p.m.
" 7	Derby-Heanor	9. 0 p.m.	Heanor-Derby	9. 0 p.m.
" 8	Derby-Nottingham	9.30 p.m.	Nottingham-Derby	9. 7 p.m.
" 9	Derby-Spondon	9. 4 p.m.	Spondon-Derby	8.56 p.m.
" 13	Derby-Ockbrook	9. 4 p.m.	Ockbrook-Derby	9.36 p.m.
" 15	Derby-Mickleover	8.45 p.m.	Mickleover-Derby	9. 8 p.m.
" 18	Derby-Tutbury	9. 0 p.m.	Tutbury-Derby	9. 0 p.m.
" 19	Derby-Melbourne	8.40 p.m.	Melbourne-Derby	8.45 p.m.
" 21	Derby-Ashby	8.40 p.m.	Ashby-Derby	8. 5 p.m.
" 22	Derby-Swadlincote	8.10 p.m.	Swadlincote-Derby	8.40 p.m.
			Swadlincote-Melbourne	9.20 p.m.
" 24	Derby-Ilkeston	8.30 p.m.	Ilkeston-Derby	8.30 p.m.
" 26	Derby-Ilkeston	8.45 p.m.	Ilkeston-Derby	8.45 p.m.
" 27	Derby-Ilkeston	9.15 p.m.	Ilkeston-Derby	9.15 p.m.
" 31	Derby-Ashbourne	9. 0 p.m.	Ashbourne-Derby	9.15 p.m.
" 130	Derby-Ashbourne	9.30 p.m.	Ashbourne-Derby	8.15 p.m.
" 38	Derby-Quarndon	9.30 p.m.	Quarndon-Derby	9. 5 p.m.
" 33	Derby-Uttoxeter	7.30 p.m.	Uttoxeter-Derby	8.15 p.m.
	Ashbourne-Uttox	8.15 p.m.	Uttoxeter-Ashbourne	9.15 p.m.
" 34	Derby-Cas Doning.	7.50 p.m.	Cas. Donington-Derby	8.45 p.m.
" 37	Derby-Wirksworth	8.30, 9. 0 p.m.	Wirksworth-Derby	7.50 p.m.
"	Ashbourne-Leek	6.7, 8.52 p.m.	Leek-Ashbourne ...	6.55, 9.40 p.m.
" 47	Hatton-Burton	7. 5 p.m.	Burton-Hatton	8. 0 p.m.
" 48	Burton-Rolleston	5.40 p.m.	Rolleston-Burton	6. 0 p.m.
" 49	Derby-Cavendish	8.55 p.m.	Cavendish-Derby	9.25 p.m.
" 55	Derby-Heanor	8.30 p.m.	Heanor-Derby	8.45 p.m.
" 56	Derby-Allestree	9. 0 p.m.	Allestree-Derby	9.30 p.m.
" 57	Derby-Allestree	8.35 p.m.	Allestree-Derby	9. 0 p.m.
" 90	Derby-Belper	8. 5 p.m.	Belper-Derby	7. 0 p.m.
" 91 and 92	Belper-Ripley	8.30 p.m.	Ripley-Belper	9. 0 p.m.
" 93	Belper-Ripley	9. 0 p.m.	Ripley-Belper	9.30 p.m.
" 94	Belper-Ripley	8.30 p.m.	Ripley-Belper	9. 0 p.m.
" 96	Belper-Ripley	8.15 p.m.	Ripley-Belper	9. 0 p.m.
" 98	Ripley-Crich	7.45 p.m.	Crich-Ripley	9. 0 p.m.
" 98	Belper-Heanor	5.30 p.m.	Heanor-Belper	6. 0 p.m.
" 99	Belper-K.T.B.	7. 5 p.m.	K.T.B.-Belper	7.42 p.m.
" 100	Alfreton-Mansfield	8.30 p.m.	Mansfield-Alfreton	9.15 p.m.
" 104	Alfreton-Belper	8.30 p.m.	Belper-Alfreton	7.45 p.m.
" 157	Belper-Crich	7.35 p.m.	Crich-Belper	9. 0 p.m.
" 159	K.T.B.-Heanor	7.30 p.m.	Heanor-K.T.B.	8. 0 p.m.
" 160	Belper-Heanor ...	6.10 p.m.	Heanor-Belper	7. 0 p.m.

NO EXCURSIONS OR TOURS WILL BE OPERATED UNTIL FURTHER NOTICE

Plans made earlier were brought into instant effect, as shown by this advertisement published on 8th September, 1939, following outbreak of war on the 3rd. The cutback was subsequently found to be too severe and some services were soon reinstated.

Judging by the white markings on the front wings, and the lack of wartime headlamp masks, this photograph was probably taken soon after the end of the war, particularly as the white markings have become badly faded. However, 413, RC 7923, was one of the last batch of single deckers to pre-war specification delivered in 1940. An SOS SON with Willowbrook B34F bodywork, it was one of a batch of fourteen, and is seen in Derby.

they had previously run at a loss! He did also say, however, that there were many inconveniences to the travelling public and that they were in the position of having to leave people behind.

The last buses to peacetime specification arrived in 1940, and these were a further fourteen SOS SONs, numbered 412-25, RC 7922-35, and identical to those received in 1939. They were the last buses built by Midland Red for another operator. Withdrawn in 1954, bus 417 was found in a field near Melton Mowbray in 1978 and rebuilt to a very high standard in the Central Works. It is preserved and licensed to PCV standard, fitted with a tachograph and used for private hire and occasional special services. There were also ten more Daimler COG5 double deckers which were numbered 1072-81, RC 7936-45, and similar to the previous years deliveries, except for a different type of front entrance. They were delivered in grey primer. It had been intended to order six SOS coaches, as well, but there were second thoughts about this, perhaps due to the expectation of war at the time when orders were being placed in mid 1939.

Probably the Company was lucky to have received these new vehicles, for many manufacturer's efforts were switched to war production at an early stage. Indeed, the Daimler works in Coventry was bombed in 1940 and production ceased entirely for a time, until it could be restarted at a requisitioned factory elsewhere. No further vehicles were to arrive until 1943.

A great wartime problem for the Company was overcrowding of its vehicles, especially in wet weather when the many people who normally cycled to work would use buses instead, and crowd out the regular travellers. In order to assist, the Ministry of Transport relaxed the standing passengers regulations from 25% of seating capacity (maximum 5) to 33% of seating capacity, (maximum 8).

Great efforts were made to try to get employers to stagger their working hours to spread the load. Adverts were placed in the local press explaining that staff had been called up and vehicles taken by the military authorities, or requisitioned for ambulances, and that additional services could not be run for these reasons. It was to little avail.

Mr Ferry met employers at the weekly lunch of the Derby Rotarians and explained all the problems. There was a shortage of drivers and the Government would take buses for use at short notice. 51% of conductors were new to the job. There had been a decrease in the number of passengers of 3.1%, but the mileage run had gone down by 36%. Many people had given up their cars due to petrol rationing and now needed to use the buses.

The Company wrote to all the large employers explaining the problems and seeking suggestions. Most people wanted to start work at 8.00am and the company had 82 buses operating out of Derby depot at 7.30, but by 10.00am there were only seven, as off peak mileage was minimised to save fuel. Staff had to work split shifts to deal with this and, owing to the shortage of drivers, some journeys could only be covered in overtime, which put a strain on the staff. The hope was that if some employers would start at 7.00am, it would be possible to bring in many more people with the same number of buses, but there was little response to the pleas.

In order to assist in dealing with the shortage of staff, many women were taken on to work as conductors. Although this seems unremarkable today, in those days many women traditionally did not work, and this social change started partly as a result of wartime experiences.

Certainly, many women at the time did not want to take on bus work, and the manager of the Derby Employment Exchange reported difficulties in filling part time vacancies for conductresses desperately needed by Trent and Derby Corporation because, he said, many women felt they were too superior. How times have changed!

This cheerful group of conductresses, were amongst the first to join the Company when this photograph was taken in 1941 in the parking area at Derby Central Bus Station. They enjoyed the work, which was interesting and varied. However, it was not without difficulties, for the blackout caused problems in handling cash and tickets, and buses were overcrowded at peak times. Conductress Ellen Paradise tries the cab of this SOS SON for size, but women were not generally employed as drivers, for steering required great effort, as there was no power assistance in those days.

The employment of women necessitated certain changes, and additional accommodation was rented at Derby Central Bus Station for the women to use, and additional toilets had to be provided at depots. The uniform adopted for the women consisted of a light brown dust coat with red trim, together with navy blue skirt, cap and greatcoat.

During 1940, the entire 1931 batch of SOS IM6s 120-35, and IM4s, 470-481, numbering 28 were passed to the War Department, and a further 19 from the 1932 and 1933 batches also went the same way. Many of these were converted to ambulances and all but six eventually finished up with Midland Red. In addition, the SOS CODs, originally numbered 450-66, but later 200-16 were also withdrawn and passed direct to Midland Red. This loss totalled sixty four vehicles although it is fair to say that many were seen as surplus to requirements following the last new deliveries and, by the standards of their year of manufacture, they were quite elderly.

In November, 1940, the service of W E Wells of Aston on Trent was taken over and this ran from Derby to Weston on Trent. The purchase price was nominally £3,000, but there was a proviso that the Company would pay in addition 25% of the amount by which the first twelve months takings exceeded the purchase price. The most likely explanation for this was that with the increased level of wartime traffic, it was difficult to predict the takings accurately, especially as there was an army camp at Weston, which generated additional traffic. No vehicles were taken over, and Trent gave the service the number 40.

The proposal for a new garage at Belper has already been mentioned, and although a contract was let for this and construction started, progress was increasingly frustrated by the lack of the necessary materials. In view of this, the contract was terminated and the project was placed in abeyance until conditions were more favourable. In addition, the two small garages in Argyll Road, Ripley, acquired with the business of A J Daley, were requisitioned by the War Department in October, 1940, and the Company's garage at Shipley was requisitioned for use by the Ministry of Aircraft production.

The Government continued to requisition buildings for war purposes, and in March 1941, the ground floor of the depot at Kent Street, Nottingham was taken for use by the Air Ministry. Vehicles also were requisitioned, with six QLs being taken by the Ministry of War Transport in April, 1941 and sixty other buses being taken by the Army in July.

The problems of overcrowding continued, and in August, 1941, the Minister of War Transport issued the Standing Passengers Order, which allowed single deck vehicles that had been specially adapted and had been approved by the Regional Transport Commissioner to carry up to 30 standing passengers, instead of 8, as previously.

The adaptation consisted of perimeter seating and

Early in the War, a number of redundant vehicles were converted into ambulances, including this 1929 Madam, and initially ten of the Company's vehicles were so treated. The vehicles were able to carry two sitting cases and ten stretcher cases, the latter being carried on metal frames designed by the Chief Engineer, Mr R C Hunt. Metal framing was also obtained by Mr Hunt to enable a number of vehicles to be converted throughout the East Midlands. The rather severe looking gentleman, standing on the step, is Mr J H Stirk who was the first Chairman of the East Midlands Traffic Commissioners, appointed following the 1930 Road Traffic Act. However, by the time that this photograph was taken, he had assumed the wartime role of Regional Transport Commissioner for the North Midlands region, which included the Counties of Derbyshire, Nottinghamshire, Lincolnshire, Leicestershire, Northamptonshire and Rutland.

uprated springs to carry the additional load, and Trent had their first such conversion, one of the Brush bodied SOS DONs of 1935, in service by the middle of September, 1941, being one of the first companies to do so.

Initially, ten such conversions were to be carried out, but only 5, Brush bodied SOS DONs 343,4,5 & 8 of 1935, together with Duple bodied AEC Regal 702 of 1937 have been identified as so treated, although there probably were others. After conversion, the DONs seated 30 and the AEC seated 31, so there was minimal loss of seating, for a near doubling of carrying capacity. In this form, the vehicles were nicknamed "invasion barges" by the crews.

In a further attempt to ease overcrowding problems, the Company introduced a permit scheme from Monday 29th September, 1941, with the aim of giving priority to essential travellers. A list was published of services on which, generally, only permit holders would be carried, although exceptions were made for certain non permit holders, such as school children going to and from school, and servicemen and others going to and from duty.

The permit scheme had been approved by the Regional Transport Commissioner, following a trial run on Trent's Nottingham-Mansfield service which had demonstrated the public's willingness to be registered for travel.

The scheme was welcomed by war workers and by early October, some 36,000 permits had been issued, with applications still being received. Shoppers and others who had hitherto travelled at the peak times quickly learned not to attempt this, because the permits were checked by special volunteers as passengers entered the vehicle. Complete new vehicles continued to be impossible to obtain, but an order was placed with Willowbrook for twelve double deck bodies for 1942/3 delivery and fitting to existing single deck bus and coach chassis.

This Brush bodied DON of 1936 was one of a number of single deckers which were converted to perimeter seating, greatly increasing the carrying capacity. The existing pairs of seats were re-arranged along each side of the bus, and additional vertical stanchions provided, although the grab rails on the overhead luggage racks also provided support for those standing. Three of the road staff demonstrate the use of the new layout, which seems rather reminiscent of the London Underground!

In December, 1941, vehicle relief was at hand, because an agreement with London Transport had been entered into for the hire of eight of their vehicles at a cost of £25 per month plus tyre mileage, and the London vehicles received on hire were ST845/55/62/88/904/14/8 and 994. They were based at Derby, but ran to other centres of operation, including Alfreton and Nottingham.

The London ST type was an early 1930s petrol engine version of the AEC Regent, and these particular vehicles had 54 seat rear entrance bodywork some by Tilling and some by Dodson. They had a set back front to the upper deck, with open rear staircases, and must have looked decidedly old fashioned to Trent passengers, used to the modern appearance of the bodywork on Trent's own double deckers, although the AEC chassis were good performers.

Licensing of London buses at that time was in the hands of the Metropolitan Police who were extremely conservative and held back considerably the development of bus design in the capital - insisting on open drivers' cabs, for example, long after the universal adoption of windscreens in the provinces. The vehicles however, provided welcome assistance to Trent, and were retained for some time, returning to London in March and April of 1944, after deliveries had been received of new utility buses.

In May 1942, an order was placed with Willowbrook for a further three double deck bodies, making a total of fifteen in all. When these were ready, they were fitted to the 1938 Daimler COG5/40s which previously had single deck bus bodies (500-8) or coach bodies (637-42), which

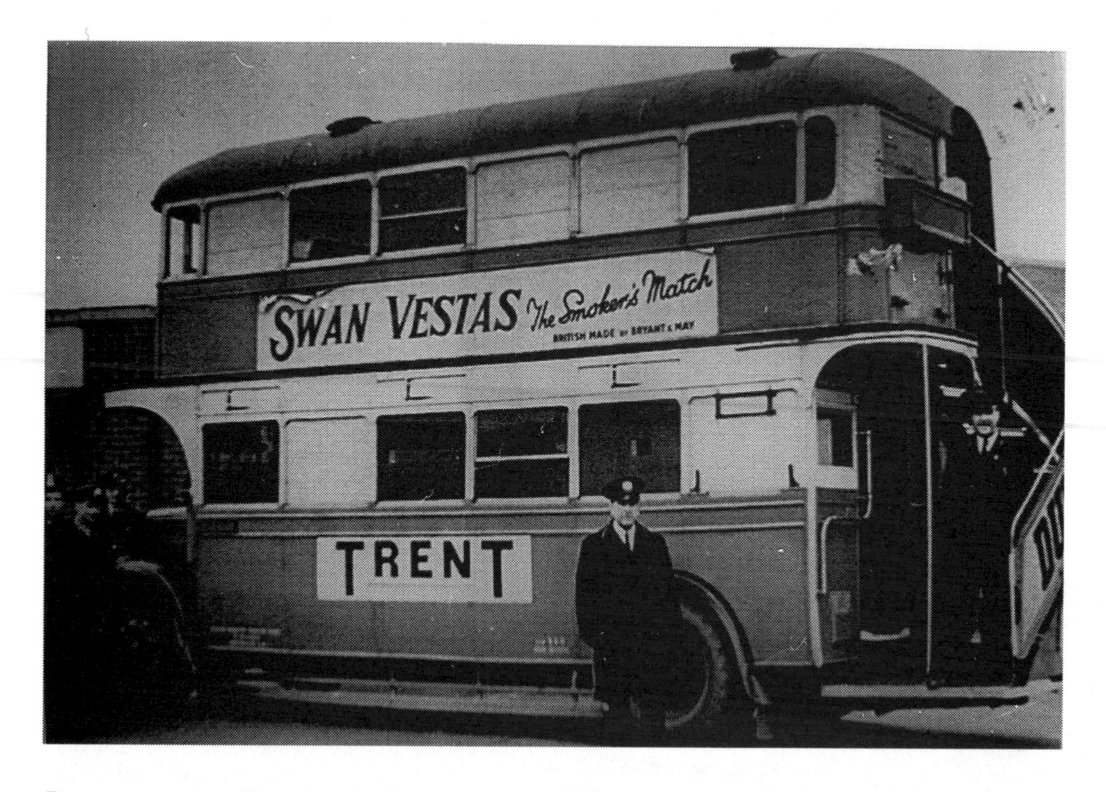

Passengers travelling in this bus, London Transport ST 888, GJ 2064, seen in Derby's Central Bus Station, must have thought its appearance rather old-fashioned compared with Trent's FEDDs, Daimlers and AEC Regents that they were used to travelling on. However, the AEC Regent chassis was familiar to staff, and the eight vehicles, taken on hire in 1942, provided welcome assistance. Note the paper fleetname sticker, pasted over the London Transport fleetname. Similar stickers had previously been used on vehicles taken over with the businesses of small operators.

were then given fleetnumbers 1088-96, in the case of 500-8, and 1082-87 for 637-42. The new bodies had 56 seats, compared with the 35 of the buses and 31 of the coaches, and were to the government utility specification, steel panelling, minimum radiussed panelling, all intended to minimise the use of labour and scarce materials. However, they had upholstered seats, compared with the wooden slatted seats, which were later part of the utility specification. The chassis were shortened from the original, since the maximum permitted length for a double decker at that time was 26' 0" (7.93m) compared with 27'6" (8.38m) for single deckers.

The bodies removed from 500-8 were sold to the original Enterprise and Silver Dawn company at Scunthorpe and fitted to other chassis. The six coaches were taken into Great Northern Road Works, where the body mountings were loosened. The vehicles were then driven gently to Belper Depot, where the bodies were removed and placed on timbers spanning between oil drums for storage for the duration of the war, and the new utility bodies were then fitted to the chassis.

A new scheme known as the British Omnibus Publicity Committee was set up to co-ordinate publicity and the Company was represented on this by Mr Howley or Mr Power. Some vehicles were given a sticker with a white single decker bus on a black background and the words "British Buses" beneath.

With effect from April 12th, 1942, the Ministry of War Transport made an Order that passengers should form a queue two deep when six or more passengers were waiting at a stopping place, whether there was a queue sign or not. This Order remained in force long after the war and was not, in fact, rescinded until 1996!

In August, 1942, a further eight vehicles were taken on hire from London Transport, and these were ST329/39/427/96/612/31/781 and 1009. All except the last of these had more modern bodies than those hired earlier, still having the set back upper deck front, but with an enclosed staircase. Some returned to London in March and April, 1944, but four were retained until May, 1945.

In 1942, Nottingham Corporation made an application to the Minister for War Transport for powers to run trolleybuses along Wollaton Road and Russell Drive, which was an extension of the existing route on the western outskirts of Nottingham. Trent and Midland General objected to this proposal, because they already served the route with their joint service. A Public Inquiry was held in Autumn, 1942, and the Minister found generally in the Corporation's favour, but subject to their offering the two companies a financial interest in the new service.

At the instigation of the Regional Transport Commissioner, a meeting took place in January, 1943 between the Commissioner, the Corporation and the two bus companies, but no agreement could be reached about the three parties having a combined interest in the new service. By June, 1943, the Ministry of War Transport had drawn up some draft Heads of Proposals for the continuance of the Companies' existing through bus service between Cotmanhay, Ilkeston and Nottingham, by

One effect of wartime restrictions was insistence on stopping only at recognised points, backed up by Government Order. Appropriate publicity was given by means of newspaper advertisements like this one, published on behalf of Trent, Midland General and Barton. All three companies were members of the British Omnibus Publicity Committee, which had adopted the symbol of a single deck bus with the words "British Buses" shown at the foot of the advertisement. Although the outline of this symbol was replicated on the bus stop sign in the advertisement, the operators continued to use their standard pattern of sign.

A further eight AEC Regents arrived on hire from London Transport in August, 1941. All but one of these had a more modern style of bodywork featuring a closed staircase, including ST 631, GN 2030, seen here at Alfreton Bus Station.

the Companies, and for the provision of shuttle services between Nottingham and Balloon Houses by the Companies and the Corporation.

The Ministry stressed their view that the service should be provided by trolleybuses, in order to economise on the use of imported fuel. The Minister indicated that he was prepared to authorise an extension of the Corporation trolley system from the junction of Ilkeston Road and Middleton Boulevard, to Balloon Houses, subject to conditions which included:-

i) Midland General would buy at an already agreed figure Trent's interests in the existing service between Nottingham, Trowell, Ilkeston and Cotmanhay.

ii) Midland General, or Notts and Derby if trolleybuses were used, would retain the whole of the existing through service between Nottingham and Cotmanhay,

iii) The Corporation would retain the whole of the existing service between Nottingham City Centre and Middleton Boulevard.

iv) The Corporation and Midland General/Notts and Derby would provide half each of the new shuttle service between Nottingham and Balloon Houses.

Midland General, who already ran trolleys through the associated Notts and Derby Traction had decided that they wished to operate trolleybuses between Nottingham and Ilkeston but, as Trent were not in a position to do so, they sold their share in the service to Midland General for £8,000. In the event, the trolleybus extension never took place, because the Corporation were unwilling to grant running powers for Company trolleybuses to use Corporation overhead! Also, when Mount Street bus station opened in Nottingham, this shortened the bus journey, compared to the former terminus at Huntingdon Street, and considerable mileage was saved. This was a contributory factor in enabling the existing bus service to be improved, and this started from 3rd October, 1943, when the new bus station opened. On the same date, Trent's share in the existing service passed to Midland General, but Trent vehicles continued to run on the service, on hire to Midland General, until January, 1944.

Towards the end of 1942, it was decided to order thirty Bristol type gas producer trailers at a total cost of £3750, and to house these an extension was built on to the back of Meadow Road depot. Probably this was not a particularly willing purchase, but the idea of running vehicles on gas was seen as a way of saving liquid fuel which had to be imported, and the Government directed that all the territorial companies should run a number of vehicles on gas. The idea had been developed by the Tilling Group, most of whose subsidiaries ran in flattish rural areas and did not suffer the problems running with gas as acutely as those operators running in more densely populated or hilly areas.

Usually, the equipment to generate the gas was carried on a trailer towed behind the vehicle which, when anthracite was burned in a retort produced coal gas which could power vehicles. The effect on performance was disastrous and vehicles using the fuel had to be confined as far as possible to routes with no significant hills. Five gallons of petrol were carried for starting, but if the bus wouldn't go, some drivers would turn over to petrol, which was strictly against the rules, and care was needed to ensure that the petrol didn't run out!

In June, 1943, the Nottingham District Traffic Superintendent reported that traffic had been lost on the 07.30 journey from Derby to Nottingham, because a producer gas vehicle was being used and this made the bus run exceptionally late. As a result, people were making other arrangements and, in particular, were tending to use the rival Barton service.

There is, of course, a steep hill when entering Nottingham from Derby, and also leaving Derby, past the Cemetery. Although the rest of the route has no significant hills travelling east, the route was not really suitable for producer gas vehicles because of these two hills. In the westbound direction, there is a hill out of Sandiacre.

In the event, ten trailers were ordered from the Bristol Tramways & Carriage Company, and nineteen from Wylie Harris Ltd, but the order to the latter was reduced to eight. In 1944 a further eleven were to be ordered, but before they had been delivered, the Ministry of War Transport announced that operators were no longer to be required to use producer gas, and any vehicles which had been converted could be altered back

The first Trent vehicle to wartime utility specification was this Daimler CWG5 with 56 seat Duple body, which arrived in June, 1943. Despite the form of construction and spartan design, the vehicle put in a full service life with the Company, remaining until May, 1956. By the time this post war view of 1097, RC 8320, was taken at Alfreton Bus Station, the tiny wartime headlights originally fitted had been replaced by standard units, and a different style of livery had been adopted, but the appearance was otherwise largely original.

again to liquid fuel. Thus ended a measure which probably caused a great deal of difficulty, but provided only very limited benefit. However, it was said that the small number of vehicles converted saved some 1400 gallons of petrol per month.

The vehicles converted were petrol engine IM4s in the 220 onwards series, and IM6s in the 136 onwards series. They were used on routes to Matlock and to Mickleover, as well as the Derby-Nottingham service.

Around the turn of the year, reservations were placed with AEC for 35 double deck chassis, 30 single deck chassis and 6 coach chassis. Twenty double deck bodies were ordered from Weymann, and fifteen double deck and twenty nine single deck bodies were ordered from Willowbrook, leaving one single deck bus chassis and six coach chassis spare. In the event, no bodies were ever received from Weymann, although the other orders were filled in various ways, but the Company was obviously trying to secure its position for the future.

A side event to affect the Company during the year was a change in the nature of the holding company, Tilling and British Automobile Traction Co, Ltd, which was split into its Tilling and BAT parts. In many ways this was not surprising, for with the different personalities involved from the two sides, and the different styles of the two organisations, relations were not always easy.

The original amalgamation had taken place before the 1930 Road Traffic Act when matters were less controlled and it was said to have been felt useful to have better co-ordination by joint control. Circumstances had now changed, and it was felt desirable to have separate management, so the individual territorial companies were separated into two new holding companies, BET Omnibus Services Ltd, controlled by BET, and Tilling Motor Services Ltd, controlled by Thomas Tilling.

Mostly, the companies returned to their original holding company and Trent thus remained firmly on the BET side. Little difference was noticed, since BET had traditionally left control with local management, providing that costs and profits were kept in line.

A further double deck utility body was ordered from Willowbrook and when it was ready, in 1943, it was of lowbridge layout, with sunken gangway on the offside, and was fitted onto the pioneer Daimler COG5/40, 1208, the body from which was sold to Hulley's of Baslow who fitted it to an AEC Regal chassis. In its new form the Daimler received the fleet number 1300, which started a fresh series because it was the first vehicle in the fleet with the lowbridge layout.

In addition to this, and also in 1943, the first complete vehicles to utility specification were received. Only two manufacturers, Daimler and Guy were building double deck buses at this stage in the war, although Bristol were to join in towards the end. Fortunately, those allocated to Trent were all built by Daimler and had either Gardner or AEC engines, so they fitted in quite well. The first to arrive were 1097/8, Gardner engined Daimler CWG5s with Duple 56 seat highbridge bodywork, featuring upholstered seats. These were soon followed by 1301-8, AEC engined Daimler CWA6s with 55 seat bodywork to lowbridge configuration, also by Duple, but with wooden slatted seats, as a further wartime economy. No vehicles were withdrawn due to their arrival and, indeed, other than those converted to ambulances, or taken for military service, there were few normal

Despite the utility design of the bodywork fitted to this Daimler CWA6, the bodybuilder, C H Roe, continued to fit the teak waist rail, which was for so many years an instant identifying characteristic of their production. New in 1944, 1103, RC 8398 was photographed in post war livery at Nottingham, in largely unaltered condition.

withdrawals during the war years, until near the end.

As mentioned earlier, on 3rd October, 1943, a new municipal bus station opened in Mount Street, Nottingham, which was an addition to the existing facility at Huntingdon Street. Services 8, Nottingham-Derby, 61, Nottingham-Mansfield and 60, Nottingham-Hucknall were transferred to the new station. This gave the Company's local management some difficulty, because service 84, Nottingham-Sutton in Ashfield, via Hucknall remained at Huntingdon Street. Whereas under the previous arrangement passengers for Hucknall could easily be divided between the two services, this advantage was now lost.

On 14th October, 1943, Mr O C Power died. He had, as previously mentioned, been Traffic Manager at Midland Red, for many years but had, in addition, brought his experience to bear in over twenty years as a Director of Trent. Thus, the direct association with Midland Red came to an end although, of course, both companies remained BET subsidiaries.

At the turn of the year, the fifteen SOS FEDD double deckers were converted from petrol to diesel by fitting AEC 7.7 litre diesel engines in place of the previous SOS petrol units. This improved the fuel consumption, and also their performance, which had previously been rather sluggish. Carlyle Works supplied strengthening pieces for the chassis, to cope with the additional vibration from the diesel engine.

In 1944, a further twelve utility Daimler CWA6s were obtained, and these were 1303-5, RC 8391-3, with Brush lowbridge 55 seat bodies, 1099-1106, RC 8394-401, with Roe 56 seat highbridge bodies, and 1107, RC 8402, with Brush 56 seat highbridge bodywork.

Towards the end of the year, consideration again turned to future vehicle requirements and the forward orders were amended to 15 AEC double deckers with Willowbrook bodies and fifty AEC single deckers, also with Willowbrook bodies. Six AEC single deck chassis were also ordered without bodies, to be fitted with existing bodies previously removed from Daimler chassis, already in storage. In addition, it was decided that the bodies on the twelve existing SOS ON coaches would be overhauled by Willowbrook, and they would be fitted with AEC diesel engines.

On 13th November, 1944, Barton had taken over the business of E & H Frakes of Castle Donnington. This included a garage, a service between Castle Donnington and Long Eaton, and a service from Castle Donnington to Derby, which was suspended at the time. Barton incorporated the Long Eaton service with their existing 3B service to Nottingham but, in March 1945 the goodwill of the Derby service, and the garage were sold to Trent, although the actual purchase completion of the garage did not take place until 23rd January, 1946.

From April, 1945, improved services were started from the Blagreaves Lane area to Derby, and a direct service introduced from Barrow on Trent, via Normanton Road, Cavendish and Sunnyhill on Fridays and Saturdays. These changes were to serve the increased housing development in the Blagreaves Lane area, but were only the first of a number of changes to serve this area.

The war with Germany came to an end on 8th May, 1945, and Japan surrendered on 15th August, 1945, bringing to an end six years of struggle. Further utility Daimlers were received, although the bodywork on these was to a more relaxed style with rounded domes and other features, such as upholstered seats, whilst still retaining the same basic outline.

Thirteen were received during 1945, these being 1108-11, RC 8464-7, with Duple highbridge 56 seat bodies, 1309-12, RC 8480-3, with Duple 55 seat lowbridge bodywork, 1112-15, RC 8530-3, with Brush highbridge 56 seat body work and 1116, RC 8570, one more Duple highbridge, the last utility vehicle. 1112-3, with Daimler engines were the only CWD6s to be received, and 1114-6 were CWA6Ds, which had a rear axle of Daimler's own make, rather than the Kirkstall unit previously used.

In October, 1945, T A Lewis Ltd, of East Bridgford was taken over, with services East Bridgford-Nottingham, via Radcliffe on Trent, East Bridgford-Newark and Excursions from East Bridgford. The services took Trent route numbers 68 and 81, respectively. Five vehicles were also included, but these were not operated, being immediately resold to Robin Hood Transport, Ltd.

In November, Mr R J Howley, CBE resigned as Chairman, although remaining on the Board. He had been in at the beginning, and had been Chairman since 1929. His place was taken by Mr R P Beddow who had, at one time, been Company Secretary.

A final event to close the year was the arrival, just before Christmas, of the first six post-war AEC Regal chassis, ready to receive the stored coach bodies from the pre-war Daimlers.

With the war over, there was much to be done by way of fleet renewal and reinstatement of services suspended during the war. The next volume will tell the story of the fleet renewal, of many new vehicles and the rehabilitation and rebodying of old ones. A new, simplified livery was introduced. Early post war vehicles were all built by AEC, but in the early fifties there was a change to Leyland.

Immediately after the war, there was an enormous increase in traffic, reaching its peak in the early fifties, before beginning a long, slow decline as people bought televisions and stayed at home for entertainment, or bought cars so they no longer needed the buses.

Later, the Company was taken into state ownership, when BET sold its UK bus interests to the Government, and remained so for nearly twenty years, before returning once again to private ownership and achieving national recognition for high standards of customer service. There were very few small takeovers, but part of North Western was absorbed, all of Midland General and, eventually, even the fiercely independent Barton became a sister company, with further service rationalisation and close working with Trent.

But all of that is another story....

The Vehicles

The Trent fleet was always comparatively standardised, in the sense of significant batches of identical vehicles. In the early days, the fleet started to develop with Tilling-Stevens vehicles and BET body styles were used. There was a varied selection in the early twenties, followed by complete standardisation on SOS models with their rather idiosyncratic styling but undoubted performance qualities. Later, although SOS chassis continued to be used, Trent went their own way with bodywork, and more mainstream body styles were fitted, built by manufacturers of their own choosing. As Midland Red needed more of their production for themselves, Trent turned to AEC for chassis with standardised body styles by Weymann and Willowbrook, with a small contribution by Duple. However, these were of some interest because they did not follow the BET standard of the day.

The double deckers were to a design which was supplied mainly to Trent and, although seemingly on Weymann's standard frames, were significantly different in appearance from similar, but metal framed bodywork by the same supplier which was built for neighbouring Midland General, also on AEC chassis. The single deckers were based on a design first supplied to the Company by Brush, on an experimental Daimler COG5 chassis. The style of that body seems to have been adopted as standard by Trent, and supplied to no other operator.

After AEC, many Daimlers were bought, which was unusual for a BET company, although SOS also supplied some further single deck and coach chassis, but none with bodies to their own design. By the time that war broke out, the fleet was becoming very standardised in appearance, although some variety was brought about by the different chassis used, and doubtless this standardisation would have continued, had the war not intervened.

In wartime, after outstanding peacetime orders had been completed, only utility specification vehicles could be obtained, but here the Company was particularly fortunate.The Government had decided that Guy and Daimler would supply the nation's requirements for double deck bodies during the war, although Bristol also came in towards the end. Guy supplied by far the larger quantity, but Trent was able secure all of its chassis allocations from Daimler and the vehicles fitted in well with the existing fleet.

The following selection of photographs endeavours to show a good cross section of the vehicles supplied to the company from the beginning to 1945, which is the end of the period covered by this volume. It also shows a selection of vehicles acquired or operated by the many smaller businesses, which were taken over by Trent during, the period covered.

Inevitably, there are some gaps in the coverage, due to the passage of time, but most types operated have been illustrated. The war years have proved a particular problem, as photography of buses was difficult during that time. Not only was film in short supply, but also photographers were liable to attract the attention of the authorities and be called upon to provide an explanation of the purpose of their activities! Thus, most pictures of wartime buses in this volume show the vehicles in their post war condition.

Soon after the start of CCHL's service between Derby and Ashbourne, this Commer WP was registered CH 405 on 23rd October, 1909. It was photographed in wintry conditions, early in 1910 on the Ashbourne-Derby road, when very lightly loaded. The vehicle, which was painted green and white with white coachlining, did not stay with CCHL long enough to join the Trent fleet, but was converted to a lorry and sold to a London firm. These Commers had a pre-selector gearbox and each gear was selected on a horizontal quadrant below the steering wheel, the change then being effected by dipping the clutch, but could also be achieved using the throttle lever, or automatically by the action of the governor on the engine speed, The internal mechanism was not dissimilar to a conventional gearbox, but with a special operating mechanism, and had no resemblance to the epicyclic gearbox developed by W G Wilson in later years, which could also be preselector and, later, automatically controlled.

The Early Fleet
Commercial Car Hirers and Trent

As described and illustrated in the text, the early vehicles were all Commers. Later a number of Maudslays were purchased, but these were soon sold to the War Office for use in the First War, leaving the fleet reduced to just two vehicles.

This well known photograph shows LE 9601, a Commer WP with Scammell & Nephew B22C bodywork which was new in 1911, and passed to Trent in 1913 as one of their first vehicles. Inside, there was a partition behind the entrance, with a sliding door, providing a rear saloon for non-smokers, and the centre entrance was guarded by a foldable trellis gate. Note the name J C Moth, Secretary on the lower panel between the driver and conductor. It was CCHL's practice to identify their vehicles by names, and LE 9601 was named "Willow", thus following the established practice that the names usually began with the letter W. Note also the number 9, on the bonnet side. The vehicle was withdrawn by Trent in 1915, and returned to CCHL, finally becoming a lorry in 1917. The bodybuilders, Scammell and Nephew were based at Spittalfields, London and later became well known at Watford as Scammell Lorries Ltd.

Trent's first new vehicles were a batch of six Commer WP 36hp with bodywork of unknown make registered CH 892-7 and all new in January, 1914. Livery was French Grey and CH 897 was the last one.

The first bulk order placed by the Company was initially for six, but later increased to twelve, Maudslay 40hp with bodywork by Brush. D110, CH 1058 pauses en route for Belper when new.

The first Tilling-Stevens chassis received the Brush bodies removed from the 1914 Maudslays sold to the War Office. This June, 1921 picture, shows D 107, new in 1916, carrying one of the Brush bodies. Driver Len Everett and Conductress Gladys Oliver stand in Heanor Market Place either side of Mr Hunt, the Town's fishmonger. A full load of passengers look on and await departure for Derby.

Tilling-Stevens to the Rescue!

With just two Commers left, the Company was desperate for vehicles, but fortunately the Tilling-Stevens came to the rescue as it employed petrol-electric transmission that did not find favour with the Army, and so the type was not wanted for the war. Over a period of eight years, or so, Tilling-Stevens was the only make purchased and these vehicles undoubtedly helped the Company to progress its early development. Over the years, a variety of body styles and makes were fitted, and there was a major body swapping exercise during 1920, as new bodies were received, and the original ones were overhauled for further use. In those days, the registration number tended to stay with the body, rather than being specifically related to the chassis, as would happen today. Whilst lists exist in the Company's records, they are incomplete and it is, in many cases, impossible to discern the full picture. All information in relation to this is therefore, presented at face value within the limitation of what is available.In later years, many vehicles were converted to standard transmission, using SOS components and were known as "Tilling B-Type".Most, if not all, were fitted with pneumatic tyres, as well.

Mystery surrounds the figures 12 and 10, painted on the back of Tilling-Stevens CH 1224. However, this rare view shows the back of one of the Holmes Bros bodies on D104, which retained its original registration number due to receiving a new body. The previous body became a temporary spare. Although not very clear in this particular picture, we see the early use of the "TMT" garter on the back of the vehicle, beneath the destination board.

The business like interior of the bodywork fitted to the Tilling-Stevens. The leather cushions and backrests, doubtless filled with horsehair, look pretty firm and not the type of place you would wish to sit for too long, especially having regard to the quality of ride which would have been provided by the solid tyred wheels! Note the wooden seat frames with grab handles, the slatted floor and the inward folding half-drop window.

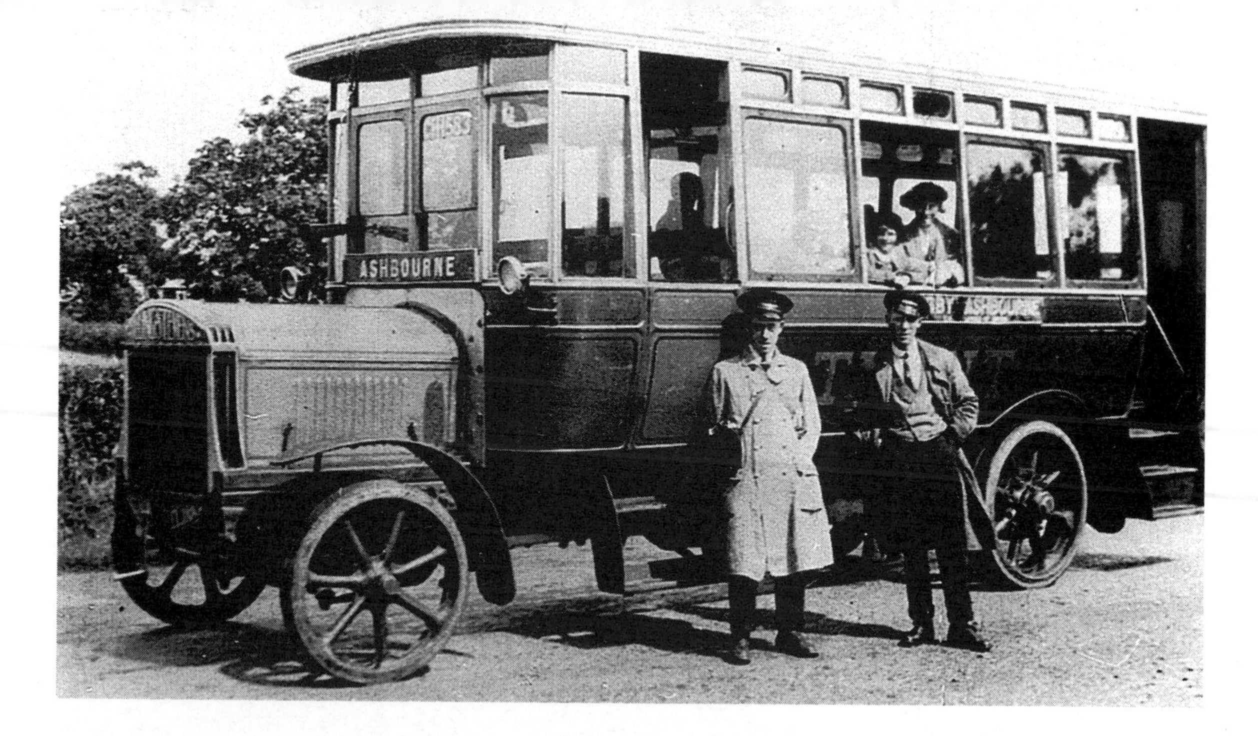

Compare this view of D118, CH 1583, with that on page 76, shown earlier. This vehicle, another Tilling-Stevens TS3 has one of the later style bodies built by Birch, or by Holmes Bros. Although still built on similar carpentry principles, the curved front panels, with the windscreen seeming to "wrap around" the front gives a more pleasing appearance. The bus carries destination boards for the historic Ashbourne service.

A number of Tilling Stevens were fitted with charabanc bodies and converted to "B Type" with a standard clutch and gearbox in place of the petrol electric transmission. One such was D140, registration number not confirmed, but seen here with Birch bodywork, waiting a private hire party, outside Derby's Station Inn in Midland Road. The individual doors for each row of seats, and the foldback hood, are typical of the period

From 1923 onwards, several of the original fleet of Tilling Stevens TS3s were rebuilt into one form or another. As already mentioned, some were rebuilt with conventional clutch and gearbox. Others were rebuilt to forward control and fitted with new bodywork, as shown by this photograph showing TS 2566, after rebodying, by which time it had been numbered 401. Like other bodies of the time, the Brush 32-seat bodywork was well proportioned, but the whole vehicle continued to look crude due to the solid tyres. Later, most of the surviving solid tyred vehicles were fitted with pneumatics which represented a major advancement. Note the use of the number P3 immediately behind the front bulkhead. This is thought to have been a running number related to the duty schedule, and somewhat akin to London practice which continues today. Their use by Trent does not seem to have lasted long, being fitted to vehicles from about 1924 to about 1929/30. The rear view of shows the large, twin rear lights, well ahead of their time, for in later years, vehicles tended to have a single light to the offside, before modern lighting standards came into force. Also visible are the full drop windows, open along the nearside, and a clear view of the TMT garter on the rear panel. The large windows are noteworthy, as is the registration number directly on the glass surface using signwriting or, more probably, transfers, in a style that was used on new vehicles for many years.

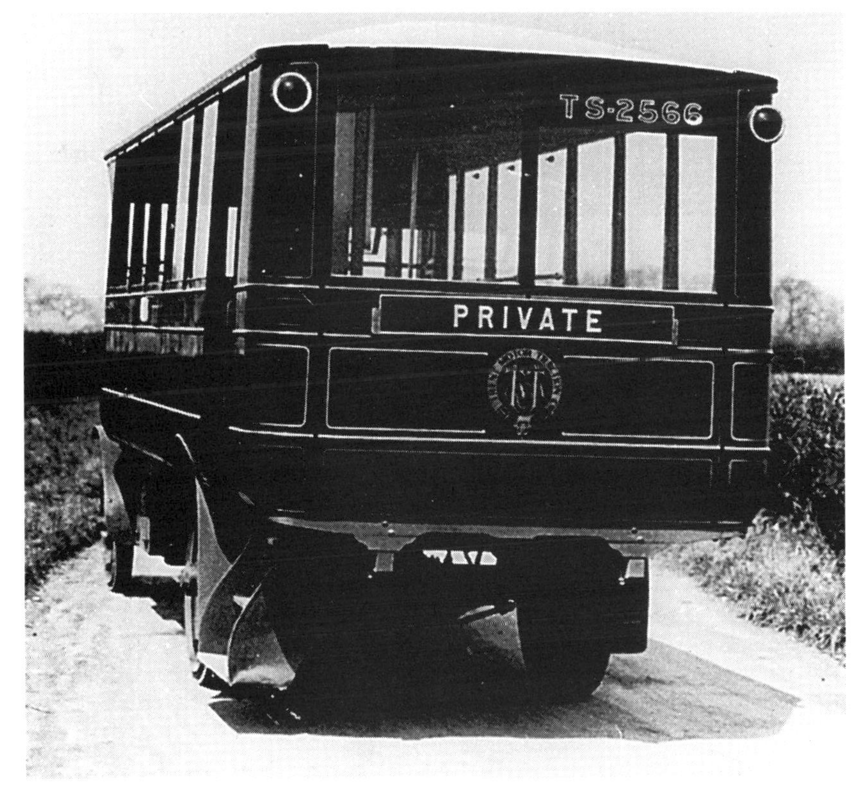

A view of Thornycroft J CH 2972, after conversion to forward control and fitted with a new single deck bus body, probably built by Brush. The pressed steel wheels are particularly noteworthy, as these were used from an early date by Thornycroft, in preference to the cast wheels more commonly used by other manufacturers at the time. The Thornycroft J chassis had originally been designed as a lorry chassis and had a 4 cylinder engine developing 40hp, driving through a cone clutch and four speed gearbox. The footbrake operated on a drum fitted at the back of the gearbox, whilst the handbrake operated directly at the rear wheels. Four of the chassis received double deck bodywork, by Birch, whilst still retaining normal control layout - see the photograph on page 24.

Thornycrofts and Vulcans.

After standardising on Tilling Stevens for some years, the opportunity arose to purchase war surplus vehicles from the Army Mechanical Transport Depot at Slough, Bucks. Thirteen Thornycroft chassis were bought and these were lengthened, refurbished and fitted with new bodies, with one being cannibalised for spares. In addition, as the Tilling Stevens were somewhat slow and ponderous, something nippy was needed to compete with the lightweight vehicles used by the small operators. Four small Vulcans were bought to cater for this need.

This photograph shows one of the Thornycroft Js, CH 2972, soon after acquisition, when it was fitted with a Birch charabanc body. Later, the vehicle was rebuilt and fitted with a saloon body, as shown opposite.

One of the Vulcan VSDs bought in 1922, to fight off competition from small operators. These were the first vehicles in the fleet with pneumatic tyres from new, and they proved highly satisfactory in combating the lighter vehicles used by the independents. The Vulcans had a 3.7 litre 4 cylinder engine driving through a 4-speed gearbox and proved nippy and economical. Other major operators, such as Ribble and Southdown bought similar vehicles to beat the small operators.

In 1924, Tilling-Stevens were chosen once again for new vehicles, which were the first to be delivered in the Company's new BET light red livery, adopted in that year. There were ten each of single and double deck models, all with Brush bodies and based on the TS6 model, this being a longer development of the TS3 with forward control layout, as illustrated by this view of 204 (CH 4066). Note the cab door, hinged along the front edge, and the quite heavily raked steering column protruding through the front panel to a steering box ahead of the front wheels. Other driver's equipment is the bulb horn, on the front of the cab, and the rather amusing hand signal, which could be swung outwards when required from inside the cab.

More Tilling-Stevens, and some lightweight Daimlers

After the Thornycrofts and Vulcans, there was a return to Tilling-Stevens. Also new, lightweight Daimlers with conventional transmission arrived and these were a major step forward, but only a foretaste of what was to come later.

In later life, many of the Tilling Stevens TS6s were rebuilt with a split propeller shaft and disc wheels fitted with pneumatic tyres. One such was CH 4077, caught by the camera enjoying an extended life as a showman's van at Nottingham's famous Goose Fair in October, 1935. This was a popular use in earlier times for buses no longer suitable for bus fleets, but with life still left in them. The Tilling Stevens were especially popular for this work, since the dynamo could power and light the roundabouts.

This specially posed shot of 201 (CH 4063), illustrates the high build of the 57-seat bodywork with a quite hefty second step up to the platform. The solid tyres suggest a crude appearance although the vehicles were actually quite well proportioned and featured the five bay construction which became the established layout for double deckers for a great many years. The Dunlop advertisement on the staircase decency screen is typical of the period. The upper deck construction of the Brush built body, consisting of wooden planks over a frame, was fairly crude and, in reality, little more than an enclosure built on top of a single deck body. Almost certainly, this picture was taken when the vehicle was some years old, as metal panels have been fixed over the upper deck side panels. This vehicle remained in the fleet, largely unaltered save for conversion to pneumatic tyres, until withdrawn in 1932.

Vehicle standards took a major leap forward, with the arrival in 1925 of a batch of fifteen Daimler CMs with Ransomes B32F bodywork, which were the first full size vehicles with pneumatic tyres. Although reverting to normal control, and retaining a high build, they were of a rather sleeker appearance than earlier vehicles, and this was accentuated by the steel disc wheels with pneumatic tyres. 808 (CH 4855) at the Ransomes Works, prior to delivery.

The smooth lines and superb paint finish of the Ransomes bodywork are clearly evident in this further view of 808. The Daimler CMs had a peculiar characteristic when the engine was switched off. The crew would walk away to get hot water to brew tea a cup of tea in their Billy can at the terminus, and as they did so, the remaining unburned petrol in the engine cylinders would explode with a loud report, startling horses and passers by. Apparently, the Police were called on more than one occasion to investigate the disturbance, but no charges were brought, since they couldn't establish that anyone had done anything illegal!

This interior shot of FM 3536, a Daimler CM with the same bodywork as those supplied to Trent, but delivered to the Wrexham & District Transport Co, Ltd illustrates the form of construction used with lightweight framing featuring strengthening gussets, and no interior lining to the upper sections. The seats, whilst still fairly basic in design, appear to offer greater comfort than those fitted to the Tilling Stevens shown earlier. The bodies weighed only 3tons 15cwts (3,810kg) and this, coupled with the quality Daimler sleeve valve engine, no doubt made the vehicles lively performers.

After the arrival of the first few SOSs in 1925/26, when five of the Daimler CMs gave up their bodies for fitting to new SOS S type chassis, new Davidson charabanc bodies were fitted instead. The vehicles concerned were renumbered 851-5. The first, 851, CH 4853, is shown in its new guise about to depart on a private hire from somewhere near Trent Bridge. Many people wore hats in those days, and one cannot but wonder why they didn't blow off in the airflow as the open vehicle gathered speed. Although nominally limited to 20mph, no doubt the Daimler chassis was eminently suitable for such work and travelled at a speed well in excess of that figure.

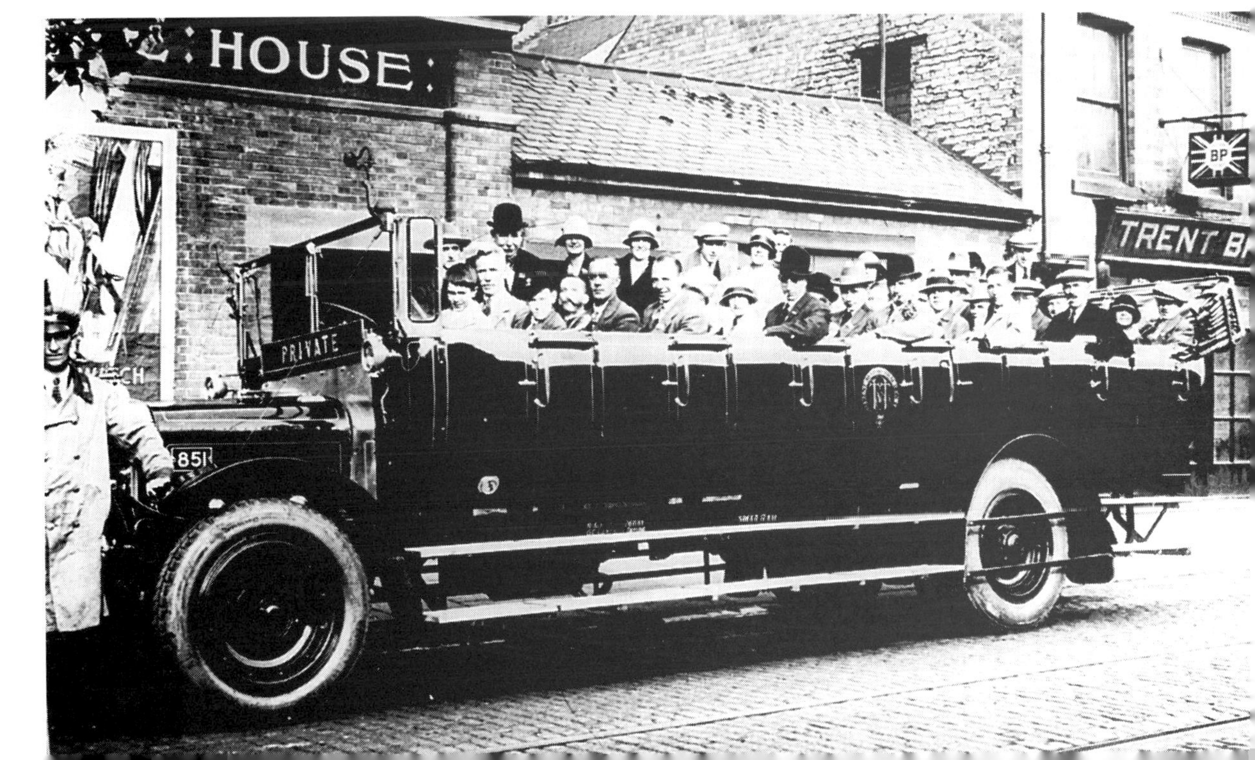

919 (CH 5430) was an SOS Standard with Ransomes bodywork to Midland Red design. In many ways, this seems a backward step in appearance compared with the earlier Daimler CMs - Wyndham-Shire was no follower of fashion and always had his own ideas about bus design! The vehicles, however, were light, nippy, reliable and just what was needed at the time. Clearly this vehicle was built for Midland Red and that Company's name is just visible cast into the radiator top tank. However, a plate with the Trent name was fitted over this before entering service, and this applied to a number of SOS models bought by Trent.

The SOS Revolution Begins!

In 1925, the SOS revolution began! Midland Red had been developing their own make of vehicle under the able guidance of their Chief Engineer, L G Wyndham-Shire, and the result was the Standard SOS, or S type, as they later became known. Wyndham-Shire had developed this model from the Tilling-Stevens TS3 (which explains the similarity in the radiator design) but used a conventional gearbox and plate clutch, in place of the petrol electric transmission. Trent took two, CH 4946/7, in 1925, and a further thirty, CH 5423-53, in 1926. The last five received bodies removed from the 1924 Daimler CMs.

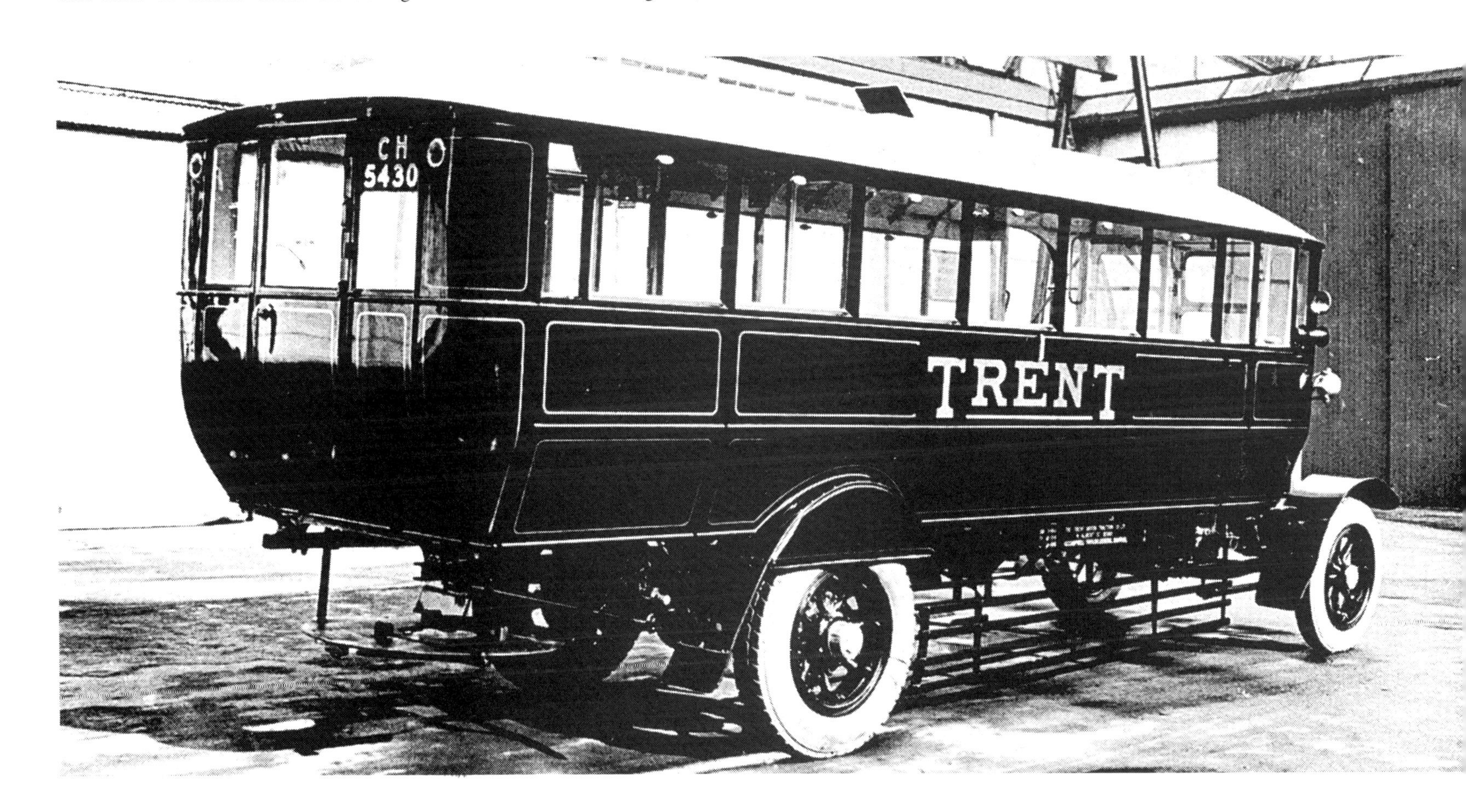

The Shire designed bodywork had a fairly unrefined appearance, partly due to the detailing, but also because of the sharp inward taper of the plywood rocker panels and the resulting edge running the length of the vehicle, which also led to an uncomfortable join with the smoothly curved rear panels. Note once again the high build, also the deep lifeguard rails, the half spats over the rear wheels and the good sized rear lights. SOS vehicles were to become the Trent standard for the next fifteen years, or so.

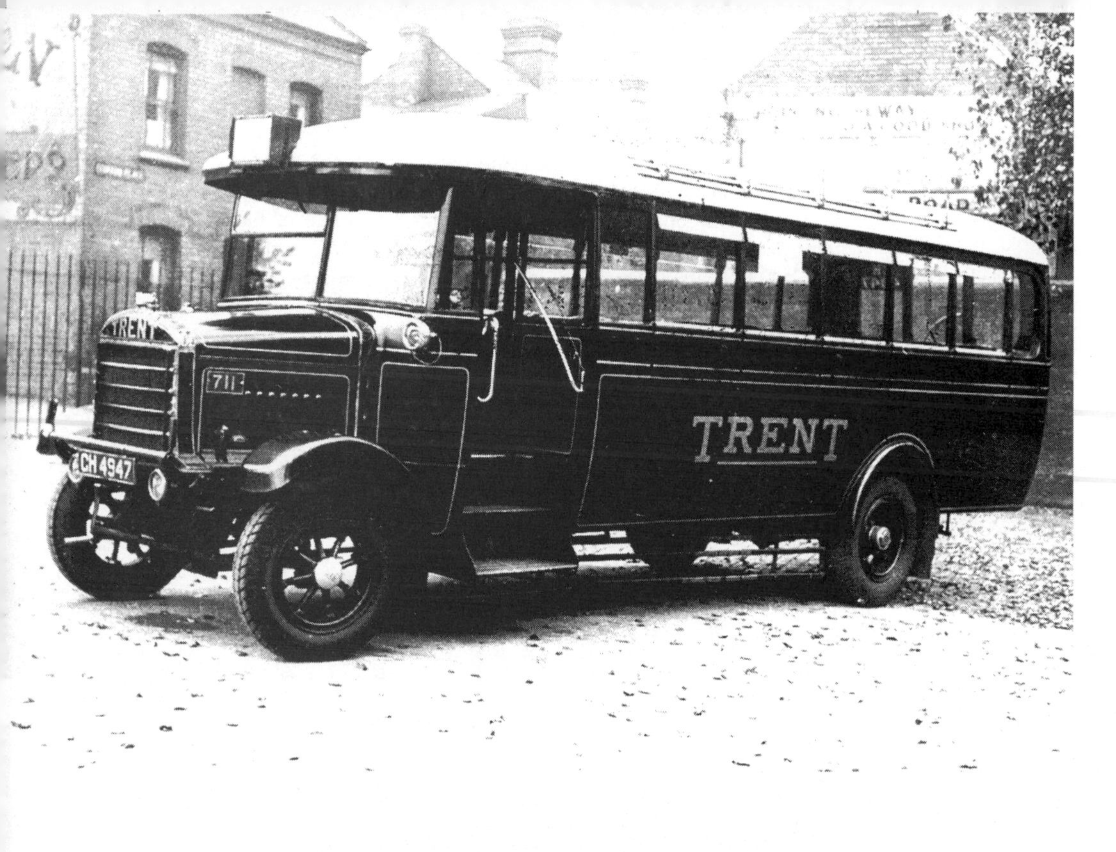

In 1930, twenty-one Standards were rebuilt and rebodied followed by the remaining eleven in 1931. The result was something of a transformation, as the new 30 seat bodies were well proportioned, rounded and attractive - quite stylish, in fact. The mechanical specification remained largely unchanged, although smaller wheels were fitted, which resulted in a slightly lower step height.

This autumnal view, taken at Nottingham's Huntingdon Street Bus Station in October 1933, shows CH 4947, one of the advance pair of Standards delivered in 1925, after conversion to ODD type and rebodying by Midland Red, using United parts. Originally numbered 900 when new, it was renumbered 711 upon rebodying.The box above the front peak was a later addition to carry a route number stencil and, apart from spoiling the lines of the vehicle, this must have been difficult to change, requiring the crew to climb onto the bonnet.

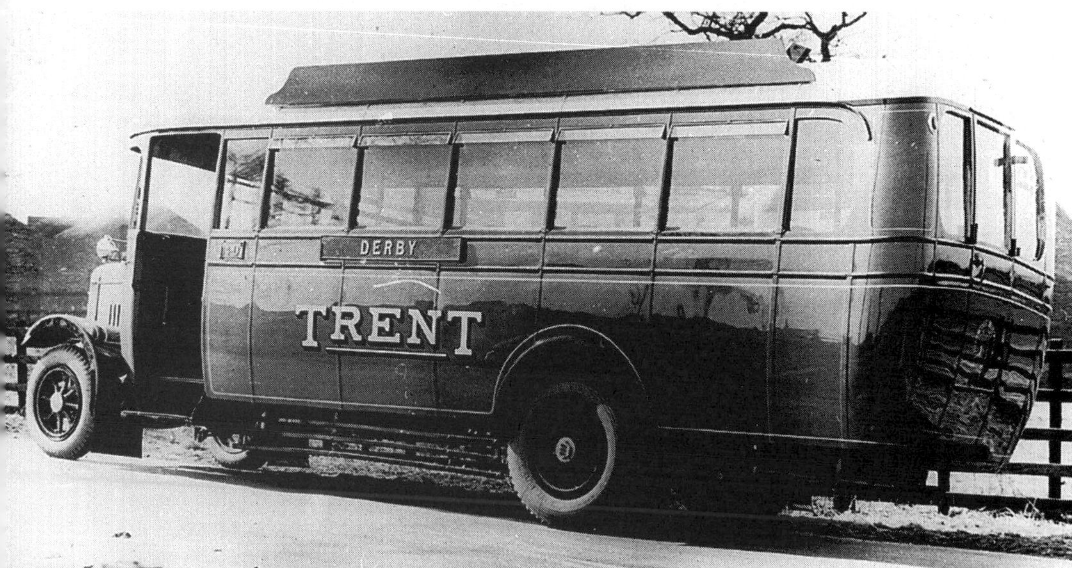

Twelve of the first twenty-one new bodies were built by United at their coach factory at Lowestoft, later to become Eastern Coach Works, the remainder being assembled by Midland Red at Carlyle Works. In 1931, the remaining eleven vehicles were similarly treated, but received bodies to identical design, built by Brush of Loughbough. This view of Brush bodied CH 5446 shows the red paint carried up the rear dome as far as the window line - note the additional moulding connecting the side and rear windows at their top edge. Others had the white carried down the rear dome as far as the waistrail. Although fitted for service, with advertisement boards and destination added, the vehicle was evidently still awaiting fleet number plates .

The SOSs clearly made a good impression, for 1927 deliveries of service buses consisted of twenty-five SOS Q types with B37F bodies by Brush. These were a further development of the SOS FS type, which Trent never bought until ten used examples were acquired from Midland Red in 1935. The FS was essentially a forward control version of the S, which seated 34, compared with the 26 of the S. The Q type took this further, by shortening the cab and allowing the engine to protrude slightly into the saloon, where it was covered by a specially shaped plate. The engine and gearbox were relocated off centre, towards the nearside. The use of angled plywood rocker panels was carried forward from the S type. Note the multi bay window layout, the rear wheel spats, the angled destination board, over the bonnet, and the route number stencil over the cab. 954 (CH 6234) at Nottingham Huntingdon Street Bus Station in the early thirties.

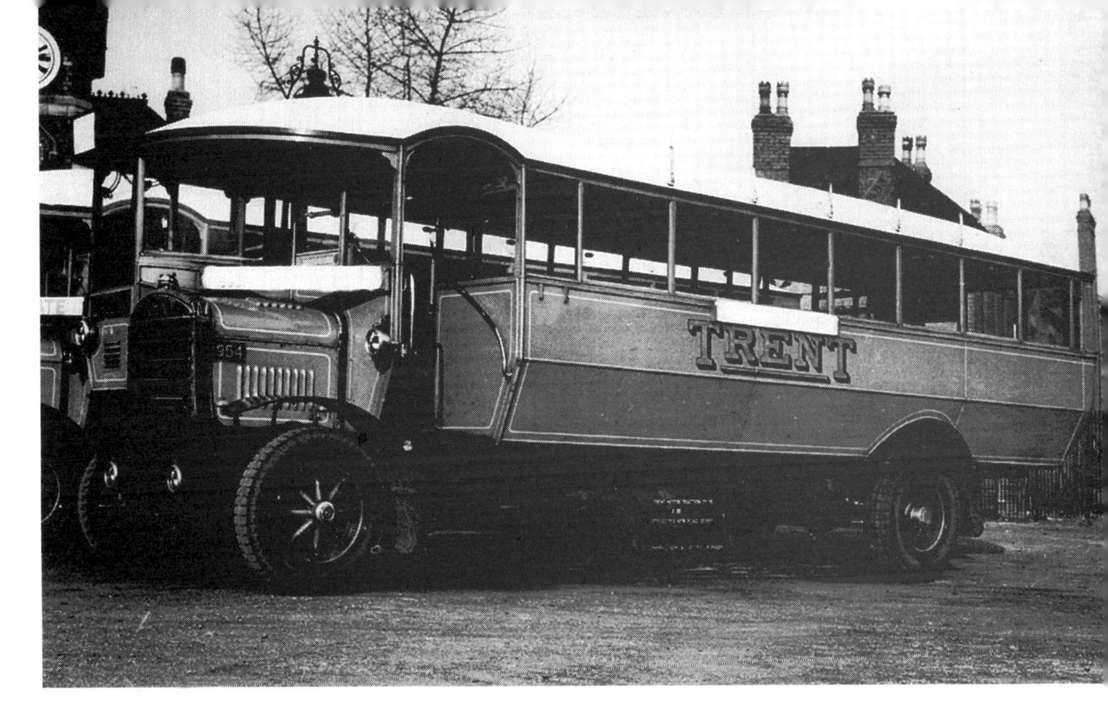

This official shot of 958 shows clearly the offset engine and radiator but, despite this, the cab dimensions still look cramped. The Trent plate screwed onto the radiator top tank, doubtless obscures the Midland Red title beneath, and the stencil box above the cab would normally have been used for the route number, rather than the Trent sign. The whole appearance is clearly designed for practicality, with little concession to style except, perhaps, for the rounded shape of the front canopy. The Qs had rear wheel brakes only and were prone to skidding under moderate braking on poor surfaces, because of this.

Interior view of bus no 970 (CH 6251), showing the tongue and groove timber roof (covered on the outside with waterproofing fabric, treated with white lead paint), the clear glass lighting units and the continuous bell pull. Note also the intermediate bulkhead and the timber frame seats. The seat covering was leather, brown when new but later treated to change the colour to plum to match the seats in later deliveries. Non-smokers were asked not to sit in the seats behind the bulkhead when other seats were available.

In 1933, the Qs were rebuilt and their appearance considerably improved. Carried out by Trent, the work involved fitting curved rocker panels, improved mudguards, without spats in the case of those at the back, relocation of the route number stencil beneath the canopy, and the addition of a dark red waistband. However, no brakes were fitted to the front wheels! This, despite the fact that Midland Red were able to fit hydraulic brakes on the front wheels of their examples. 957 (CH 6238) at Nottingham in 1933, soon after the work was completed.

The charabanc equivalent of the Q was the QC, portrayed here by 603, CH 6259, one of five delivered in 1927 with Carlyle bodywork. Note the normal control layout and the deep spats over the rear wheels, together with the use of the Trent garter on the side, in preference to the standard fleet name. These features were all intended to provide a more genteel appearance then the workaday buses, although the mechanical specification of the two types of chassis was not greatly different. The batch of vehicles remained in the fleet until 1936, which meant that they gave a good period of service at a time of rapid change in vehicle design, although of they would not have seen heavy use, generally being used only during the summer months, when the fold back roof was doubtless popular. Petrol was 1/2d (5.9p) a gallon when this picture was taken outside the old Derby Vulcanising Co premises in London Road, evidently at the start of a staff outing. The period advertising hoarding is an interesting backdrop, worthy of study in itself.

The main new vehicle deliveries in 1928 were no less than thirty-eight SOS QLs, with the bodywork order being split evenly between Brush and Ransomes. 537, CH 7706, was photographed outside the Ransomes works prior to delivery. The spoked wheels have now given way to modern pressed steel wheels of smaller diameter giving a lower ride height. However, the Shire designed body style is largely unaltered from that of the Qs delivered in the previous year. Note also that twin rear wheels were now fitted and the route number stencil was fitted beneath the front canopy, rather than above the cab as originally on the Qs.

One of the Brush bodied examples photographed in the layover area at Nottingham Huntingdon Street Bus Station in August, 1933. The destination boards, angled over the bonnet and in slots along the side, are very much in the Trent style of the day. The destination was in red, with the intermediate points in black lettering. One wonders how effective they were at night, with no visible lighting. Like the Q, shown earlier, a dark red waistband had been applied.

Like the Q before, the QL had a coach equivalent, and Trent took three of these QLCs, with Short bodywork, in 1928. 650, CH 7145, was photographed at Skegness, on a private hire outing in July, 1929. The radiator is very similar in appearance to the Tilling Stevens Petrol Electrics and also the early SOSs which, of course, were derived from the Tilling Stevens. Note the words "Motor Services" cast into the bottom tank, in accordance with Midland Red practice, at the time.

For 1929, there was further development of the SOS, for the M type was introduced, and buses of this type came to be known as 'Madams'. The build was much lower, and the appearance was much improved by the fitting of full front wings, evenly spaced, larger windows requiring fewer pillars and curved sides, in place of the angular panels of the previous models. The interior was more comfortable, with bucket seats being featured. Bodywork was by Brush, and 417, CH 8114, was photographed at Nottingham, in April, 1933.

The rear view of Madam 420 illustrates to good effect the pressed metal number plate, which was a feature of the fleet from around 1924 until 1962 and which had the background painted in a particular colour to signify the depot to which the vehicle was allocated. The "target" type of advertisement on the emergency door became a feature around the time that these vehicles were new.

The seventeen service buses delivered in 1930 were Brush bodied SOS COD type, nominally designed by Mr P G Stone-Clarke, the Trent Company's Chief Engineer of the day. The COD chassis was a variation on the Madam, and the bodywork took the Madam style a little further in terms of appearance by reducing the number of bays from seven to six. It also eliminated the porch type of entrance and subtle radii were applied to the corners of the rear most window. Note, also, the new flat-topped radiator style. In this official view, CH 8908 is shown with its initial fleet number 458, which was changed to 208 in 1932.

CH 8902 is shown with its original number, 452, but received the number 202 in 1932, when the entire batch was re-numbered from 450-66 to 200-216 at the same time as the first batch of IM4s was re-numbered into the 2xx series, leaving only the Madams numbered in the 4xx series.In addition to the seventeen CODs built for Trent, twenty-three were built by Midland Red for their own use, and also twenty-one for PMT. Most of the Trent examples were transferred to Midland Red, during the war.

Three more QLC coaches also arrived during 1930 to join those received the previous year. They had Short bodywork of generally similar design to their predecessors. However, they featured a new radiator of smooth outline and modern appearance, although the design was not repeated on any further vehicles. This change was accompanied by new, larger headlamps, mounted at a higher level than before. They had a six cylinder engine in place of the 4cylinder unit fitted to the earlier versions, and were thus more powerful. 671, CH 8920 was photographed at Nottingham in August, 1934

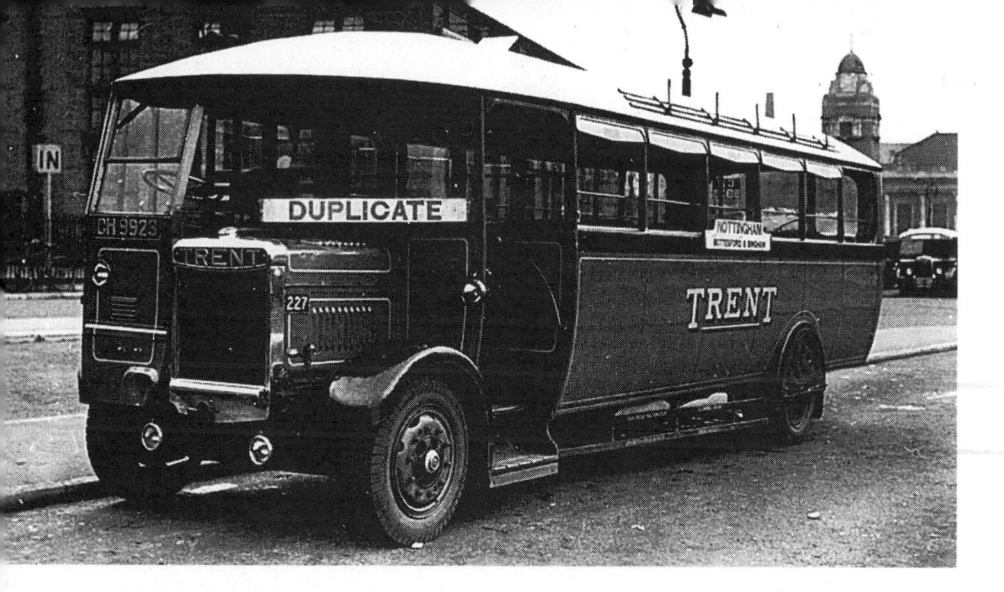

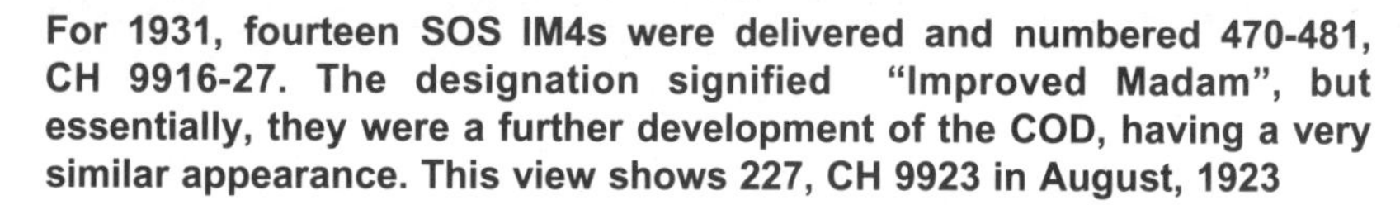

For 1931, fourteen SOS IM4s were delivered and numbered 470-481, CH 9916-27. The designation signified "Improved Madam", but essentially, they were a further development of the COD, having a very similar appearance. This view shows 227, CH 9923 in August, 1923

There were also 16 IM6s, 120-135, CH9900-15, which featured the new SOS RR2SB engine coupled to the "silent third" gearbox. They were of similar appearance to the IM4s, save for a deeper version of the new flat-topped radiator. Compare this rear view with that of the original M shown previously. The general proportions are similar, but the roof and windows are more curvaceous.

Further IM4s followed in 1932 and 235, RC410, is pictured in a remarkable afterlife when some sixteen years old. In the post war period, London Transport experienced a severe vehicle shortage, before bulk deliveries of the classic RT type got into full swing. Private operators were engaged to assist, and one such supplied the former Trent vehicle for use on Route 96, running between Putney Common and Aldgate, in 1948, the bus having been sold by Trent in January, 1947. As might be expected, the Trent nameplate had been removed from the radiator top tank, and a sticker reading " On Hire To London Transport Executive" is just visible along the lower edge of the front bulkhead window.

The driver still sat over the petrol tank on the IM4, as shown clearly by this view of 254, RC 539, which was delivered a few months after the vehicle in the previous picture. This led to the unusual arrangement of the cab door, which was hinged from the front offside corner of the body. Note the ventilation flap, open in the roof, and the usual frame for the side advertisements over the windows.

There were also ten six cylinder IM6s delivered in 1932, and the bodywork on these was to the same design and 32 seats capacity as the IM4s, although built by Short, rather than Brush. The additional power from the larger engine was intended to be used on longer distance services, but when this photograph was taken, in July, 1935, 145, RC 910, had only run in on the short service from Hucknall.

The twentyfive IM4s delivered in 1933 show little change from their predecessors, although fitted with Short bodywork. 272, RC 1291 looked work worn in Nottingham, when awaiting a spell of duty on service 68 to Cotmanhay, operated jointly with Midland General, in September, 1938. In the background, a Barton Leyland Lion and Leyland Cub await their respective duties.

Sister vehicle 271 was nearing the end of its service life when photographed in August, 1948. It was withdrawn in Autumn, 1949, having put in a creditable 16 years service.

This photograph shows to good effect the attractive lines of the first SOS ON types delivered to Trent in 1934. They marked a turning point, for they were the first vehicles for many years that did not have bodywork to the rather dated designs of Midland Red. Indeed, although many further SOS chassis were bought, there were only two further batches of vehicles with bodies to Midland Red's designs, and Trent vehicles began to take on a more mainstream appearance. The body design was known as the Duple "Rodney" type and, visible through the windows, note the high backed seats and curtained windows, which were complimented by an interior heating system for the winter. This batch of ON chassis supplied to Trent brought a more conventional layout around the cab with the cab door placed directly in front of the bulkhead, the petrol tank having been located below the floor of the saloon, in what was by then considered the conventional position. However, Midland Red persisted with the petrol tank under the driver's seat arrangement for its own deliveries and, indeed, Trent took further examples to this layout, but with bus bodywork.The vehicles had the SOS RR2LB 6cylinder petrol engine and the SOS "silent third" gearbox. They were superb and saw use on the Company's more prestigious routes, such as Manchester and, as this view in which 684, RC 1804, is about to leave Nottingham for Derby via Sandiacre. Barton competed end to end on this route, but went via Long Eaton and used Leyland Lions on their service. It is a great pity that these vehicles did not survive into the preservation era, but the entire batch were fitted with new Willowbrook bus bodies and AEC 7.7 litre diesel engines, as part of the post-war refurbishment programme.

Six ON type coaches, 625-30, RC 2546-51, arrived in 1935, with Duple coach bodies incorporating some of the design features of the dual-purpose vehicles delivered in the previous year, but lacking the subtlety and attractiveness of the earlier vehicles, despite the curved roofline and stepped waist rail, intended to make them more coach like. Fitted with 31 seats when new, the seating capacity of the batch was increased to 35 in 1938. Traditionally, SOS chassis had been light in weight and designed to carry lightweight bodywork, but the body on these vehicles was well appointed, and therefore rather heavy. As a result, the engines were prone to over-heating when used on Scottish tours during the summer months, despite the larger radiator that accompanied the six-cylinder engine. Streamlined paint schemes were becoming very fashionable in the mid-thirties, and this batch of vehicles introduced the idea to the Trent fleet, starting a trend that was to last until the war. The last of the batch, 630, RC 2551 at Nottingham, awaiting excursion duties in May, 1935, soon after delivery.

Diesel power entered the fleet in a serious way with the arrival of thirty SOS DON with Brush bodywork in 1935, the change in chassis designation signifying the change in engine type. Midland Red had not yet developed a diesel unit of its own, so the 7.7 litre AEC unit was used. However, the petrol SOS unit used previously had been very short, and the AEC unit was much longer. Thus, there was six inches (152mm) less length in the saloon, which kept the seating capacity to a maximum of 36, rather then 38, as had been possible on the petrol engine models built for Midland Red use. The appearance was much improved when compared with the IM models, featuring radiused window pans and a generally co-ordinated appearance, although the narrow cab with the windscreen seeming to sag to the offside still had a rather old fashioned look. Although roller blinds had been used to show destinations for some years on coaches, they at last appeared on this batch of buses, and the angled board over the bonnet began to be superseded, but the stencil beneath the canopy for the route number continued in use.The batch, numbered 300-29, RC 2700-29, was split in two, the first 15 having seats for thirty-six and standard external livery, as shown by 307, RC 2707, when new.

In contrast, 300, RC 2700 was photographed, very late in life and looking distinctly work worn, in March, 1952 shortly before withdrawal. Note the removal of the moulded waistline, and the rear wheel spats, also the simplified post-war livery. It is parked on Derby Cattle Market in Meadow Road. This was adjacent to the Central Bus Station and was, for many years, used as a layover area for spare buses, especially those allocated to Uttoxeter New Road Depot, which was then a running depot, to minimise dead mileage. The area is now entirely obliterated by the Inner Ring Road, built in 1969/70.

The second fifteen of the batch seated only thirty-four and externally carried the streamlined livery first seen on the coaches delivered earlier in the year. They also featured a slightly superior type of seat, and were thus of a dual-purpose nature. These views well illustrate the general styling features of both types of vehicle, and also the streamlined livery used. The views show 315, RC 2715, when new.

This interior view of the same vehicle shows comfortable seats and lining panels covered in moquette, the colour of which was probably based around a plum shade, in line with the leather fitted to earlier vehicles. Note the registration number on the rear window, which relied on the interior lights for illumination. This was common practice on buses for many years, but it meant that the interior lights had always to be on at night, even when running with no passengers, although on some vehicles, one or two suitably placed interior lights were wired in with the side and tail lights, to overcome this.

The Daimler COG5SD with Brush body delivered in 1935. Featuring the Gardner engine, which was to become legendary for its frugal fuel consumption, high torque and power output, the vehicle did not lead to any business for Daimler until bulk orders were placed for delivery in 1938, following further purchases of SOSs and some large batches of AECs. The right hand picture shows the unusual, but modern appearance of the back of the vehicle.

After a period of some three or four years with no double deckers in the fleet, the type returned in 1936 with the arrival of fifteen SOS FEDDs with Metro-Cammell metal framed bodywork. The type letters signified "Front Entrance Double Decker", and the bodywork, designed by Midland Red, was quite attractively proportioned save for the rather narrow cab similar to that found on SOS saloons, which allowed access to virtually the whole of the top of the engine. Although rather angular, the radiator, with its Trent plate screwed to the top tank, neat SOS letters and centre bright strip was a quite neatly executed design. They were the last vehicles for Trent with Midland Red designed bodywork.

The petrol tank beneath the driver's seat, and the front hinged cab door were both carried over from the saloons, as shown by 1008, RC 3330 when new.

Sister vehicle 1011, RC 3333, was photographed at Nottingham Huntingdon Street in September, 1936, when nearly new. At that time, the vehicles had the SOS RR2LB petrol engine coupled to the "silent third" gearbox and were rather underpowered, but in 1943 the entire batch were fitted with AEC 7.7 litre diesels which improved the performance and fuel consumption to good effect.

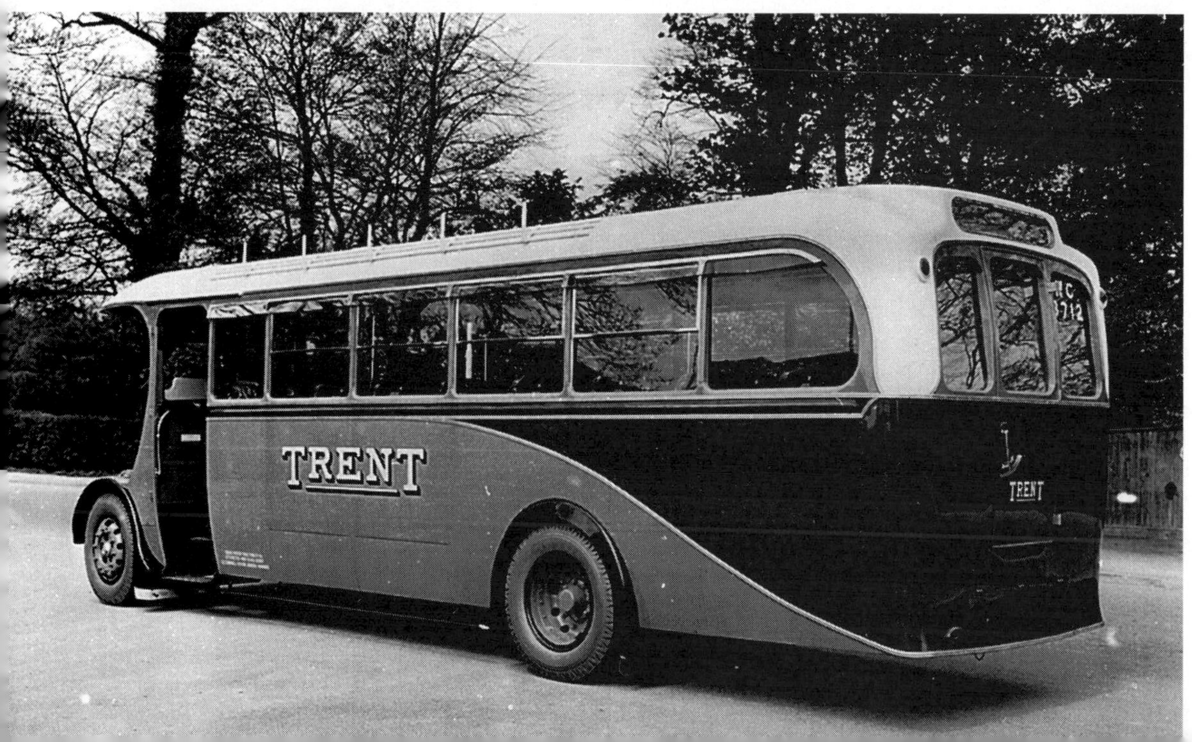

In the first part of the 1930s, many small operators were taken over, and many non-standard vehicles entered the fleet. To eliminate most of these, and continue modernisation of the fleet, no less than forty SOS DONs were purchased in 1936. All were bodied by Brush to a design the principal characteristics of which Trent henceforth adopted as standard until the early years of the war, and had built by Willowbrook and Duple, as well as Brush. It was similar to that on the Daimler COG5SD, RC 3210, delivered the previous year.The design was quite well proportioned, although the front had rather a square appearance, to match the angular SOS radiator. The squared off rear dome, together with the raised rear destination box, provided slightly jarring notes in an otherwise well executed design. They marked an end to the slightly eccentric Midland Red designs and, as with the ONs delivered in 1934, had a conventional cab layout, with the fuel tank located beneath the floor on the offside. These views show 341, RC 3712, without fleetnumber plates fitted, when new. Many were rebodied by Willowbrook, after the war.

The year's coaches were six ON type, retaining the RR2LB petrol engine for quieter operation, and fitted with Duple C31F bodywork. Having regard to the overheating problems experienced with previous models of similar type, efforts were made to keep the weight down, and they turned the scales at a creditable 5tons 19cwt (6045kg). They featured the streamline livery, and also the raised "TMT" device featured on some of the contemporary DONs. Note the provision of semaphore trafficators.

The interior was well finished, although the use of rails across the top of alternate seats is noteworthy on a coach and detracts from the sumptuous appearance. The gap in the overhead luggage rack marks the location of the emergency exit - a good place to sit for extra legroom, but perhaps at the risk of feeling draughts!

The interior of the Regals had a well-finished appearance, with moquette on the rear window surrounds and parcel rack inserts, in addition to the well-upholstered seats.

A change of Vehicle Policy - AECs in favour, SOS in decline.

1937 marked a change in vehicle policy, and the beginning of the end of supply by Midland Red. No dissatisfaction with the latter's products was recorded, but both Companies needed vehicles in increasing numbers, and it is probable that Midland Red could not supply the entire requirement. It was natural, therefore, that it should meet its own requirements, and that the other companies to whom it supplied vehicles, including PMT and Northern General, as well as Trent, should purchase proprietary chassis, although Northern was also well known for building some of its own vehicles. Deliveries to Trent that year consisted entirely of AEC chassis, fifty in number, featuring the AEC 7.7litre diesel engine coupled to an AEC pre-selector gearbox of the Wilson type.

There were twenty AEC Regal chassis, for which the body order was split equally between Duple and Willowbrook, each producing a style of generally similar character to that built by Brush on the previous year's deliveries of DONs, but with many detail differences that significantly affected the appearance. In addition to the re-arrangement of the window bays, the destination box was incorporated into the roof contours, which had a downward slope giving a softer appearance.704, RC 4605, with Duple body was photographed in August, 1938 at Derby. The Madam, waiting behind, 428, CH 8130, was new in 1929, and the vehicles are thus separated in age by some seven years, but the contrast in appearance is remarkable.

711, RC 4612 of the second batch with Willowbrook bodywork, at Derby in September, 1949, after removal of the streamline mouldings, and shortly before withdrawal for chassis refurbishment and rebodying. Compared with the Duple version, the Willowbrook bodies featured a rather deeper windscreen and rounded canopy to the entrance, resulting in a slightly better appearance. They began an association between the two companies which was to last for many years, Willowbrook becoming a regular body supplier to Trent until the end of the BET years. Indeed, a number of bodies were later supplied to Trent as part of a bulk multi-operator order during its period of nationalised ownership.

Contemporary with the Regals were thirty Regent deckers with fifty-four seat front entrance bodywork by Weymann of Addlestone. As the official front view shows, the traditional style of AEC radiator, which always looked imposing, complemented the style of the Weymann bodywork quite effectively. Note the width marker on the nearside front wing, and the continued use of stencils for the route number, with roller blind for the destination at front and rear. the upper left view shows 1029, RC 4633, at Nottingham, whilst the lower view shows 1016, RC 4622 at Derby, both taken on 7th September, 1938.

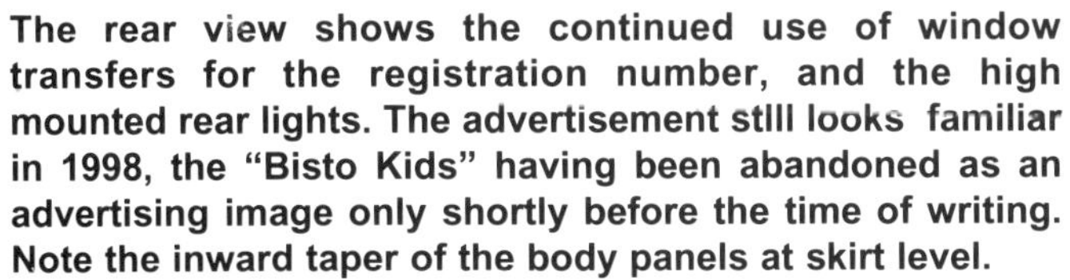

The rear view shows the continued use of window transfers for the registration number, and the high mounted rear lights. The advertisement still looks familiar in 1998, the “Bisto Kids” having been abandoned as an advertising image only shortly before the time of writing. Note the inward taper of the body panels at skirt level.

Although well proportioned externally, they appeared a little spartan internally, particularly on the upper deck, where the seat covering was leather rather than moquette. Note also the single skin roof construction. The use of a single seat adjacent to the heel arch compares with later practice of using a bench seat in this location, and resulted in a reduction in seating capacity.

Six coaches with Duple coachwork were purchased in1938 . These looked similar to the SOS ONs of 1936, although they had a slightly softer profile to the rear dome. One wonders what the Company's excursion and coach cruise passengers thought about the sound and vibration from the rugged 5 cylinder Gardner diesel engine, compared with the six cylinder petrol SOS units powering the coaches they were used to. 641, RC 5992 was undertaking a spell as an exhibition coach promoting the Company's programme of "Luxury Coach Cruises" in Derby Bus Station, giving potential passengers a chance to step aboard and inspect the high standard being offered. At that time, a 12 days Coach Cruise to the Scottish Highlands and John o' Groats from Nottingham or Derby cost 19 Guineas (£19-95). The guinea was an anachronistic denomination for which there was, by that time, no coin, but it had the value of £1 1s 0d, or £1-05, in today's coinage. This price included first class hotel accommodation, meals, gratuities and "the services of an experienced guide." It is worth remembering that although this seems a low figure, wages were low and the fares were substantial sums of money, which could only be afforded by the well heeled, such as business and professional people, rather than what would then have been considered ordinary working people. The Company's programme covered most tourist areas in the country, including the Lake District, Devon and Cornwall, the South Coast and Isle of Wight, the Yorkshire Dales, and others.

Further change - Daimlers to the Fore.

1938 brought a further change of policy, for Daimler was now favoured with a bulk order for single and double deck buses, and single deck coaches. These featured the Gardner 5LW engine which, like the AECs of the previous year, was coupled to a Wilson type preselector gearbox, although this time of Daimler manufacture. (The design of Walter George Wilson had been patented and was widely licensed to a number of vehicle manufacturers over the years. However, Daimler pioneered its use on buses, and AEC initially used units of Daimler manufacture, before obtaining its own rights for this purpose. The Riley private car was also noted for making extensive use of units employing the Wilson principles and, of course, Daimler also built private cars, as well as buses, and these used similar units also. Later gearboxes of the Wilson type used in buses, from the mid fifties onwards, were controlled semi-automatically, whereby the gear-change pedal was eliminated and the change was effected by the use of a small lever controlling the gearbox either pneumatically, or electro-pneumatically. In some cases, such as the London Transport /AEC Routemaster, operation was made fully automatic.

The nine single deck Daimlers, 500-508, received Willowbrook 35 seat bodies of appearance similar to the previous year's AEC Regals, save for a slightly deeper windscreen and minor details. However, the characteristic Daimler radiator design and lack of wheel nut rings gave the vehicles a slightly more rugged appearance. As related in the text, the bodies were removed in 1943, when the whole batch were fitted with utility double deck bodies, also by Willowbrook. The redundant saloon bodies were sold to the original Enterprise and Silver Dawn Company, of Scunthorpe, Lincs. This photograph shows the first of the batch, which arrived a few months earlier than the rest, with fleetnumber 600, although this was never carried in service.

The bodies on the double deckers were similar in appearance to those on the previous year's AECs, although the destination boxes were slightly deeper, with room for bigger lettering. The Autovac unit, for many years a characteristic of Daimler vehicles, and a curse to paint shop staff since the paint brush could not properly get behind it at repaint time, was carried on the front bulkhead, next to the bonnet.This August, 1948 view shows 1055, RC 6004, in the new, simplified postwar livery, at Nottingham.

The final SOSs supplied to the Company were two batches of SON models. These were fitted with the SOS K series diesel engine, rather than the AEC 7.7 litre unit fitted to the DONs delivered in 1936, and this was coupled to an Aphon model gearbox by ZF of Germany. The Willowbrook body followed what was, by then, the established standard style, although there were detailed differences, such as the window spacing, and, also, the emergency exit, which was in the back, resulting in a three panel back window and a reduction in capacity of one seat, compared with the Daimlers, received in 1938. All the SONs featured a new style radiator, with a pressed aluminium shell, resulting in a significant improvement in appearance compared with previous SOSs. This official view shows 401, RC 7090, when new. The diamond "TMT" device had been adopted for some vehicles in 1936.

More Daimlers, the return of SOS, and the last vehicles to peacetime specification

For 1939, a further twelve Daimler COG5 double deckers were received, but the single deck and coach orders reverted once again to SOS, with six SON coaches and twelve SON saloons being received. 1940 marked the receipt of the last buses to peacetime specification, the very last SOSs and, indeed, the last new vehicles until 1943. The Company was fortunate to receive these deliveries but the vehicles followed the pattern, which had become established over a period, of standard designs from established suppliers. The Daimlers were amongst the last chassis built before enemy bombing of Coventry destroyed the factory, causing production to be transferred to Wolverhampton after a period. The SOSs were particularly significant as they were numerically the last production SOS chassis built, although a small number of experimental vehicles were built during the war, using parts from pre-war chassis. They were also the last chassis supplied by Midland Red to another operator, although it did, of course, continue building vehicles for its own use until 1970. One of the batch, 417, RC7927, is preserved by the Company and occasionally used in service, having been carefully restored to full PCV standard.During the war years, L G Wyndham-Shire, the Chief Engineer of Midland Red, retired in 1940 and O C Power the Traffic Manager and also, it will be recalled, a Director of Trent, died suddenly, in 1943. This brought to an end the unusual arrangement of a company with no General Manager, and D M Sinclair was appointed first Chief Engineer, and then General Manager, following the death of Mr Power. Like Wyndham-Shire, Sinclair was a talented engineer, and he had been Assistant Chief Engineer at Northern General, which Company had also built its own vehicles. D M Sinclair continued and developed the Shire tradition of innovation, Midland Red beating all the mainstream manufacturers in getting an underfloor engine prototype single decker into service. However, there were no more vehicles built for other operators, and those built for Midland Red's own use were built, not as SOS, but under the "BMMO" name, these being the initials of the Company's then full title, "Birmingham and Midland Motor Omnibus Co Ltd".

The double deckers were numbered 1060-1071, RC 7071-82, and were identical to the previous year's deliveries, except that they incorporated a still deeper destination box, allowing the display of intermediate points, as well as the final destination. This August, 1948 view show 1071, RC7082, in a short-lived all-red postwar livery, by which time the destination box had been masked to a single line.

The six coaches were also mounted on the newly introduced SOS SON chassis, having functional coachwork by Willowbrook of Loughborough. When new, the vehicles had a livery style similar to the other coaches and many of the single deck buses in the fleet, with the streamline feature and diamond TMT device as a fleetname style. However, by the time that this photograph was taken, after the war, the streamline moulding had been removed, and the diamond fleetname device replaced by the garter and TMT initials device, which had been used on many vehicles from the early days of the Company. 647, RC7087 awaits duty on the Skegness service.

644, RC 7084 was photographed in the coach park at Skegness in June, 1948, and shows a different style of streamline livery using modified mouldings with reversed red and cream, and a new, Gothic style of fleetname, which was used for a brief period after the war. The vehicle behind is a then newly delivered AEC Regal III with Windover coachwork.

The Daimlers were very similar to the previous deliveries, except that they had an open front entrance arrangement, with an internal sliding door at the entrance to the lower saloon. The reason for this change is not known, although the external sliding doors were prone to slamming shut under sharp braking, if left open. However, the new arrangement must have had drawbacks of its own, since the upper saloon would have been exposed to the elements, just as with an open rear platform.This photograph shows 1079, RC 7943, in post war red and ivory livery.

This close up view shows the revised entrance arrangement. Note the sliding door to the saloon and the deep entrance step. Also the large, square staircase mirror.

This post war view shows 412, RC 7922, one of the last SOSs built, parked off service in the old Derby Cattle Market. The vehicle has acquired post war livery, and the streamline mouldings have been removed. Also, a smaller form of fleetname is now used, in yellow, rather than gold, as this was cheaper. Note the red and black colour coding on the fleet numberplate, indicating allocation to Ashbourne Depot.

1085, RC 5991, a Daimler/COG5SD formerly numbered 640 when fitted with a Duple C31F body awaits departure on the Gunthorpe service, one wintry looking morning.

More Capacity Urgently Needed - Double Deck Bodies On Single Deck Chassis!

Capacity was a continual problem during the war years, especially at peak travelling times when factories, shops and offices started and finished for the day. This was aggravated in poor weather, when people who might normally walk or cycle to work wanted to use the bus.A number of solutions were adopted, but perhaps the most effective was to take the single deck bodies off the Daimler COG5 buses and coaches delivered in 1935/8 and replace them with double deck bodies! Willowbrook supplied new 56 seat double deck bodies to utility style in 1942, resulting in an extra fourteen deckers. The coach bodies were placed in store, to reappear after the war on new chassis, whilst the single deck bus bodies were sold.

1093, RC 5984, originally 505 when fitted with a Willowbrook B35F body was photographed in the parking area at Nottingham Huntingdon Street around 1950. Although to utility specification, the design was quite well executed, only the upper deck overhanging the cab striking a jarring note, almost looking as though the original cab had been retained, although this was not the case. The majority of the two batches lasted until 1953 in rebodied form, giving a useful service life.

The unique Daimler COG5 with Brush body, RC 3210, added to the fleet in 1935, continued to make history when it was rebodied in 1943, with the Company's first double deck body to the so called lowbridge layout, featuring a sunken side gangway with transverse rows of four seats on the upper deck. The vehicle was renumbered from 1208 to 1300, thus starting a new series, which continued to be used for lowbridge vehicles until 1962. It is seen in this post war view at Wetmore Road, Burton on Trent in the company of Stevenson's 17, LRE 199, a Guy Arab II with Park Royal utility body, which was that Company's first double decker when new in 1945.

The first utility vehicle to arrive was 1097, RC 8320, received in summer, 1943. The livery was the standard light red and maroon, and even the straw lining was retained, although there was a dark matt paint finish on the roof, used by most operators to make their vehicles less conspicuous to enemy aircraft overhead. Note, however, the white edging to the front wings and the lower panels, intended to make the vehicle more conspicuous on the ground in blackout conditions, and the tiny headlamps, also intended to make the vehicle less visible from above.

Wartime Utilities - Still more Daimlers

No new vehicles were received in 1941 or 1942. Many manufacturers ceased production of buses soon after the war began, as their efforts were diverted to military vehicles. However, Daimler maintained production into 1940, as already described, but ceased in that year after the factory was destroyed by enemy action. A gap followed until production resumed at a factory in Wolverhampton. In the meantime, the Government had laid down an austerity specification for buses, under which the use of labour and scare materials was minimised, whilst at the same time a serviceable product was produced. Trent was particularly fortunate, because all of its utility buses were of Daimler manufacture and thus fitted in well to the existing maintenance arrangements. The Daimler model supplied was the CW, based on the peacetime CO model already well represented in the fleet but differing in the use of more steel in place of lightweight aluminium components, which were in short supply. Initially, the engine was the Gardner 5LW, leading to the designation CWG5 and thus directly comparable. Later, the standard engine was the AEC 7.7litre, leading to the designation CWA6, but this was equally satisfactory since the Company already had many such engines, fitted to both AEC products and in the fleet of SOS DONs.Bodywork was by a variety of suppliers, who all built to there own design, but following the utility specification. This resulted in designs with a minimum of radiused panelling in order to cut out the need for skilled panel beating, wooden slatted seating, no glass in the rear emergency exit and a generally basic, or austere, specification.The following selection of photographs shows examples of all the types supplied, and it will be noted that no single deck vehicles were supplied during this time. Although Trent traditionally had a high proportion of rural services, it also served the major industrial centre of Derby and there was a need for high capacity vehicles to serve the likes of the LMS Railway and Rolls Royce, amongst others, which were heavily involved in the war effort. Nottingham also had industry and there were also the coalmines to be served, although these were less in Trent territory than that of neighbouring Midland General.

This photograph is in the Company's records, and the caption indicates that it is "Interior view of 1943 Gardner Daimler". However, there were only two wartime "Gardner Daimlers" and inspection of photographs the exterior of these reveals that the provision of the half drop windows does not match with those in this photograph, although it does match with the Duple bodied Daimler CWA6s delivered in 1945. It therefore seems more likely to be one of those, particularly as it is marked as a Duple photograph. Whichever the vehicle, the photograph conveys effectively the basic specification, and the lower panels, unlined and with body framing exposed, are clearly visible behind the first seat on the left of the picture. The ceiling and interior lights, however, appear not dissimilar to peacetime specifications.

The second vehicle of the batch was 1098, RC 8321, and this view shows the single panel destination box, which was part of the utility specification, masked to show a single line display. These vehicles were over half a ton heavier than the last Daimlers delivered to peacetime specification in 1940. They weighed 7tons 7cwts (7468kg), compared with 6tons 15cwts (6858kg) of the 1940 vehicles, demonstrating the effect of replacing aluminium with steel. The pair were the only wartime Daimlers supplied with the Gardner 5LW engine. The upper deck emergency exit was originally fully panelled, which may have been fitted with windows before entering service. Derby Bus Station saw little activity as the bus awaits its journey to Heanor, one Sunday in June,1948.

The two CWG5s were quickly followed by five CWA6s, also bodied by Duple, but built to the so-called lowbridge layout, first seen in the fleet when 1208, RC3210 was re-bodied, as described earlier. That vehicle took fleet number 1300, and the five CWA6s followed on, taking numbers 1301-2, 6-8, RC 8359-60, 78-80. The photograph shows 1301 at Derby, in April, 1953.

Unlike many companies, Trent did not rebuild large numbers of its utility bodies, confining that activity to reconstruction of accident and structural damage. When this photograph was taken, in May, 1952, the upper deck front windows had been rebuilt to incorporate glazing secured by rubber gasket, and the lower deck end windows had been converted to D shape, to provide extra strength. 1307, RC 8379, awaits duty on a Works Service at Derby.

The first vehicles received in 1944 were a further three lowbridge CWA6s, although this time with bodies by Brush. Fleet numbers allocated filled the gap left in the previous year, 1303-5, RC 8391-3, suggesting that they may, in fact, have been expected earlier, but were not received. This view, taken in August, 1948, shows 1305, RC 8393 about to take a journey to Ilkeston, in almost original condition. Bringing up the rear is a then brand new AEC Regent II with Willowbrook lowbridge body to post war design.

The next eight vehicles, received in 1944, marked a new supplier for Trent, these being bodied by Charles H Roe, of Leeds. They were of well-proportioned and clean design, having perhaps the most pleasing appearance of all the utility bodies supplied to Trent. In many ways, they showed a strong resemblance to the makers normal standard, with well rounded roof profile, deep windows and the characteristic waistrail moulding which was for many years an instant recognition feature of Roe bodywork. Most of Roe's wartime production had been to lowbridge design on Guy Arab chassis, which made these eight vehicles rare, the contract awarded by the Ministry of Supply having been for only nineteen vehicles. 1105, RC 8400 had received a repaint into the short lived all red post-war livery when this picture was taken at a remarkably rural looking Nottingham Huntingdon Street, but was otherwise in as built

A solitary Brush bodied CWA6, 1117, RC 8402, also arrived in 1944. It was photographed some time later, having received the post-war red and cream livery, but otherwise unchanged. To the right is 1301, RC 8359, a 1943 example with Duple lowbridge bodywork, in wartime grey. Behind are a Barton TD5 with Duple bodywork, a forerunner of its famous fleet of Leyland PD1 double deck coaches, and a utility Guy Arab.

By 1945, the Government had introduced a more relaxed bodywork specification and this permitted rounded domes and more ventilated side windows instead of the two previously permitted and upholstered seats. The various body builders put their own interpretations on this, and introduced some of the changes gradually. This post war view of 1108, RC 8464, the first of eight Duple bodied CWA6s delivered in 1945. Note that three half-drop windows are now fitted on the upper deck, and two on the lower. The front dome is quite rounded, although the rear dome retains the angular profile. Separate destination and three track number blinds are fitted, although it is possible that these were not fitted from new, since Trent altered the destination layouts of many utility bodies, after the war.

This view shows 1309, RC 8480, the first of four CWA6s with Duple L55R bodywork delivered in 1945. The bench seats associated with the lowbridge layout are just visible in the upper deck. In this March, 1954 view, the ventilators have been removed from the upper deck windows, larger headlamps have been fitted and there are signs of strengthening around the lower deck front and rear pillars, which are tapered. The vehicle was to see a further two years service, being withdrawn in 1956.

In 1945, Daimler introduced their new 8.6litre, six cylinder CD6, which they had been developing throughout the war. This began to be fitted to the CW chassis, together with a rear axle, also of Daimler manufacture. The model designation was CWD6 and production was interspersed with CWA6 production. Trent received just two in 1945, with Brush bodies to the new relaxed specification, and two with AEC engines and identical body-work.In this 1950s view, the first of the two, 1112, RC 8530, waits out of service in the parking area at Derby Bus Station.

The Brush relaxed design featured a very rounded rear dome, and the step below the windscreen was eliminated compared with the original Brush utility design, shown earlier. A remarkably grubby looking 1113, RC 8351, is parked at what looks like the Derby railway works, perhaps waiting to take the workforce home. The numberplate is particularly clear, because it was painted white, indicating allocation to Shipley Depot. Vehicles allocated to this depot had the numbers picked out in red paint, because they otherwise did not show well against the white background. Any vehicles transferred then to Uttoxeter New Road, for which the code was a red background had to have the paint removed from the numbers!

This view of the same vehicle, taken in Uttoxeter New Road depot, well illustrates the smooth rounded profile of the rear dome. This had a remarkable effect in softening the overall appearance of the vehicles, the lack of louvres over the side windows also contributing to this effect.

The very last utility received was 1116, RC 8570, a CWA6D with Duple body to that company's fully relaxed specification. Note the rounded front and rear domes, multiple sliding vents in the side windows, together with separate destination and route number boxes. Despite the relaxation, the tiny wartime headlights were still fitted, although the black out regulations had been withdrawn at Christmas, 1944. This was the last double deck body that Duple supplied to Trent, although the bodybuilder supplied some attractive double deck designs to other operators, notably Red and White and Barton.The CWA6D designation simply meant that the new Daimler rear axle was fitted, as well as an AEC engine. Vehicles so designated were effectively CWD6s, but with an AEC engine.

This ex Phipps vehicle lasted some twenty-one months in the Trent fleet, until September, 1930. TO 6098 took fleetnumber 1251 and was a Chevrolet LM with 20 seat bodywork of unknown make. The six wheel configuration was not a factory product, but was a conversion carried out by the Longframe Six-wheeler Construction Co to increase the load carrying capacity to 2 Tons (2032kg) which enabled a seating capacity of twenty, rather than the more usual fourteen of a four wheel version.This picture was evidently taken at the time of withdrawal by Trent, since there is clear evidence on the front cantrail of the standard Trent stencil route number box having been removed - note the water stain and the redundant electrical wire hanging beneath.

Independents taken over.

As related in the text, there were many small operators taken over by the Company during the course of its development. A number of photographs of the vehicles operated by these companies, many of which were taken into the Trent fleet for a time, have been found, and a selection is included here to round off the photographic story. A number of others have been used to illustrate the text.Non-standard vehicles tended to be kept for only a fairly short period of time, although the quality makes, such as Leyland, AEC and, especially, Dennis tended to stay for longer.

W & A Clarke, trading as Clarke's Bus Service,

and operating between Nottingham and Ilkeston were taken over in July, 1925. Three Daimlers were involved and were operated for a time by Trent. They included this Y type with Bartle body new in 1923, which lasted but a few months with Trent.

J T Gregson & Sons

ran between Nottingham and Burton Joyce via Gedling and sold their business to Trent in March, 1929. The take-over included three small Reos and this one, TO 4822 which was new in 1927, took fleet number 1052 in the Trent fleet, lasting until 1930. Note that it was fitted with Trent's standard box for the route number stencil beneath the canopy. The legal lettering shows the Company's address as 10, Albert Street, Derby, rather than Uttoxeter New Road, as later.

George Phipps' District Omnibus Service, Horsley Woodhouse

was sold to Trent in January, 1929, and fourteen vehicles changed hands, together with the garage. This little 14 seat Talbot, R 9323 took fleet number 1255 but, by the standards of the day it was quite old, having been new in 1922 and was sold very quickly. See also the vehicle pictured on page 126.

George Chapman & Sons of Belper

sold his eleven vehicle business to Trent in March, 1929. Included was RA 4571 this Dennis 30cwt with Willowbrook B18F body, which had been new in 1927. Receiving fleet number 1350, the vehicle lasted with Trent until 1931. In typical Trent style, a stencil box for the route number has been fitted below the front canopy.

Higgs & Waller (Melbourne) Ltd

competed vigorously with Trent on the Derby-Melbourne-Swadlincote route, eventually selling out in April, 1929. The sale included four AECs, which rather put the Trent fleet to shame as they included heaters in their specification, unlike Trent vehicles of the time. The front folding doors, operated on this AEC Type 5 by a lever in the driver's cab, were another refinement that Trent's SOSs did not have until later. However, the vehicles ran on solid tyres, so it is unsurprising that they lasted with the Company for only a very short time.

L H Dutton of Radcliffe on Trent, trading as Dutton's Motor Service

and operating between Nottingham and Radcliffe and Nottingham and Granby, sold his business to Trent in December, 1929. One of the Dutton's of Radcliffe Thornycrofts in service. RR 3005 was photographed with driver at Trinity Square, Nottingham, in 1927.

This superb period shot shows the L H Dutton of Radcliffe on Trent fleet lined up outside the garage on the A52 just east of Radcliffe. Identifiable nearest the camera are two Thornycrofts and a Chevrolet. So far as is known, none of the vehicles passed to Trent, but a garage is still on the site at the time of writing. A further Dutton's of Radcliffe vehicle is shown on the previous page.

E Bramley & Sons of Cotmanhay, trading as Prince of Wales Service

and running between Nottingham and Cotmanhay, via Ilkeston was taken over by Trent, jointly with the Midland General subsidiaries Williamson's and Dawson's Enterprise, in March 1930. This De Dion with Vickers B20F body, RA 3915, was included in the three vehicles which passed to Trent. It received fleetnumber 1361, and lasted until 1932, before withdrawal. The location of the photograph, used for other photographs of Trent vehicles, suggests that it was taken just after acquisition by Trent. This tends to be confirmed by the fact that the Prince of Wales feathers, used by Bramley as what would nowadays be termed a logo and originally positioned on the panel below the second window, had been removed. However, the Trent fleetnumber and legal lettering were not yet in place, and the Prince of Wales fleetname was still in position over the windscreen.

Turner & Wagg of Derby, trading as Wagg's Super Service
was another competitor to Trent on the Derby-Melbourne and Swadlincote service. The Company bought the business in August, 1930, including two Daimler CF6s and this ADC 423 with Willowbrook B32F body. CH 7783 was new in 1928 and took fleet number 100. It lasted with Trent until 1934.

H D Bayliss & Sons, of Ashbourne
became a significant operator on the Ashbourne-Derby corridor, as related in the text. This Leyland Lion LT2, RB 2059, with Davidson B 32F bodywork was new in 1930 and became fleet number 1309 in the Trent fleet. It remained with the Company until 1936.

The paper fleetname sticker on RB 1535, this 1930 Dennis GL, is typical of the way things were dealt with when a take-over occurred. The legal lettering had been altered and doubtless the vehicle would be in the paintshop at Uttoxeter New Road before long, although it lasted with Trent only until 1932, as fleetnumber 1352.

This Commer, RB 187 was new in 1929 and took fleetnumber 1204, lasting with Trent until 1934. Driver J W "Dickie" Bird stands with his machine during a break in service at the height of the competitive activity between the two operators.

Reynolds Bros of Bulwell was taken over in February, 1931, jointly with Nottingham Corporation. Ten vehicles were involved, of which five Leylands passed to Trent and five Gilfords, including this one, passed to the Corporation. The vehicle saw little time with the Corporation, being withdrawn soon after it was acquired. In contrast, the Leylands that Trent received lasted several years. Probably, Trent could use single deckers, whereas the Corporation's need was limited due to its entirely urban operating area. It perhaps agreed to take the Gilfords, which were essentially a lightweight chassis, for early disposal.

Mason's Bus Service
Owner J W Longdon of Derby sold his business to Trent in March, 1932, but no vehicles were involved. Albion CH 6734 was photographed outside St Werburgh's Church in Cheapside, Derby, for many years a departure point before the Central Bus Station opened. The crew transferred to Trent, conductor W F " Billy" Bull having a long career with Trent, later transferring to Central Works at Uttoxeter New Road as a painter.

H O Oxenham of Borrowash, who traded as Orange Coaches,

sold to Trent in May 1932 at the same time as colleague operators E G Buxton (Vincent's Reliance) and F H Rolstone (Vincent's Devonian) who all ran together on the Derby-Ockbrook via Borrowash route. Once again, no vehicles changed hands, but this delightful picture shows an unidentified Gilford of Oxenham & Sons. Location is Cock Pitt Hill, Derby, long before the development of the Eagle Centre, and the position must be somewhere in the traffic lanes on the north west side of today's Cock Pitt Roundabout.

Blue Bus Services (Derby) Ltd,

run by Messrs Whitehall & Brannan, sold their Derby-Ilkeston service to Trent in May, 1934. The sale included no vehicles, but one of the vehicles which had bee used on the service was CH 3669, a 1923 Fiat with body by Derby coachbuilders Sanderson & Holmes. However, it had long gone when the business was sold to Trent.

A Slater & Sons of Mayfield

sold their Ashbourne-Uttoxeter service and their excursions to Trent in January, 1935. As related in the text, no vehicles changed hands, but this Gilford, RF 5032, Slater's fleet number 1 was used on the service.

Dutton's Unity Service Ltd, of Nottingham

was a significant operator on the Nottingham-Sutton-in-Ashfield corridor and sold to Trent with effect from November 1935. This was the same family as Dutton's of Radcliffe on Trent, and Leonard Dutton was a Director of Unity and owned the Radcliffe operation. This photospread shows some of the Unity fleet, outside their Kent Street Nottingham premises, which passed to Trent with the business. A photograph of a former Dutton's vehicle appears on page 54.

Dennis Lancet I, ATV 4, with Willowbrook C32F body (shown top left) was referred to by Trent as a Dennis de luxe and one result of its entering the fleet was that Trent was able to reduce its order for SOS coaches by one unit, such was their opinion of the Dennis. The vehicle took fleet number 1212 initially, although renumbered in 1936 to 1230. In view of the coach status, a number in the 6XX would have seemed more appropriate, but acquired vehicles were normally numbered in the 12XX/13XX series at that time. It was new in 1935, just before the take-over, and remained with Trent until 1945.

Another Lancet I (shown lower left) was ATV 746, also new in 1935, and fitted with a Willowbrook DP35F body. Initially numbered 1210, it was renumbered 1232 in 1936 and remained in service with Trent until 1946.

An older Dutton vehicle acquired
was TV 7472, this 1932 TSM B10A with Willowbrook
B32F body. Initially numbered 1217,it became 1213 in 1936.
It had only a short life with Trent, being withdrawn in 1936.

This 1932 AEC Regal,
TV 8971, initially took fleet number 1215 in
the Trent fleet, but was renumbered 1204 in 1936. Bodywork
was Brush B32F, and the vehicle remained with Trent until 1940.

A J Daley & Sons of Ripley, trading as Pippin Service

sold to Trent in October, 1935. Eight vehicles changed hands, including RB 1102; a 1930 TSM B10A2, which initially took Trent fleet number 1228, but was renumbered 1218 in 1936 and withdrawn soon afterwards.

R E Horspool of Loughborough

sold his group of services based on that town to Trent with effect from December, 1935. Four vehicles were involved, including JU 3060, a 1933 Dennis Lancet I with C32F body built locally by Willowbrook. The Horspool vehicles must have looked quite distinctive in their yellow livery, with dark relief, and the Dennis radiator used at that time made this vehicle particularly imposing. Trent kept the vehicle until 1946, following which it passed to South Notts of Gotham, for further service.

C E Salt's Red Star Service,

of Duffield, serving the Derby-Belper route was sold to Trent in January, 1936. These three vehicles were included in the sale. Nearest the camera is CH 9305, a 1930 Gilford 168SD with Willowbrook B26F body which took fleet number 1207 but was soon withdrawn. Note the Gruss air springs either side of the radiator, which were a prominent feature of later Gilfords. Just visible behind are two Dennis Lancet Is, also Willowbrook bodied, which fared rather better, lasting until 1945 and 1946.

A J Walters & Son, of Derby,

ran a works service between Allenton and the Celanese Works at Spondon, which Trent purchased with effect from January, 1938. Trent bought no vehicles, but one of Walters' vehicles is shown here following a serious accident. It is CH 7044, a 1927 Bean, with Willowbrook B18F body. The photograph was taken at the former Reeve, Burgess coachworks at Pilsley near Chesterfield (it was known as Reeve and Kenning at the time), who doubtless undertook the extensive repairs needed.

Fleet List, 1913-1945. Please see also Additional Notes on Page 154.

Year to Stock	Fleet No	Registration No	Chassis	Body	Layout	Year W'drwn.	Remarks (Rb - Rebodied, Rn - Renumbered)	Add'l Note
1913		CH 537	Commer WP 32hp			1917	Ex CCHL, new 1911	
1913		CH 673	Commer WP 36hp				Ex CCHL, new 1912	
1913		CH 832	Scout 20hp			1918	Ex CCHL, new 1913	
1913	Wrexham	CH 850	Commer WP 36hp			1915	Ex CCHL, new 1913	
1913	Willow	LE 9601	Commer WP 36hp	Scammell & Nephew	B22C	by 1915	Ex CCHL, new 1911	
1913	?	?	Commer WP	?	?	?		
1914	?	CH 892-7	Commer WP 36hp	?	?	by 1915		
1914	D101	CH 930	Maudslay 40hp	CCHL		1915	Chassis to War Office	
1914	D102-3	CH 992-3	Maudslay 40hp	Brush		1915	Chassis to War Office	
1914	D104-12	CH 1004-5/11-2/ 28/46/58-9/74	Maudslay 40hp	Brush		1915	Chassis to War Office	
1915	D100	CH 1195 CH 1432 (3/20)	Tilling Stevens TS3	?		1929	Rb Birch B28R, 9/20. Conv to B2 type, Rn 100 by 12/26	1
1915	D101	CH 1198 CH 1437 (3/20)	Tilling Stevens TS3	Brush	B28R	1929	Rb Brush B32R, Rn 450 and conv to forward control by 1925.	1
1915	D102	CH 1200 Ch 1224 (3/20)	Tilling Stevens TS3	Brush	B28R	1933	Rn 132 by 12/26. Conv to B1 Type and Rn 765 by 12/29. Rn 905 by 12/30	1
1915	D103	CH 1209 CH 1348 (3/20)	Tilling Stevens TS3	Brush	B28R	?	Rb Birch B28R, 5/20.	1
1915	D104	CH 1224 CH 1287 (3/20)	Tilling Stevens TS3	Brush	B28R	1929	Rb Birch Ch29, 3/20. Rn 50 by 12/26	1
1915	D105	CH 1276 CH 1314 (3/20)	Tilling Stevens TS3	Brush	B28R	1930	Rb ? Ch29. Rn 55 by 12/26	1
1915	D106	CH 1287 CH 1198 (3/20)	Tilling Stevens TS3	Brush	B28R	1929	Conv to B2 Type and Rn 106 by 1926	1
1916	D107	CH 1314 CH 1419 (3/20)	Tilling Stevens TS3	Brush	B28R	1929	Rb Brush B32R, Rn 404 and converted to forward control by 1925.	1
1916	D108	CH 1336 CH 1276 (3/20)	Tilling Stevens TS3	Brush	B28R	1933	Rn D105 by 3/20. Rb Birch B26R by 1921 Rn 1?? by 12/26. Conv to B1 Type and Rn 759 by 12/29. Rn 917 by 12/30	1
1916	D109	CH 1348 CH 1209 (3/20)	Tilling Stevens TS3	Brush	B28R	1929	Rb Birch B28R 3/20. Conv to B2 Type and Rn 103 by 12/26.	1
1916	D110	CH 1351 CH 1200 (3/20)	Tilling Stevens TS3	Brush	B28R	1929	Rb Holmes B28R by 1920. Rn 1?? by 12/26. Conv to B1 Type and Rn 756 by 12/29. Rn 909 by 12/30.	1
1916	D111	CH 1373 CH 1351 (3/20)	Tilling Stevens TS3	Brush	B28R	1929	Rb Brush B32R, Rn 403 and conv to forward control by 1925.	1
1916	D112	CH 1419 CH 1336 (3/20)	Tilling Stevens TS3	Brush	B28R	1933	Rb Birch B28R, 8/20. Rn 1?? by 12/26. Conv to B1 Type and Rn 757 by 12/29. Rn 903 by 12/30.	1

Year to Stock	Fleet No	Registration No	Chassis	Body	Layout	Year W'drwn.	Remarks (Rb - Rebodied, Rn - Renumbered)	Add'l Note
1917	D113	CH 1432 CH 1195 (3/20)	Tilling Stevens TS3	?	?	1933	Rn 160, by 12/26. Conv to B1 Type and Rn 760 by 12/29. Rn 902 by 12/30.	1
1917	D114	CH 1437 CH 1373 (3/20)	Tilling Stevens TS3	?	?	1933	Rb Birch B28R, 7/20. Rn 128 By 12/26 Conv to B1 Type and Rn 770 by 12/29. Rn 918 by 12/30.	1
1917	?	R 2716	Star	?	B???	1919	Ex Harrison, Ashbourne, new 1915	
1918	D115	CH 1492	Tilling Stevens TS3	?	?	1933	Rb Birch B28R, 10/20. Conv to B1 Type and Rn 755 by 12/29. Rn 911 by 12/30.	1
1919	D116	CH 1578 CH 1677 (3/20)	Tilling Stevens TS3	Holmes	B28R	1933	Rb ? B26R by 1922.Rn 1?? by 12/26. Conv to B1 Type, Rn 762 by 12/29. Rn 912 by 12/30.	1
1919	D117	CH 1583 CH 1578 (3/20)	Tilling Stevens TS3	Holmes	B28R	1929	Rn 117, in 1924(?). Rb Brush B32R, Rn 405 and conv to forward control by 1925.	1
1919	D118	CH 1600 CH 1583 (3/20)	Tilling Stevens TS3	Holmes	B28R	1933	Rn 102 by 12/26. Conv to B1 Type and Rn 766 by 12/29. Rn 913 by 12/30.	1
1919	D119	CH 1620 CH 1600 (3/20)	Tilling Stevens TS3	Rebuilt Brush? (Originally fitted to D106.)	B28R	1929	Conv to B2 Type and Rn 102 by 12/26.	1
1919	D120	CH 1624 CH 1620 (3/20)	Tilling Stevens TS3	Holmes	B28R	1929	Rb Brush B32R, Rn 402 and conv to forward control by 1925.	1
1919	D121	CH 1677 CH 1624 (3/20)	Tilling Stevens TS3	Holmes	B28R	1930	Rb Birch(?) Ch29, (1921?). Rn 56 by 12/26.	1
1919	D122	CH 1763	Tilling Stevens TS3	Holmes	B28R	?	?	1
1919	D123	CH 1793	Tilling Stevens TS3	Brush (Originally fitted to D102.)	B28R	1933	Rb Birch B26R, conv to B1 Type and Rn 761 by 12/29. Rn 914 by 12/30.	1
1919	D124	CH 1769	Tilling Stevens TS3	Holmes	B28R	?	?	1
1919	D125	CH 1784	Tilling Stevens TS3	Holmes	B28R	1933	Rb Holmes B28R from D121, Rn 156 by 12/26. Conv to B1 Type and Rn 767 by 12/29. Rn 908 by 12/30.	1
1919	D126	CH 1789	Tilling Stevens TS3	Holmes	B28R	1929	Rn 106 by 12/26. Conv to B2 Type and Rn 105 by 12/29.	1
1920	D127	CH 1833	Tilling Stevens TS3	Brush (Originally fitted to D108.)	B28R	1929	Body rebuilt. Previously fitted to D108 Rn 400, conv to forward control by ?	1
1920	D128	CH 1834	Tilling Stevens TS3	Holmes	B28R	1933	Rb Birch B28R from D130, Rn 130 by 12/26. Conv to B1 Type and Rn 769 by 12/29. Rn 900 by 12/30.	1
1920	D129	CH 1905	Tilling Stevens TS3	Birch	B28R	1929	Conv to B2 Type and Rn 104 by 12/29.	1
1920	D130	CH 1906	Tilling Stevens TS3	Birch	B28R	1929	Rn 114 by 12/26. Conv to B1 Type and Rn 768 by 12/29. Rn 919 by 1930. Conv to Lorry 12, 1930.	1
1920	D131	CH 1936	Tilling Stevens TS3	Birch	B28R	1930	Rn 52 by 12/26.	1
1920	D132	CH 1937	Tilling Stevens TS3	Birch	B28R	1933	Rb Brush B28R from D105.Conv to B1 Type and Rn 764 by 12/29.Rn 907 by 12/30.	1

Year to Stock	Fleet No	Registration No	Chassis	Body	Layout	Year W'drwn.	Remarks (Rb - Rebodied, Rn - Renumbered)	Add'l Note
1920	D133	CH 1953	Tilling Stevens TS3	?	?	1933	Chassis s/hand. Rn 1?? by 12/26. Rb ? B26R, conv to B1 Type and Rn 758 by 12/29. Rn 916 by 12/30.	1
1920	D134	CH 1963	Tilling Stevens TS3	Birch	B28R	1928	?	1
1920	D135	CH 1964	Tilling Stevens TS3	Birch	B28R	1929	Conv to B2 Type and Rn 101 by 1926.	1
1920	D136	CH 1976	Tilling Stevens TS3	Birch	B28R	1928	?	1
1920	D137	CH 1977	Tilling Stevens TS3	Birch	Ch26	1930	Rn 52 by 12/26.	1
1920	D138	CH 2041	Tilling Stevens TS3	Birch	Ch29	1933	Rn 1?? by 12/26 Rb Birch B28R from D137, conv to B1 Type and Rn 763 by 12/29. Rn 901 by 12/30.	1
1920	D139	KN 8686	Tilling Stevens TS3	Birch	Ch29	1930	Rn 53 by 12/26.	1
1920	D140?	TS 2566	Tilling Stevens TS3	Birch	Ch29	1929	Rb ? B32R, Rn 401 and conv to forward control by unknown date.	1
1920	D141?	TS 2568	Tilling Stevens TS3	Birch	Ch29	1930	Rn 54 by 12/26.	1
1920	D142?	TS 2570	Tilling Stevens TS3	?	Ch?	1929		1
1921	V143	CH 2786	Vulcan VSD	Birch	B22R	1927	Rn 601, 1924	
1921	V144	CH 2787	Vulcan VSD	Birch	B22R	1926	Rn 602, 1924	
1922	T146?	CH 2913	Thornycroft J	Birch	OT46R	1927		2
1922	T147?	CH 2972	Thornycroft J	?	Ch?	1928	Conv to forward control and Rb Brush B32R around 1924.	2
1922	T148?	CH 3001	Thornycroft J	?	Ch?	1929	Conv to forward control, Rb Brush B32R and rn 700, around 1924.	2
1922	T149?	CH 3002	Thornycroft J	?	Ch?	1927		2
1922	T150?	CH 3020	Thornycroft J	?	Ch?	1927		2
1922	T151	CH 3076	Thornycroft J	Birch	OT46R	1927		2
1922	T152	CH 3097	Thornycroft J	Birch	OT46R	1927		2
1922	T153?	CH 3112	Thornycroft J	Birch	OT46R	1927		2
1922	T154?	CH 3140	Thornycroft J	?	Ch?	1928		2
1922	V155?	CH 2939	Vulcan VSD	Birch	B22R	1926	Rn 603, 1924	
1922	V156?	CH 2973	Vulcan VSD	Birch	B22R	1926	Rn 604, 1924	
1922	T157?	CH 3141	Thornycroft J	?	Ch?	1927		2
1922	T158	CH 3185	Thornycroft J	?	B?	1927		2
1922	T159?	CH 3202	Thornycroft J	?	B?			2
1923	T160	DP 2119	Thornycroft J	Brush	B26R	1927	Ex Thames Valley 9, new 1919	3
1923	T161	DP 2120	Thornycroft J	Brush	B26R	1927	Ex Thames Valley 10, new 1919	3
1923	T162	DP 2121	Thornycroft J	Brush	B26R	1927	Ex Thames Valley 11, new 1919	3
1923	T163	DP 2599	Thornycroft J	Tilling	B26R	1927	Ex Thames Valley 27, new 1920	3
1923	D164	AL 8430	Tilling Stevens TS3A	Brush	B33R	1932	Ex Clayton, Nottingham, new 1921. Conv to B1 type and rn 752 by 12/28. Rn 920 by 12/30. Conv to lorry 11 by 10/31.	1
1923	D165	AL 8431	Tilling Stevens TS3A	Brush	B33R	1933	Ex Clayton, Nottingham, new 1921. Conv to B1 type, rn 751 by 12/28. Rn 910 by 12/30.	1

Year to Stock	Fleet No	Registration No	Chassis	Body	Layout	Year W'drwn.	Remarks (Rb - Rebodied, Rn - Renumbered)	Add'l Note
1923	D166	AL 8432	Tilling Stevens TS3A	Brush	B33R	1933	Ex Clayton, Nottingham, new 1921. Conv to B1 type and rn 750 by 12/28.	1
1923	D167	AL 8433	Tilling Stevens TS3A	Brush	B33R	1933	Ex Clayton, Nottingham, new 1921. Conv to B1 type and rn 753 by 12/28. Rn 904 by 12/30.	1
1923	D168	CH 3805	Tilling Stevens TS3	Brush		1933	Rn 109, 1924. Converted to B1 Type and Rn 754 by 12/28. Rn 915 by 12/30.	1
1924	200-9	CH 4062-5/72 67/6/73-5	Tilling Stevens TS6	Brush	OT57R	1931-2	Converted to pneumatic tyres, 1928.	
1924	300-9	CH 4076-85	Tilling Stevens TS6 Long Saloon	Brush	B37R	1931-2	Converted to pneumatic tyres, 1928.	
1925	800,2,4,5 or 9.	CH 4853	Daimler CM	Ransomes	B31F		Rb Davidson Ch32, Rn851, 1925 Rb Ex BMMO B31F, Rn 810, 1931	4
1925	800,2,4,5 or 9.	CH 4857	Daimler CM	Ransomes	B31F	1932	Rb Davidson Ch32, Rn852, 1925 Rb Ex BMMO B31F, Rn 811, 1931	4
1925	800,2,4,5 or 9.	CH 4852	Daimler CM	Ransomes	B31F		Rb Davidson Ch32, Rn853, 1925 Rb Ex BMMO B31F, Rn 812, 1931	4
1925	800,2,4,5 or 9.	CH 4858	Daimler CM	Ransomes	B31F	1932	Rb Davidson Ch32, Rn854, 1925. Rb Ransomes B31F, Ex 921, Rn 813, 1931.	4
1925	800,2,4,5 or 9.	CH 4864	Daimler CM	Ransomes	B31F	1932	Rb Davidson Ch32, Rn855, 1925 Rb Ransomes B31F, Ex 920,	4
1925	801	CH 4859	Daimler CM	Ransomes	B31F	1932	Rb Ransomes B31F, ex 922, 1931	4
1925	803	CH 4854	Daimler CM	Ransomes	B31F	1933	Rb ex BMMO B31F, 1930.	4
1925	806	CH 4862	Daimler CM	Ransomes	B31F	1933	Rb ex BMMO B31F, 1930.	4
1925	807	CH 4863	Daimler CM	Ransomes	B31F	1933	Rb Ransomes B31F, ex 923, 1931.	4
1925	808	CH 4855	Daimler CM	Ransomes	B31F	1932	Rb ex BMMO B31F, 1930.	4
1925	810	CH 4856	Daimler CM	Ransomes	B31F		Rn 800, 1926. Rb ex BMMO B31F, 1930.	4
1925	811	CH 4860	Daimler CM	Ransomes	B31F	1932	Rn 802, 1926.Rb ex BMMO B31F, 1930.	4
1925	812	CH 4861	Daimler CM	Ransomes	B31F	1932	Rn 804, 1926.Rb Ransomes B31F ex 925, 1931.	4
1925	813	CH 4865	Daimler CM	Ransomes	B31F	1932	Rn 805, 1926. Rb Ransomes B31F ex924, 1931.	4
1925	814	CH 4866	Daimler CM	Ransomes	B31F	1933	Rn 809, 1926. Rb Ransomes B31F, ex 926, 1931.	4
1925	?	AU 7140	Daimler Y		B26	1925	Ex Clarke, Nottingham, new 1923	
1925	850	AU 7445	Daimler CB		B26	1931	Ex Clarke, Nottingham, new 1923 Rb Garford Ch18, Ex PET, 1926	
1925	?	AU 8316	Daimler Y			1926	Ex Clarke, Nottingham, new 1923	
1925	900	CH 4947	SOS S	Ransomes	B31F	1936	Rn 711, 1930.	5
1925	901	CH 4946	SOS S	Ransomes	B31F	1936	Rn 707, 1930.	5
1926	902	CH 5423	SOS S	Ransomes	B31F	1936	Rn 718, 1930.	5
1926	903	CH 5433	SOS S	Ransomes	B31F	1936	Rn 719,1930.	5
1926	904	CH 5434	SOS S	Ransomes	B31F	1936	Rn 709, 1930.	5

Year to Stock	Fleet No	Registration No	Chassis	Body	Layout	Year W'drwn.	Remarks (Rb - Rebodied, Rn - Renumbered)	Add'l Note
1926	905	CH 5424	SOS S	Ransomes	B31F	1936	Rn 702, 1930.	5
1926	906	CH 5426	SOS S	Ransomes	B31F	1936?	Rn 708, 1930.	5
1926	907	CH 5425	SOS S	Ransomes	B31F	1936	Rn 720, 1930.	5
1926	908	CH 5435	SOS S	Ransomes	B31F	1936	Rn 704, 1930.	5
1926	909	CH 5436	SOS S	Ransomes	B31F	1936	Rn 712, 1930.	5
1926	910	CH 5428	SOS S	Ransomes	B31F	1936	Rn 703, 1930.	5
1926	911	CH 5427	SOS S	Ransomes	B31F	1936	Rn 715, 1930.	5
1926	912	CH 5438	SOS S	Ransomes	B31F	1936	Rn 716, 1930.	5
1926	913	CH 5437	SOS S	Ransomes	B31F	1936	Rn 700, 1930.	5
1926	914	CH 5429	SOS S	Ransomes	B31F	1936	Rn 717, 1930.	5
1926	915	CH 5439	SOS S	Ransomes	B31F	1936	Rn 710, 1930.	5
1926	916	CH 5432	SOS S	Ransomes	B31F	1936	Rn 714, 1930.	5
1926	917	CH 5431	SOS S	Ransomes	B31F	1935	Rn 705, 1930.	5
1926	918	CH 5440	SOS S	Ransomes	B31F	1936	Rn 706, 1930.	5
1926	919	CH 5430	SOS S	Ransomes	B31F	1936	Rn 701 1930.	5
1926	920	CH 5441	SOS S	Ransomes	B31F	1936	Rn 713, 1930.	5
1926	921	CH 5442	SOS S	Ransomes	B31F	1936	Rn 721, Rb Brush B26F, 1931.	6
1926	922	CH 5443	SOS S	Ransomes	B31F	1936	Rn 722, Rb Brush B26F, 1931.	6
1926	923	CH 5445	SOS S	Ransomes	B31F	1936	Rn 723, Rb Brush B26F, 1931.	6
1926	924	CH 5444	SOS S	Ransomes	B31F	1936	Rn 724, Rb Brush B26F, 1931.	6
1926	925	CH 5447	SOS S	Ransomes	B31F	1936	Rn 725, Rb Brush B26F, 1931.	6
1926	926	CH 5446	SOS S	Ransomes	B31F	1936	Rn 726, Rb Brush B26F,1931.	6
1926	927	CH 5448	SOS S	Ransomes	B31F	1936	Body ex 809. Rn 727, Rb Brush B26F, 1931.	6
1926	928	CH 5449	SOS S	Ransomes	B31F	1936	Body ex 802. Rn 728, Rb Brush B26F, 1931.	6
1926	929	CH 5451	SOS S	Ransomes	B31F	1936	Body ex 800. Rn 729, Rb Brush B26F, 1931.	6
1926	930	CH 5452	SOS S	Ransomes	B31F	1936	Body ex 804. Rn 730, Rb Brush B26F, 1931.	6
1926	931	CH 5453	SOS S	Ransomes	B31F	1936	Body ex 805. Rn 731, Rb Brush B26F, 1931.	6
1927	950-3	CH 6231-2/5-6	SOS Q	Brush	B37F	1944-5		
1927	954	CH 6234	SOS Q	Brush	B37F	1941		
1927	955-6	CH 6233/7	SOS Q	Brush	B37F	1945		
1927	957	CH 6238	SOS Q	Brush	B37F	1941		
1927	958-60	CH 6239/40/2	SOS Q	Brush	B37F	1945		
1927	961	CH 6241	SOS Q	Brush	B37F	1945	Conv to ambulance, 1939.	
1927	962-3	CH 6243-4	SOS Q	Brush	B37F	1945		
1927	964	CH 6246	SOS Q	Brush	B37F	1941		
1927	965	CH 6245	SOS Q	Brush	B37F	1945	Conv to ambulance, 1939.	
1927	966	CH 6247	SOS Q	Brush	B37F	1945		
1927	967-8	CH 6248-9	SOS Q	Brush	B37F	1941		
1927	969	CH 6250	SOS Q	Brush	B37F	1945	Conv to ambulance, 1939.	
1927	970-1	CH 6251-2	SOS Q	Brush	B37F	1945		
1927	972	CH 6253	SOS Q	Brush	B37F	1941		
1927	973	CH 6254	SOS Q	Brush	B37F	1945	Conv to ambulance, 1939.	

Year to Stock	Fleet No	Registration No	Chassis	Body	Layout	Year W'drwn.	Remarks (Rb - Rebodied, Rn - Renumbered)	Add'l Note
1927	974	CH 6255	SOS Q	Brush	B37F	1945		
1927	600-4	CH 6256-60	SOS QC	Carlyle	Ch30	1936		
1928	500-6	CH 7129/33/30 34/6/8/40	SOS QL	Brush	B37F	1937		
1928	507	CH 7141	SOS QL	Ransomes	B37F	1937		
1928	509-13	CH 7132/1/5/7/9	SOS QL	Brush	B37F	1937		
1928	514-5	CH 7142-3	SOS QL	Ransomes	B37F	1937		
1928	650-2	CH 7144/6/5	SOS QLC	Short	C30F	1936-7		
1928	508/16-7	CH 7700/2/1	SOS QL	Ransomes	B37F	1937		
1928	518-9	CH 7748/51	SOS QL	Brush	B37F	1937		
1928	520	CH 7704	SOS QL	Ransomes	B37F	1937		
1928	521	CH 7750	SOS QL	Brush	B37F	1937		
1928	522	CH 7703	SOS QL	Ransomes	B37F	1937		
1928	523	CH 7753	SOS QL	Brush	B37F	1937		
1928	524	CH 7707	SOS QL	Ransomes	B37F	1937		
1928	525-6	CH 7752/4	SOS QL	Brush	B37F	1937		
1928	527	CH 7708	SOS QL	Ransomes	B37F	1937		
1928	528-9	CH 7755-6	SOS QL	Brush	B37F	1937		
1928	530	CH 7710	SOS QL	Ransomes	B37F	1937		
1928	531	CH 7749	SOS QL	Brush	B37F	1937		
1928	532-3	CH 7705/9	SOS QL	Ransomes	B37F	1937		
1928	534	CH 7757	SOS QL	Brush	B37F	1937		
1928	535-7	CH 7711-2/6	SOS QL	Ransomes	B37F	1937		
1928	1000	HD 2619	AEC 411	?	B30F	1930	Ex Retford MS, new 1926	
1928	1001-2	HD 2684-5	AEC 411	?	B30F	1930	Ex Retford MS, new 1926	
1928	1003-4	HD 2712/4	AEC 413	?	B30F	1930	Ex Retford MS, new 1926	
1928	1005	HD 2760	AEC 414	?	B26	1929	Ex Retford MS, new 1926	
1928	1006	TW 1833	AEC 413	?	B30F	1929	Ex Retford MS, new 1926	
1928	1050	RR 6425	Reo	?	B14F	1931	Ex Gregson, new 1927	
1928	1051	RR 8495	Reo FAX	?	B20F	1931	Ex Gregson, new 1928	
1928	1052	TO 4822	Reo	?	B20F	1931	Ex Gregson, new 1927	
1929	1200	RA 199	Chevrolet X	?	B14	1929	Ex Phipps, new 1926	
1929	1201	RA 513	Chevrolet X	?	B14	1929	Ex Phipps, new 1926	
1929	1202	RA 1429	Chevrolet X	?	B14	1929	Ex Phipps, new 1927	
1929	1203	RA 1728	Chevrolet LM	?	B14	1929	Ex Phipps, new 1927	
1929	1204	RA 2576	Chevrolet LM	?	B14	1931	Ex Phipps, new 1927. Conv to lorry A7	
1929	1205	RA 3817	Chevrolet LM	?	B14	1929	Ex Phipps, new 1927	
1929	1206	RA 5102	Chevrolet LO	?	B14	1931	Ex Phipps, new 1928	
1929	1250	RA 5767	Chevrolet LM	?	B20	1930	Ex Phipps, new 1927	
1929	1251	TO 6098	Chevrolet LM 6 wheeler	?	B20	1930	Ex Phipps, new 1927	
1252	1252	RA 4858	Chevrolet LM 6 wheeler	?	B20	1930	Ex Phipps, new 1928	
1929	1253	RA 4261	Chevrolet LM 6 wheeler	?	B20	1930	Ex Phipps, new 1927	

Year to Stock	Fleet No	Registration No	Chassis	Body	Layout	Year W'drwn.	Remarks (Rb - Rebodied, Rn - Renumbered)	Add'l Note
1929	1254	RA 6458	GMC	?	B20	1930	Ex Phipps, new 1928	
1929	1255	R 9323	Talbot	?	B14	1929	Ex Phipps, new 1922	
1929	1300	RA 7080	Leyland Lion PLSC3	Leyland	B32F	1934	Ex Phipps, new 1928	
1929	1301	RA 6795	Leyland Lion PLSC1	Leyland	B32F	1934	Ex Chapman, new 1928	
1929	1302	RA 3023	Leyland Lion PLSC1	Leyland	B32F	1934	Ex Chapman, new 1927	
1929	1303	RA 735	Leyland Lion PLSC1	Leyland	B32F	1934	Ex Chapman, new 1926	
1929	1350	RA 4571	Dennis 30cwt	Willowbrook	B18	1931	Ex Chapman, new 1927	
1929	1351	RA 4375	Dennis 30cwt	Willowbrook	B18	1931	Ex Chapman, new 1927	
1929	1352	NU 8559	Dennis 50cwt	?		1929	Ex Chapman, new 1929	
1929	1353	NU 8446	Dennis 50cwt	?		1929	Ex Chapman, new 1929	
1929	1400	R 6766	Commer 3P	?	B25	1929	Ex Chapman, new 1921	
1929	1401	RA 1226	Commer 2P	?	B26	1929	Ex Chapman, new 1926	
1929	1450	NU 6880	Karrier	?	B26	1929	Ex Chapman, new 1925	
1929	1451?	NU 9719	Dodge	?		1931	Ex Chapman, new 1926. Conv to lorry D5 1929.	
1929	1005	WB 4261	AEC 411 Renown	?	B30	1930	Ex Higgs & Waller, new 1925	
1929	1006	NU 2290	AEC 503	?	B34	1929	Ex Higgs & Waller, new 1924	
1929	1007	NU 5055	AEC 503	?	B34	1929	Ex Higgs & Waller, new 1925	
1929	1008	NU 3451	AEC 503	?	B34	1929	Ex Higgs & Waller, new 1924	
1929	400-5	CH 8101/3/2/5/11	SOS M	Short	B34F	1938		
1929	406-7	CH 8113/5	SOS M	Short	B34F	1945	Conv to ambulance, 1939.	
1929	408	CH 8117	SOS M	Short	B34F	1938		
1929	409	CH 8119	SOS M	Short	B34F	1929	Destroyed by fire	
1929	410-1	CH 8121/3	SOS M	Short	B34F	1945	Conv to ambulance, 1939.	
1929	412-3	CH 8125/06	SOS M	Short	B34F	1938-39		
1929	414	CH 8107	SOS M	Short	B34F	1945	Conv to ambulance, 1939.	
1929	415	CH 8104	SOS M	Short	B34F	1937		
1929	416	CH 8109	SOS M	Short	B34F	1945	Conv to ambulance, 1939.	
1929	417-21	CH 8110/2/4/6/8	SOS M	Short	B34F	1938		
1929	422	CH 8120	SOS M	Short	B34F	1945	Conv to ambulance, 1939.	
1929	423-4	CH 8122/4	SOS M	Short	B34F	1938		
1929	425-7	CH 8126-8	SOS M	Short	B34F	1945	Conv to ambulance, 1939.	
1929	428-9	CH 8130/29	SOS M	Short	B34F	1938		
1929	1304	RA 6798	Leyland Lioness PLC1		B26	1933	Ex Turner, Findern. new 1928	
1930	409	CH 8917	SOS M	Short	B34F	1938		
1930	670-2	CH 8919-20/18	SOS QLC	Short	C30F	1937		
1930	450-6	CH 8900-6	SOS COD	Brush	B34F	1940	Rn 200-6, 1932	
1930	457	CH 8907	SOS COD	Brush	B34F	1947	Rn 207, 1932	
1930	458-63	CH 8908-13	SOS COD	Brush	B34F	1940	Rn 208-13, 1932	
1930	464	CH 8914	SOS COD	Brush	B34F	1947	Rn 214, 1932	
1930	465-6	CH 8915-6	SOS COD	Brush	B34F	1940	Rn 215-6, 1932	
1930	1305	RA 9409	Leyland Tiger TS2	?	B30	1934	Ex Bramley, new 1929	

Year to Stock	Fleet No	Registration No	Chassis	Body	Layout	Year W'drwn.	Remarks (Rb - Rebodied, Rn - Renumbered)	Add'l Note
1930	1360	RA 5539	De Dion	?	B20	1932	Ex Bramley, new 1928	
1930	1361	RA 3915	De Dion	?	B20	1932	Ex Bramley, new 1927	
1930	100	CH 7783	ADC 423	Willowbrook	B32F	1934	Ex Wagg, new 1928	
1930	101	CH 8358	Daimler CF6	Willowbrook	B32F	1934	Ex Wagg, new 1929	
1930	102	CH 8635	Daimler CF6	?	B32F	1934	Ex Wagg, new 1929	
1930	1200	RA 3025	Albion PK26	?	?32?	1931	Ex Bayliss, new 1927	
1930	1201	RA 3692	Albion PK	?	?28?	1933	Ex Bayliss, new 1927	
1930	1202	RA 4964	Albion PJ	?	?24?	1934	Ex Bayliss, new 1928	
1930	1203	RA 9329	Bristol B	W J Smith	B31F	1934	Ex Bayliss, new 1929	
1930	1204	RB 187	Commer 4PE	?	?30?	1934	Ex Bayliss, new 1929	
1930	1306	RA 5365	Leyland Lion PLSC3	Leyland	B34F	1934	Ex Bayliss, new 1927	
1930	1307	RA 6602	Leyland Lion PLSC3	Leyland	B32F	1934	Ex Bayliss, new 1928	
1930	1308	RA 7323	Leyland Lion PLSC3	?	B30F	1934	Ex Bayliss, new 1928	
1930	1309	RB 2059	Leyland Lion LT2	Davidson	B32F	1936	Ex Bayliss, new 1930	
1930	1352	RB 1535	Dennis GL	?	B18F	1932	Ex Bayliss, new 1930	
1930	1353	RB 2061	Dennis GL	?	B18F	1932	Ex Bayliss, new 1930	
1931	1310	CH 9750	Leyland Lion LT2	Leyland	B32	1936	Ex Reynolds Bros, new 1931 and first registered by Trent.	
1931	1311	TV 2791	Leyland Lion LT2	Leyland	B35	1935	Ex Reynolds Bros, new 1930	
1931	1312	TV 2207	Leyland Tiger TS2	Leyland	B32	1934	Ex Reynolds Bros, new 1930	
1931	1313	TV1005	Leyland Lion LT1	Leyland	B32	1935	Ex Reynolds Bros, new 1929	
1931	1314	TO 9058	Leyland Lion PLSC3	Leyland	B32F	1934	Ex Reynolds Bros, new 1929	
1931	120-35	CH 9900-15	SOS IM6	Short	B34F	1940	Sold to War Dept, then BMMO	7
1931	470	CH 9916	SOS IM4	Short	B34F	1947	Rn 220 by 1/1932	
1931	471-81	CH 9917-27	SOS IM4	Short	B34F	1940	Rn 221-31 by 1/1932	8
1932	1205	WN 340	Tilling Stevens Express B10A	?	B32	1932	Ex Poundall, Belper, new 1927	
1932	1206	YV 2982	Tilling Stevens Express B10A	?	B32	1932	Ex Poundall, Belper, new 1928	
1932	1207	RA 7069	Tilling Stevens Express B10A	?	B32F	1937	Ex Barlow, new 1928. Rn 1211,1936	
1932	232	RC 407	SOS IM4	Brush	B34F	1940		8
1932	233-5	RC 408-10	SOS IM4	Brush	B34F	1947		
1932	236	RC 411	SOS IM4	Brush	B34F	1940	Sold to War Dept, then BMMO	7
1932	237-40	RC 412-5	SOS IM4	Brush	B34F	1948-9		
1932	241-2	RC 416-7	SOS IM4	Brush	B34F	1940	Sold to War Dept, then BMMO	7
1932	243-7	RC 418-22	SOS IM4	Brush	B34F	1947-9		
1932	248	RC 423	SOS IM4	Brush	B34F	1940	Sold to War Dept, then BMMO	7
1932	249-51	RC 424-6	SOS IM4	Brush	B34F	1947-9		
1932	252	RC 537	SOS IM4	Brush	B34F	1940	Sold to War Dept, then BMMO	7
1932	253-6	RC 538-41	SOS IM4	Brush	B34F	1948-9		
1932	136-9	RC 901-4	SOS IM6	Short	B34F	1948		
1932	140	RC 905	SOS IM6	Short	B34F	1940	Sold to War Dept, then BMMO	7
1932	141-5	RC 906-10	SOS IM6	Short	B34F	1948		
1933	257-61	RC 1276-80	SOS IM4	Short	B34F	1948-9		

Year to Stock	Fleet No	Registration No	Chassis	Body	Layout	Year W'drwn.	Remarks (Rb - Rebodied, Rn - Renumbered)	Add'l Note
1933	262-4	RC 1281-3	SOS IM4	Short	B34F	1940	Sold to War Dept, then BMMO	7
1933	265	RC 1284	SOS IM4	Short	B34F	1952	Fitted with Gardner 4LW engine, possibly from new. Converted to tree cutter no 22, and used in this form until 1959.	
1933	266	RC 1285	SOS IM4	Short	B34F	1940	Sold to War Dept, then BMMO	7
1933	267	RC 1286	SOS IM4	Short	B34F	1949		
1933	268	RC 1287	SOS IM4	Short	B34F	1940	Sold to War Dept, then BMMO	7
1933	269-71	RC 1288-90	SOS IM4	Short	B34F	1949		
1933	272	RC 1291	SOS IM4	Short	B34F	1940	Sold to War Dept, then BMMO	7
1933	273	RC 1292	SOS IM4	Short	B34F	1949		
1933	274	RC 1293	SOS IM4	Short	B34F	1940	Sold to War Dept, then BMMO	7
1933	275	RC 1294	SOS IM4	Short	B34F	1947		
1933	276-9	RC 1295-8	SOS IM4	Short	B34F	1940	Sold to War Dept, then BMMO	7
1933	280-1	RC 1299-300	SOS IM4	Short	B34F	1949		
1933	1201	CH 9637	Guy Conquest	Guy	B32	1933	Ex Rhodes, new 1930	
1933	1202	CH 8447	Dennis EV	Wilkinson	B32	1933	Ex Rhodes, new 1929	
1933	1205	CH 8668	Dennis G	Wilkinson	B19	1933	Ex Rhodes, new 1929	
1933	1206	CH 7268	Dennis G	Wilkinson	B18	1933	Ex Rhodes, new 1929	
1933	1208	CH 6739	Dennis 30cwt	Wilkinson	B14	1933	Ex Rhodes, new 1927	
1934	680-91	RC 1800-11	SOS ON	Duple	DP32R	1955	Rb and rn, see note	9
1934	1201	VO 7858	Albion PH49	J Taylor	B20F	1938	Ex Retford Coachways, new 1932 Rn 1223, 2/1936	
1934	1202	VO 5594	AEC Regal	J Taylor	B32F	1938	Ex Retford Coachways, new 1931 Rn 1201, 2/1936. Conv to lorry, 1938.	
1935	1203	RB 4341	Morris Commercial Dictator HF6	?	B32F	1936	Ex North, Derby, new 1931. Rn 1237, 1936.	
1935	1204	RB 7174	Morris Commercial Dictator HF6	?	B32F	1936	Ex North, Derby, new 1932.Rn 1238, 1936.	
1935	1205	VT 34	Tilling Stevens Express B10A	Willowbrook (new 1933)	B32F	1936	Ex Kingfisher, chassis new 1927 Rn 1209, 2/1936	10
1935	1206	VT580	Tilling Stevens Express B10A	Willowbrook (new 1933)	B32F	1936	Ex Kingfisher, chassis new 1927 Rn 1210, 2/1936	10
1935	1208	RC 3210	Daimler COG5SD	Brush	B32F	1954	Rb Willowbrook UL55R, rn 1300, 1943.	11
1935	625-6	RC 2546-7	SOS ON	Duple	C31F	1946	Converted to C35F, 1938	
1935	627-30	RC 2548-51	SOS ON	Duple	C31F	1948	Converted to C35F, 1938	
1935	300-14	RC 2700-14	SOS DON	Brush	B36F	1951-3		
1935	315-29	RC 2715-29	SOS DON	Brush	B34F	1950-3		12
1935	800	HA 3547	SOS FS	Brush	B34F	1937	Ex BMMO 591, new 1926.	13
1935	801	HA 3553	SOS FS	Brush	B34F	1936	Ex BMMO 597, new 1926. Destroyed by fire.	13
1935	802	HA 3573	SOS FS	Brush	B34F	1952	Ex BMMO 624, new 1926. Converted to tuition bus No 15, 1937. Used until 1952.	13
1935	803	HA 3577	SOS FS	Brush	B34F	1936	Ex BMMO 631, new 1926.	13
1935	804	HA 3586	SOS FS	Brush	B34F	1936	Ex BMMO 644, new 1926.	13
1935	805	HA 3546	SOS FS	Brush	B34F	1937	Ex BMMO 589, new 1926.	13

Year to Stock	Fleet No	Registration No	Chassis	Body	Layout	Year W'drwn.	Remarks (Rb - Rebodied, Rn - Renumbered)	Add'l Note
1935	806	HA 3578	SOS FS	Brush	B34F	1937	Ex BMMO 633, new 1926.	13
1935	807	HA 3582	SOS FS	Brush	B34F	1937	Ex BMMO 640, new 1926.	13
1935	808	HA 3583	SOS FS	Brush	B34F	1936	Ex BMMO 638, new 1926.	13
1935	809	HA 3588	SOS FS	Brush	B34F	1937	Ex BMMO 647, new 1926.	13
1935	1225	RB 4393	Morris Commercial Dictator		B32F	1936	Ex Stevenson, Little Eaton, new 1931. Rn 1236, 2/1936	
1935	1226	RB 6738	Dennis Lancet I	Willowbrook	C32F	1945	Ex Stevenson, Little Eaton, new 1932. Rn 1229, 2/1936	
1935	1209	BTO 389	Dennis Lancet I	Willowbrook	C32F	1945	Ex Dutton (Unity), Nottingham, new 1935. Rn 1233, 2/1936	
1935	1210	ATV 746	Dennis Lancet I	Willowbrook	C35F	1947	Ex Dutton (Unity), Nottingham new 1935. Rn 1232, 2/1936	
1935	1211	ATV 301	Dennis Lancet I	Yeates	DP36F	1947	Ex Dutton (Unity), new 1934 Rn 1231, 2/1936	
1935	1212	ATV 4	Dennis Lancet I	Willowbrook	C32F	1945	Ex Dutton (Unity), new 1935 Rn 1230, 2/1936	
1935	1213	ATO 209	AEC Regal 4	Willowbrook	DP32F	1940	Ex Dutton (Unity), new 1934 Rn 1202, 2/1936	
1935	1214	AAU 86	AEC Regal 4	Willowbrook	DP32F	1940	Ex Dutton (Unity), new 1934 Rn 1203, 2/1936	
1935	1215	TV 8971	AEC Regal 4	Brush	B32F	1940	Ex Dutton (Unity), new 1933 Rn 1204, 2/1936	
1935	1216	TV 7917	Tilling Stevens B49A7	Willowbrook	B32F	1936	Ex Dutton (Unity), new 1933 Rn 1212, 2/1936	
1935	1217	TV 7472	Tilling Stevens B49A7	Willowbrook	B32F	1936	Ex Dutton (Unity), new 1932 Rn 1213, 2/1936	
1935	1218	TV 6765	Tilling Stevens B49A7	Beadle	B32F	1936	Ex Dutton (Unity), new 1932 Rn 1214, 2/1936	
1935	1219	TV 6036	Tilling Stevens B49A7	Willowbrook	B32F	1936	Ex Dutton (Unity), new 1932 Rn 1215, 2/1936	
1935	1220	TV 5363	Tilling Stevens Express B10A2	Willowbrook	B32F	1936	Ex Dutton (Unity), new 1931 Rn 1216, 2/1936	
1935	1221	TV 4505	Tilling Stevens Express B10A2	Dixon or W J Smith	B32F	1936	Ex Dutton (Unity), new 1931 Rn 1217,2/1936	
1935	1222	TV 2250	GMC	Bracebridge	B20F	1936	Ex Dutton (Unity), new 1930 Rn 1239, 2/1936	
1935	1223	TV 1908	GMC T30	Rainford	B20F	1936	Ex Dutton (Unity), new 1930 Rn 1240, 2/1936	
1935	1224	TV 1057	GMC T42	Rainford	B24F	1936	Ex Dutton (Unity), new 19?? Rn 1241, 2/1936	
1935	1235	JU 3060	Dennis Lancet I	Willowbrook	C32F	1947	Ex Horspool, new 1934. Rn 1228, 2/1936	
1935	1236	UT 8948	Maudslay ML3E	Willowbrook	B32F	1936	Ex Horspool, new 1932. Rn 1224, 2/1936	

Year to Stock	Fleet No	Registration No	Chassis	Body	Layout	Year W'drwn.	Remarks (Rb - Rebodied, Rn - Renumbered)	Add'l Note
1935	1237	JU 652	Maudslay ML3X	Willowbrook	B32F	1936	Ex Horspool, new 1931. Rn 1225, 2/1936	
1935	1238	UT 7854	Gilford AS6	Willowbrook	B20F	1936	Ex Horspool, new 1930. Rn 1206, 2/1936	
1935	1227	RB 7897	AEC Regal	Willowbrook	B32F	1940	Ex Daley, new 1933. Rn 1205, 2/1936. Converted to Lorry 12.	
1935	1228	RB 1102	Tilling Stevens Express B10A2		B32F	1936	Ex Daley, new 1930. Rn 1218, 2/1936.	
1935	1229	UV 4215	Tilling Stevens Express B10A2		B32F	1936	Ex Daley, new 1929. Rn 1219, 2/1936	
1935	1230	RA 8698	Tilling Stevens Express		B32	1936	Ex Daley, new 19?? Rn 1220, 2/1936.	
1935	1231	UU 3170	Tilling Stevens Express B10A		B32R	1937	Ex Daley, new 1929. Rn 1221, 2/1936	
1935	1232	RA 7662	Dennis G		B18F	1936	Ex Daley, new 1929. Rn 1235, 2/1936	
1935	1233	RA 6957	Tilling Stevens Express B10A2		B32F	1936	Ex Daley, new 1928. Rn 1222, 2/1936	
1935	1234	NU 9413	Dennis 30cwt		B14	1936	Ex Daley, new 1926. Rn 1234, 2/1936	
1936	1239	RB 473	Guy		B20	1936	Ex Partlow & Tarlton,new 1930 Rn 1242, 2/1936.	
1936	1240	RB 5420	Guy		?32?	1936	Ex Partlow & Tarlton,new 1931 Rn 1243, 2/1936	
1936	1241	RB 7610	Guy		B20	1936	Ex Partlow & Tarlton,new 1932 Rn 1244, 2/1936.	
1936	1000-14	RC 3322-36	SOS FEDD	Metro Cammell	H56F	1950-1	1002 damaged by fire, w'drn 1948.	
1936	1239	CH 9305	Gilford 168SD	Willowbrook	B26F	1936	Ex Salt, new 1931. Rn 1207, 2/1936.	
1936	1240	RB 8452	Dennis Lancet I	Willowbrook	C32F	1945	Ex Salt, new 1933. Rn 1226, 2/1936.	
1936	1241	BNU 809	Dennis Lancet I	Willowbrook	DP38F	1947	Ex Salt, new 1935. Rn 1227, 2/1936.	
1936	330-1	RC 3701-2	SOS DON	Brush	B36F	1951-3		
1936	332	RC 3703	SOS DON	Brush	B36F	1958	Rb W'brook B35F, rn512, 1949	
1936	333-4	RC 3704-5	SOS DON	Brush	B36F	1952-3		
1936	335	RC 3706	SOS DON	Brush	B36F	1958	Rb W'brook B35F, rn513, 1949	
1936	336	RC 3707	SOS DON	Brush	B36F	1942	Destroyed by fire	
1936	337	RC 3708	SOS DON	Brush	B36F	1958	Rb W'brook B35F, rn514, 1949	
1936	338	RC 3709	SOS DON	Brush	B36F	1958	Rb W'brook B35F, rn515, 1949	
1936	339	RC 3710	SOS DON	Brush	B36F	1958	Rb W'brook B35F, rn516, 1949	
1936	340	RC 3711	SOS DON	Brush	B36F	1953		
1936	341	RC 3712	SOS DON	Brush	B36F	1958	Rb W'brook B35F, rn517, 1949	
1936	342	RC 3713-17	SOS DON	Brush	B36F	1952		
1936	343-5	RC 3714-16	SOS DON	Brush	B36F	1951-3	Converted to B32F + 22 standing, 1941. Reverted to B36F, 11/1945.	
1936	346	RC 3717	SOS DON	Brush	B36F	1952		
1936	347	RC 3718	SOS DON	Brush	B36F	1958	Rb W'brook B35F, rn518, 1949	
1936	348	RC 3719	SOS DON	Brush	B36F	1958	Converted to B32F + 22 standing, 1941. Reverted to B36F, 11/1945. Rb W'brook B35F, rn 519, 1949	
1936	349-50	RC 3720-1	SOS DON	Brush	B36F	1952		
1936	351	RC 3722	SOS DON	Brush	B36F	1958	Rb W'brook B35F, rn520, 1949	
1936	352	RC 3723	SOS DON	Brush	B36F	1958	Rb W'brook B35F, rn521, 1949	

Year to Stock	Fleet No	Registration No	Chassis	Body	Layout	Year W'drwn.	Remarks (Rb - Rebodied, Rn - Renumbered)	Add'l Note
1936	353-4	RC 3724-5	SOS DON	Brush	B36F	1952-3		
1936	355	RC 3726	SOS DON	Brush	B36F	1958	Rb W'brook B35F, rn522, 1949	
1936	356	RC 3727	SOS DON	Brush	B36F	1958	Rb W'brook B35F, rn523, 1949	
1936	357	RC 3728	SOS DON	Brush	B36F	1951		
1936	358	RC 3729	SOS DON	Brush	B36F	1958	Rb W'brook B35F, rn524, 1949	
1936	359	RC 3730	SOS DON	Brush	B36F	1958	Rb W'brook B35F, rn525, 1949	
1936	360	RC 3731	SOS DON	Brush	B36F	1958	Rb W'brook B35F, rn526, 1949	
1936	361	RC 3732	SOS DON	Brush	B36F	1958	Rb W'brook B35F, rn527, 1949	
1936	362	RC 3733	SOS DON	Brush	B36F	1958	Rb W'brook B35F, rn528, 1949	
1936	363	RC 3734	SOS DON	Brush	B36F	1952	Converted to tuition bus 15	
1936	364	RC 3735	SOS DON	Brush	B36F	1958	Rb W'brook B35F, rn529, 1949	
1936	365	RC 3736	SOS DON	Brush	B36F	1952		
1936	366	RC 3737	SOS DON	Brush	B36F	1958	Rb W'brook B35F, rn530, 1949	
1936	367-8	RC 3738-9	SOS DON	Brush	B36F	1951-2		
1936	369	RC 3740	SOS DON	Brush	B36F	1958	Rb W'brook B35F, rn531, 1949	
1936	631-6	RC 3741-6	SOS ON	Duple	C31F	1948		
1937	700-2	RC 4601-3	AEC Regal	Duple	B35F	1958	Rb Willowbrook B35F, 1950	14
1937	703	RC 4604	AEC Regal	Duple	B35F	1955		14
1937	704	RC 4605	AEC Regal	Duple	B35F	1958	Rb Willowbrook B35F, 1950	14
1937	705-9	RC 4606-10	AEC Regal	Duple	B35F	1958	Rb Willowbrook B35F, 1950	
1937	710	RC 4611	AEC Regal	Willowbrook	B35F	1958	Rb Willowbrook B35F, 1950	
1937	711	RC 4612	AEC Regal	Willowbrook	B35F	1958	Rb Willowbrook B35F, 1950	
1937	712	RC 4613	AEC Regal	Willowbrook	B35F	1953		
1937	713-16	RC 4614-17	AEC Regal	Willowbrook	B35F	1958	Rb Willowbrook B35F, 1950	
1937	717	RC 4618	AEC Regal	Willowbrook	B35F	1953		
1937	718	RC 4619	AEC Regal	Willowbrook	B35F	1958	Rb Willowbrook B35F, 1950	
1937	719	RC 4620	AEC Regal	Willowbrook	B35F	1953		
1937	1015	RC 4621	AEC Regent	Weymann	H54FD	1960	Rb W'brook L55R, rn 1340,1949	
1937	1016	RC 4622	AEC Regent	Weymann	H54FD	1958	Rb W'brook H56R, 1948, rn 1162, 1957	
1937	1017	RC 4623	AEC Regent	Weymann	H54FD	1959	Rb W'brook L55R, rn 1341,1949	
1937	1018	RC 4624	AEC Regent	Weymann	H54FD	1960	Rb W'brook L55R, rn 1330,1948	
1937	1019	RC 4625	AEC Regent	Weymann	H54FD	1959	Rb W'brook L55R, rn 1342,1998	
1937	1020	RC 4626	AEC Regent	Weymann	H54FD	1959	Rb W'brook L55R, rn 1343,1949	
1937	1021	RC 4627	AEC Regent	Weymann	H54FD	1960	Rb W'brook L55R, rn 1331,1948	
1937	1022	RC 4628	AEC Regent	Weymann	H54FD	1960	Rb W'brook L55R, rn 1332,1948	
1937	1023	RC 4629	AEC Regent	Weymann	H54FD	1960	Rb W'brook L55R, rn 1333,1948	
1937	1024	RC 4630	AEC Regent	Weymann	H54FD	1960	Rb W'brook L55R, rn 1334,1948	
1937	1025	RC 4631	AEC Regent	Weymann	H54FD	1958	Rb W'brook H56R, 1948, rn 1163, 1957	
1937	1026	RC 4632	AEC Regent	Weymann	H54FD	1958	Rb W'brook H56R, 1948,rn 1164, 1957	
1937	1027	RC 4633	AEC Regent	Weymann	H54FD	1959	Rb W'brook L55R, rn 1335,1948	
1937	1028	RC 4634	AEC Regent	Weymann	H54FD	1960	Rb W'brook L55R, rn 1336,1948	
1937	1029	RC 4635	AEC Regent	Weymann	H54FD	1960	Rb W'brook L55R, rn 1344,1949	

Year to Stock	Fleet No	Registration No	Chassis	Body	Layout	Year W'drwn.	Remarks (Rb - Rebodied, Rn - Renumbered)	Add'l Note
1937	1030	RC 4636	AEC Regent	Weymann	H54FD	1959	Rb W'brook L55R, rn 1345,1949	
1937	1031	RC 4637	AEC Regent	Weymann	H54FD	1958	Rb W'brook H56R, 1948, rn 1165, 1957	
1937	1032	RC 4638	AEC Regent	Weymann	H54FD	1960	Rb W'brook L55R, rn 1337,1948	
1937	1033	RC 4639	AEC Regent	Weymann	H54FD	1960	Rb W'brook L55R, rn 1346,1949	
1937	1034	RC 4640	AEC Regent	Weymann	H54FD	1959	Rb W'brook L55R, rn 1347,1949	
1937	1035	RC 4641	AEC Regent	Weymann	H54FD	1959	Rb W'brook L55R, rn 1348,1949	
1937	1036	RC 4642	AEC Regent	Weymann	H54FD	1947		
1937	1037	RC 4643	AEC Regent	Weymann	H54FD	1958	Rb W'brook H56R, 1948,rn 1166, 1957	
1937	1038	RC 4644	AEC Regent	Weymann	H54FD	1959	Rb W'brook L55R, rn 1338,1948	
1937	1039	RC 4645	AEC Regent	Weymann	H54FD	1959	Rb W'brook L55R, rn 1349,1949	
1937	1040	RC 4646	AEC Regent	Weymann	H54FD	1959	Rb W'brook L55R, rn 1350,1949	
1937	1041	RC 4647	AEC Regent	Weymann	H54FD	1958	Rb W'brook H56R, 1948, rn 1167, 1957.	
1937	1042	RC 4648	AEC Regent	Weymann	H54FD	1960	Rb W'brook L55R, rn 1351,1949	
1937	1043	RC 4649	AEC Regent	Weymann	H54FD	1958	Rb W'brook H56R, 1948. Rn 1168, 1957.	
1937	1044	RC 4650	AEC Regent	Weymann	H54FD	1960	Rb W'brook L55R, rn 1339,1948	
1937	500	RC 5724	Daimler COG5/40	Willowbrook	B35F	1954	Rb W'brook UH56R, rn 1088	
1938	501	RC 5980	Daimler COG5/40	Willowbrook	B35F	1953	Rb W'brook UH56R,rn 1089,1942	15
1938	502	RC 5981	Daimler COG5/40	Willowbrook	B35F	1953	Rb W'brook UH56R,rn 1090,1942	15
1938	503	RC 5982	Daimler COG5/40	Willowbrook	B35F	1953	Rb W'brook UH56R,rn 1091,1942	15
1938	504	RC 5983	Daimler COG5/40	Willowbrook	B35F	1953	Rb W'brook UH56R,rn 1092,1942	15
1938	505	RC 5984	Daimler COG5/40	Willowbrook	B35F	1953	Rb W'brook UH56R,rn 1093,1942	15
1938	506	RC 5985	Daimler COG5/40	Willowbrook	B35F	1953	Rb W'brook UH56R,rn 1094,1942	15
1938	507	RC 5986	Daimler COG5/40	Willowbrook	B35F	1953	Rb W'brook UH56R,rn 1095,1942	15
1938	508	RC 5987	Daimler COG5/40	Willowbrook	B35F	1953	Rb W'brook UH56R,rn 1096,1942	15
1938	637	RC 5988	Daimler COG5/40	Duple	C31F	1953	Rb W'brook UH56R,rn 1082,1942	16
1938	638	RC 5989	Daimler COG5/40	Duple	C31F	1953	Rb W'brook UH56R,rn 1083,1942	16
1938	639	RC 5990	Daimler COG5/40	Duple	C31F	1953	Rb W'brook UH56R,rn 1084,1942	16
1938	640	RC 5991	Daimler COG5/40	Duple	C31F	1953	Rb W'brook UH56R,rn 1085,1942	16
1938	641	RC 5992	Daimler COG5/40	Duple	C31F	1953	Rb W'brook UH56R,rn 1086,1942	16
1938	642	RC 5993	Daimler COG5/40	Duple	C31F	1953	Rb W'brook UH56R,rn 1087,1942	16
1938	1045	RC 5994	Daimler COG5	Weymann	H54FD	1957	Rb W'brook H54R, 1946	
1938	1046-9	RC 5995-8	Daimler COG5	Weymann	H54FD	1957	Rb Brush H56R, 1948	
1938	1050-1	RC 5999-6000	Daimler COG5	Weymann	H54FD	1957	Rb W'brook H54R, 1946	
1938	1052-3	RC 6001-2	Daimler COG5	Weymann	H54FD	1957	Rb Brush H56R, 1948	
1938	1054	RC 6003	Daimler COG5	Weymann	H54FD	1957	Rb W'brook H54R, 1946	
1938	1055	RC 6004	Daimler COG5	Weymann	H54FD	1953		
1938	1056	RC 6005	Daimler COG5	Weymann	H54FD	1957	Rb Brush H56R, 1948	
1938	1057-8	RC 6006-7	Daimler COG5	Weymann	H54FD	1957	Rb W'brook H54R, 1946	
1938	1059	RC 6008	Daimler COG5	Weymann	H54FD	1957	Rb Brush H56R, 1948	
1939	1060	RC 7071	Daimler COG5	Weymann	H54FD	1954		
1939	1061-2	RC 7072-3	Daimler COG5	Weymann	H54FD	1956	Rb W'brook H54R, 1946	
1939	1063	RC 7074	Daimler COG5	Weymann	H54FD	1957	Rb W'brook H56R, 1948	

Year to Stock	Fleet No	Registration No	Chassis	Body	Layout	Year W'drwn.	Remarks (Rb - Rebodied, Rn - Renumbered)	Add'l Note
1939	1064-5	RC 7075-6	Daimler COG5	Weymann	H54FD	1957	Rb Brush H56R, 1948	
1939	1066	RC 7077	Daimler COG5	Weymann	H54FD	1956	Rb W'brook H54R, 1946	
1939	1067	RC 7078	Daimler COG5	Weymann	H54FD	1957	Rb W'brook H54R, 1946	
1939	1068	RC 7079	Daimler COG5	Weymann	H54FD	1957	Rb Brush H56R, 1948	
1939	1069	RC 7080	Daimler COG5	Weymann	H54FD	1958	Rb Brush H56R, 1948	
1939	1070	RC 7081	Daimler COG5	Weymann	H54FD	1957	Rb Brush H56R, 1948	
1939	1071	RC 7082	Daimler COG5	Weymann	H54FD	1954		
1939	643-8	RC 7083-8	SOS SON	Willowbrook	C31F	1954		
1939	400-11	RC 7089-100	SOS SON	Willowbrook	B34F	1954		
1940	412-25	RC 7922-35	SOS SON	Willowbrook	B34F	1954	417 preserved by Company	
1940	1072	RC 7936	Daimler COG5	Weymann	H54F	1957	Rb W'brook H56R, 1948	17
1940	1073	RC 7937	Daimler COG5	Weymann	H54F	1957	Rb Brush H56R, 1948	17
1940	1074	RC 7938	Daimler COG5	Weymann	H54F	1958	Rb W'brook H56R, 1948	17
1940	1075	RC 7939	Daimler COG5	Weymann	H54F	1957	Rb Brush H56R, 1948	17
1940	1076	RC 7940	Daimler COG5	Weymann	H54F	1958	Rb W'brook H56R, 1948	17
1940	1077-8	RC 7941-2	Daimler COG5	Weymann	H54F	1958	Rb Brush H56R, 1948	17
1940	1079	RC 7943	Daimler COG5	Weymann	H54F	1954		17
1940	1080	RC 7944	Daimler COG5	Weymann	H54F	1958	Rb W'brook H56R, 1948	17
1940	1081	RC 7945	Daimler COG5	Weymann	H54F	1958	Rb Brush H56R, 1948	17
1941-2			No vehicles received					
1943	1097-8	RC 8320-1	Daimler CWG5	Duple	UH56R	1956		
1943	1306-8	RC 8378-80	Daimler CWA6	Duple	UL55R	1956-7		
1944	1301-2	RC 8359-60	Daimler CWA6	Duple	UL55R	1956		
1944	1303-5	RC 8391-3	Daimler CWA6	Brush	UL55R	1956		
1944	1099-101	RC 8394-6	Daimler CWA6	Roe	UH56R	1956-7		
1944	1102-6	RC 8397-401	Daimler CWA6	Roe	UH56R	1956-7		
1944	1107	RC 8402	Daimler CWA6	Brush	UH56R	1957		
1945	1108-11	RC 8464-7	Daimler CWA6	Duple	UH56R	1957		
1945	1309-10	RC 8480-1	Daimler CWA6	Duple	UL55R	1956		
1945	1311	RC 8482	Daimler CWA6	Duple	UL55R	1957		
1945	1312	RC 8483	Daimler CWA6	Duple	UL55R	1956		
1945	1112-3	RC 8530-1	Daimler CWD6	Brush	UH56R	1957	1113 converted to CWA6D type, 1948	
1945	1114-15	RC 8532-3	Daimler CWA6D	Brush	UH56R	1957		
1945	1116	RC 8570	Daimler CWA6D	Duple	UH56R	1957		

This list has been prepared largely from Company records, although with the assistance of the records of the PSV Circle, which is hereby acknowledged. Readers with a particular interest in vehicles are commended to join the PSV Circle, which is the national enthusiast body for vehicle records. The early Company records are fairly limited, with early fleetlists for 1919, and 1920 only being found, and then a regular annual list for most years from 1926. In addition, some early ledgers exist, which make various references to vehicles, but not always linking types, fleetnumbers and registration numbers together, in a way that we would today. The early part of the list, especially the Tilling Stevens TS3s and Thornycrofts cannot, therefore, be guaranteed, and more information would be welcomed by the author. The list is, however, intended to be as accurate as possible with the available information. Information not found, or not positively confirmed, has been shown with a question mark.

Please see Page 154, for Additional Notes referred to on pages140 - 153

Additional Notes referred to on pages 140 to 153.

Note	Remarks
1	**Tilling Stevens TS3.** The early Tilling Stevens TS3s were the subject of some re-bodying and rebuilding around 1919-20. It seems also that a number of registrations were exchanged between vehicles. A list dated 31st December, 1919 shows all vehicles with their original registration numbers, body numbers and fleet numbers. A further list, dated 31st March, 1920, shows the vehicles with fleet numbers and body numbers as before, but with the registration numbers in a different sequence. It is known that, in the early days of motor transport, registration numbers often stayed with the bodies when these were exchanged, rather than with the chassis, as is the case today. However, as the body numbers and fleet numbers were in the same order, and matched in the same way in both lists, it does not appear that the bodies were generally swapped over and, for the same reason, it does not appear that the vehicles were renumbered either. After much thought, the two lists have been taken at face value, and it has been assumed that the registrations have been changed round, although no reason has been found for this. Accordingly, the revised registration numbers have been entered , with the date, in the appropriate column. All references to further changes, in the remarks column, relate to the vehicle with its second registration number. Clearly, if the two lists referred to are not taken at face value, then it affects the remarks relating to all twenty two vehicles. There was one additional Tilling Stevens TS3 chassis, CH 1975, which was first registered as a lorry. No information has been found to suggest that it ever operated with a bus body. Photographic evidence shows it with a lorry body and carrying fleet number 147, on a metal plate fixed to the bonnet, in the post 1924 style used for buses. The TS3s were the subject of much modification during their long operational lives. Twenty were converted to B1 Type, with conventional gearbox and clutch. Others were converted to B2 Type retaining the petrol electric transmission, but with pneumatic tyres. A number were converted to forward control and received new Brush B32R bodies. A number were also converted to double deck, possibly with ex-Midland Red bodies. Still more received charabanc bodies. A number received second hand Ransomes B31F bodies removed from SOS S Types when these were rebuilt as ODD Type and rebodied. Most, if not all, eventually ran on pneumatic tyres.
2	**Thornycroft J.** Four of these vehicles were originally supplied with Birch OT57R bodywork, whilst some had charabanc bodies and others single deck bus bodies. At least four were converted to forward control and fitted with new Brush B32R bodies, being numbered first 500/1,510/1, and later 700/1,710/1.
3	**Thornycroft J, ex Thames Valley.** The bodies on these vehicles were new in 1916, and originally fitted to Belsize chassis. DP 2120 was converted by Trent to lorry no 2, and DP 2599 to lorry no 1, both in 1927.
4	**Daimler CM.** Originally supplied with Ransomes B31F bodies, five of these vehicles gave up their bodies to new SOS S Type chassis, received new Davidson charabanc bodies, and were renumbered 851-5. Some of the remaining vehicles were then renumbered into the gaps created in the number series, in order to make a complete run. Later, in 1930-31, all received used bodies, some taken from the SOS S types, when these were rebuilt to ODD Type and rebodied, and others acquired second hand from Midland Red, which had almost certainly been removed from S Type chassis as part of the same process in that fleet. The charabancs were then renumbered again to 810-14.
5	**SOS S Type.** The first twenty-one S Types were converted to ODD Type in 1930, and fitted with new B26F bodies, built up from kits of parts supplied by United of Lowestoft. The original bodies were fitted to Tilling Stevens TS3s and Daimler CMs, and the "new" ODDs were renumbered from the 9xx series to the 7xx series.
6	**SOS S Type.** The remaining S Types were converted to ODD Type in 1931, and fitted with new B26F bodies of identical design to the previous twenty-one, but built by Brush. As with the earlier rebuilds, some of the original bodies were fitted to Tilling Stevens TS3s and Daimler CMs, and the "new" ODDs were renumbered from the 9xx series to the 7xx series.
7	**SOS IM4 and IM6, new 1931-33.** Sold to War Department, subsequently passing to BMMO.
8	**SOS IM4, new 1931 and 33.** Sold to War Department.
9	**SOS ON.** The original Duple bodies of 682-91 were upseated to DP35R in 1938. In 1946, the chassis were fitted with AEC 7.7litre diesel engines, in place of the original SOS petrol units, rebodied Willowbrook B35F and received fleetnumbers 370-81, in order. In 1949, they were renumbered to 500-11, in order.
10	**VT 34, VT 580, Tilling Stevens Express B10A.** Kingfisher acquired these from Tilstone, Stoke on Trent, but VT 580 had been new to Pritchard, Stoke on Trent.
11	**RC 3210 Daimler COG5.** Exhibited at the Commercial Motor Show at Olympia, London.
12	**323, RC 2723, SOS DON.** Used by the Company as a Booking Office at Skegness during summer seasons until 1963, following which it was replaced by a caravan. Preserved by the Lincolnshire Vintage Vehicle Society at Lincoln, although without seats, due to its previous use.
13	**SOS FS Type.** These vehicles were previously on hire from BMMO, from March, 1935, until acquisition.
14	**700-4, RC 4601-5, AEC Regal/Duple B35F.** Converted to B30F + 30 standees (perimeter seating), 1940-46.
15	**500-8, RC 5724, 5980-7, Daimler COG5/40/Willowbrook B35F.** Original bodies sold to the original Enterprise & Silver Dawn, Scunthorpe.
16	**637-42, RC 5988-93, Daimler COG5/40/Duple C35F.** Coach bodies stored during the war, and fitted to new AEC Regal chassis, 637-42, RC 8740-5, in 1946.
17	**1072-81, RC 7936-45, Daimler COG5/Weymann H54F.** The original bodies featured doors at entrance to lower saloon, rather than to the platform, which was the more usual arrangement on double deckers.

Acquired Operators, 1913 - 45. Please see also Additional Notes starting on Page 159.

Takeover or Agreement Date	Operator Name	Routes	Allocated Route No	Vehicles Acquired	Amount Paid	Add'l Note
1st Nov 1913	Commercial Car Hirers Ltd.	Derby-Ashbourne, via Brailsford Derby-Alfreton, via Ripley Alfreton-Chesterfield, via Clay Cross Derby-Melbourne Derby-Uttoxeter	- - - - -	6	£8 381	
Feb/Mar 1916	G Dawkins & W C Ballard, Alfreton.	Alfreton-Derby, via Ripley	-	1	£1 150	1
26th Feb 1917	J Harrison, Ashbourne & Derby Motor Service, Ashbourne.	Ashbourne-Derby, via Brailsford	-	1	£750	
19th Feb 1919 (wef 20th Jan 1919)	Loughborough Road Car Co, Ltd.	Loughborough-Shepshed Loughborough-Mountsorrell	- -	1 plus garage	£1 517	2
??? Jul 1922	G J Hawksworth, Tutbury.	Burton-Uttoxeter	20/21	None	?	3
25th Jul 1923	Clayton Transport & Motor Bus Co, Ltd., Nottingham.	Nottingham-Burton Joyce, via Gedling	35/36?	4	£2 400	
5th June, 1925	W & A Clarke, Clarke's Bus Service, Nottingham.	Nottingham-Ilkeston	inc into32?	3	£715	
??? Oct 1928	Retford Motor Services.	Nottingham-Doncaster via Ollerton.	36	7	£3 247	4
??? Jan 1929	J Wade, The Bean Bus Service, Nottingham.	Nottingham-East Bridgford Nottingham-Gunthorpe Nottingham-Hoveringham Nottingham-Burton Joyce-Gunthorpe-E. Bridgford-Radcliffe on Trent-W. Bridgford-Nottingham.(Circular).	33A/33B 34C inc into 34D 33A/34B	None	£145	5
21st Jan 1929	G Phipps, District Omnibus Service, Horsley Woodhouse.	Derby-Alfreton, via Ripley Derby-Heanor, via Kilburn Toll Bar and Horsley Woodhouse Derby-Ilkeston, via Morley and Smalley Cross Roads.	inc into 1 7 10?	14 plus garage	£12 500	
4th Mar 1929	George Chapman & Sons, Belper.	Derby-Belper, via Holbrook Belper-Ripley, via Ambergate and Lower Hartshay. Belper- Ripley, via Openwoodgate and Heage. Belper-Ripley, via The Lawn and Heage.	11 15 16/17 16/17	11 plus garage	£8 020	
6th Mar 1929	J T Gregson & Sons, Burton Joyce.	Nottingham-Burton Joyce, via Gedling.	34A	3	£2 100	
30th Apr 1929 (wef 24th Mar)	Higgs & Waller (Melbourne), Ltd.	Derby-Melbourne, via Chellaston	inc into 3	4	£2 765	
17th May 1929	P & G Wright,Wright Brothers, South Normanton.	Alfreton-Mansfield	inc Into 21	None	£750	
??? July 1929	Lincolnshire Road Car Co, Ltd.	Contribution towards payment of £500 which LRCC had previously made to Albert Warburton to leave their routes.	-	None	£150	
30th Sept 1929	Hubert de Tracey Wilkinson, Britannia Omnibus Service, Nottingham.	Nottingham-Gunthorpe, via Burton Joyce and Lowdham	34C	None	£145	6
??? Oct 1929	Barton Transport Ltd.	Derby-Nottingham	inc into 8	None	£600	7
22nd Oct 1929	J Turner, Eagle Motor Services, Derby.	Derby-Mickleover.	inc into 6A/B	1	£2 175	8
4th Nov 1929	G Daley, The Guy Service, Ripley.	Belper-Ripley, via Ambergate	inc into 15?	None	£45	
30th Dec 1929	L H Dutton, Dutton's Motor Service, Radcliffe on Trent.	Nottingham-Bingham, via Radcliffe on Trent. Nottingham-Granby	inc into 33C? 38	None	£650	9
18th Mar 1930	E Bramley, Prince of Wales Service, Cotmanhay.	Nottingham-Ilkeston-Cotmanhay.	32	3	£2 500	10
31st May 1930	TC Cox & T Pollard, TPS Omnibus Service, or Cox's Service, Derby.	Derby- Spondon (Celanese) via Uttoxeter Road, Slack Lane, Ashbourne Road and Brook Street. Derby-Belper, via Openwoodgate and Holbrook	? inc into 11?	None	£2 000	

Takeover or Agreement Date	Operator Name	Routes	Allocated Route No	Vehicles Acquired	Amount Paid	Add'l Note
16th Aug 1930 (wef 12th Aug)	F H Turner & G Wagg, Wagg's Super Service, Derby	Derby-Melbourne and Swadlincote.	inc into 3	3	£4 500	
24th Nov 1930 (wef 7th Dec)	H D Bayliss & Sons, Ashbourne.	Derby-Ashbourne, via Brailsford Derby-Ashbourne, via Cross o' the Hands	4B 18	11	£14 000	
28th Feb 1931 (wef 1st Mar)	Reynolds Brothers, Bulwell.	Nottingham-Hucknall, via Bulwell		5	£7 625	11
4th Dec 1931	Arthur Farnsworth, Blue Bird Service,	Mansfield-Hucknall, via Sutton in Ashfield.	30	5	£3 500	12
20th Jan 1932 (wef 7th Jan)	P & J W Poundall, Belper.	Belper-Ripley, via Openwoodgate, Kilburn and Denby	14	2	£1 350	13
9th Mar 1932 (wef 20th Mar)	J W Longdon, Mason's Bus Service, Derby.	Derby-Tutbury, extended to Church Broughton on Fridays	inc into 6C?	None	£3 150	
10th Mar 1932	Mrs L Green, Blue Glider Motor Service, Wymeswold.	Nottingham-Loughborough, via Bunny and Wymeswold.	inc into 66?	None	£250	
22nd Apr 1932 (wef 1st May)	E Barlow, Belper.	Derby-Belper, via Holbrook	11?	1	£2 900	
22nd Apr 1932 (wef 15th May)	J Clews, Spondon Ex-Servicemen's, Spondon.	Derby-Spondon Excursions from Spondon	inc into 9?	None	£1 500	14
22nd Apr 1932 (wef 15th May)	W Liewsley, Liewsley's Bus Service, Spondon.	Derby-Spondon	inc into 9?	None	£875	14
13th May 1932 (wef 5th Jun)	E G Buxton, Vincent's Reliance, Ockbrook.	Derby-Ockbrook, via Borrowash	inc into 9A?	None	£700	15
13th May 1932 (wef 5th June)	F H Rolstone, Vincent's Devonian, Ockbrook.	Derby-Ockbrook, via Borrowash	inc into 9A?	None	£300	15
13th May 1932 (wef 5th Jun)	H O Oxenham, Orange Coaches, Borrowash.	Derby-Ockbrook, via Borrowash	inc into 9A?	None	£525	15
19th July, 1932	J W Harwood, Costock.	Loughborough-Costock via Wymsewold.	?	None	£240	16
2nd Aug 1932	J C & W Severn, Severn Bros, Swanwick. G Shaw, George Shaw & Sons, Ironville. W E Topham, Leabrooks. R Fearn, Alfreton. All operating as members of Alfreton Bus Association.	Alfreton-Ripley, via Somercotes and Leabrooks.	2	None	£2 000	17
15th Aug 1932	S P Radford, Mayfield.	Ashbourne-Leek, via Waterhouses, Main Road, Caulden Low and Waterfall.	19	None	£1 350	
27th Oct 1932	City Coaches, Ltd Derby.	Covenant to withdraw application for Excursion & Tours from Derby, and closure of their business.	-	None	£175	
21st Mar 1933 (wef 9th Apr)	C W Rhodes, Rhodeland Motor Services, Derby. (Formerly Rhodes & Holland).	Derby-Wirksworth, via Allestree and Duffield.	20	5 plus garage	£6 000	
1st Jun 1933 (wef 3rd Apr)	J Henshaw & F Upton, Henshaw's Bus Service, or White Lion Service, Jacksdale.	Alfreton-Spondon, via Jacksdale and Ripley.	?	None	£275	18
12th Dec 1933	J W Taylor, Maroon Services, Whatstandwell.	Whatstandwell-Ripley, via Crich and Bull Bridge. Excursions from Whatstandwell	15A, later 21	None	£900	19
20th Apr 1934 (wef 1st Jul)	W Haywood, Boxall's Service, Cotmanhay.	Cotmanhay-Derby Excursions from Ilkeston	10C	None	£2 000	
8th May 1934 (wef 1st Jul)	Whitehall & Brannan, Blue Bus Services (Derby), Ltd.	Derby-Ilkeston, via Morley and Smalley Common. Derby-Heanor, via Morley and Smalley. Derby-Horsley	10B 55? 22	None	£9 000	
??? Jul 1934	Midland General Omnibus Co, Ltd.	Excursions from Alfreton which MGO had acquired from J H Booth, Westhouses.	-	None	£1 100	20

Takeover or Agreement Date	Operator Name	Routes	Allocated Route No	Vehicles Acquired	Amount Paid	Add'l Note
10th Aug 1934	J H Wood, Woods Omnibus Service, Riddings.	Alfreton-Ripley, via Leabrooks and Somercotes.	101	None	£275	
4th Dec 1934 (wef 9th Jun 1935)	Retford Coachways, Ltd.	Retford-Nottingham, via Tuxford	80	2	£6 003	21
31st Dec 1934	S O Stevenson, Eagle Services, Little Eaton.	Derby-Sunnyhill and Stenson, via Littleover.	49 & 50	None	£2,150	22
22nd Jan 1935	A Slater & Sons, Mayfield.	Ashbourne-Uttoxeter, via Rocester Excursions from Ashbourne and Mayfield.	51/2/3/4	None	£5 500	
14th Mar 1935	T Pollard, TP Services, Derby.	Derby(Ashbourne Road Tram Terminus)-Spondon (Celanese), via Brook Street Excursions & Tours from Derby	?	None	£2 500	
23rd Mar 1935	Kingfisher Services Ltd, Derby.	Derby-Quarndon Derby-Allestree(Lane End) Derby-Allestree(Scarsdale Avenue) Circular route, Derby-Darley Abbey-Allestree (Lane End)-Derby(direct) Excursions from Derby	56/7	2	£7 750	23
23rd March 1935 (wef 24th Mar.)	H S North Ltd, Derby.	Derby-Heanor, via Coxbench, Horsley Woodhouse Belper-Heanor, via Kilburn Toll Bar, H. Woodhouse	151/29? 55 98	2	£9 750	24
9th Apr 1935 (possibly wef 1st Feb.)	S O Stevenson, Eagle Services, Little Eaton.	Derby(LMS Siddalls Road)-Littleover, via Osmaston Road and Sunnyhill. (Works Service) Derby(LMS Siddalls Road)-Littleover Hollow, via Burton Road, Abbey Street, Wardwick and Siddalls Road. (Works Service)	? ?	None	£60	25
19th Jun 1935	F Butler, T Butler & Mrs R Butler, Kirkby in Ashfield.	Sutton in Ashfield(Portland Sq)-Annesley Woodhouse(Robin Hood),via Nuncargate, East Kirkby and Kirkby in Ashfield	81	None	£725	
28th Aug 1935 (wef 1st Nov)	Dutton's Unity Service Ltd, Nottingham.	Sutton in Ashfield-Nottingham, via Annesley Park and Moorbridge Sutton in Ashfield-Nottingham, via Annesley Loop and Moorbridge (Workmen's service) Sutton in Ashfield-Nottingham, via Sutton Junction and Bulwell Newstead-Summit Pit	84 85? 86? ?	15 plus garage	£82 500	26
17th Oct 1935 (wef 29th Dec.)	A J Daley & Sons, Pippin Services, Ripley.	Alfreton-Belper, via Pentrich Ripley-Alfreton, via Swanwick Ripley-Belper, via Bull Bridge Crich-Belper, via Bull Bridge Ambergate-Ripley, via Nether Heage Excursions & Tours from Ripley, Nether Heage and Ambergate	104 101 ? 157 158	8 plus garage	£20 000	
22nd Oct 1935	S O Stevenson, Eagle Services, Little Eaton.	Belper-Ripley, via Holbrook and Kilburn Heage-Spondon Derby-Spondon Derby-Sutton on the Hill Derby-Longford Derby-Lane Ends Derby-Trusley Derby-Hollington Derby-Longford.	99 ? ? 152 156 153 155 156 154	2	£4 850	28

Takeover or Agreement Date	Operator Name	Routes	Allocated Route No	Vehicles Acquired	Amount Paid	Add'l Note
26th Oct 1935 (wef 15th Dec)	R E Horspool, Loughborough.	L'borough-Nottingham, via Wymeswold and Bunny. Loughborough-Willoughby Loughborough Circular via Hoton, Wymeswold and Willoughby. Loughborough-Nanpantan Loughborough-Coalville Loughborough(Brush Works)-Skelthorpe Loughborough(Brush Works)-Forest Road Loughborough(Empress Works)-Knight Thorpe Road Excursions and Tours from Loughborough	 124 123	4	£6 850	27
30th Dec 1935	Partlow & Tarlton, Ltd.	Heanor-Kilburn Toll Bar, via Loscoe Chapel, Bulls Head and Denby Church	159	3	£2 850	
15th Jan 1936	C E Salt, Red Star Service, Duffield.	Derby-Belper, via Allestree and Duffield Duffield Church (Circular) via Avenue Road and Hazelwood Road (Sundays only service)	inc into 2 Possibly abandoned	3	£8 350	
??? Jan 1936	Midland General Omnibus Co, Ltd.	Excursions and Tours from Alfreton, previously operated by Alfreton Motor Transport, Ltd.	-	None	£140	
???May 1936	Midland General Omnibus Co, Ltd.	Undertaking not to pick up passengers at Derby on the Ilkeston-Blackpool express service, previously operated by Straw & Fletcher, Ilkeston.	-	None	£260	
2nd Jul 1936	A J Walters & Son, Derby.	Allenton-Spondon (Celanese), via Victory Road and Cavendish	?	None	£1 750	
9th Jul 1936	Heanor & District Omnibus Co, Ltd.	Heanor-Ilkeston, via Rose and Crown and Stanley Common	Abandoned?	None	£300	29
13th Dec 1937 (wef 2nd Jan 1938)	Birmingham & Midland Motor Omnibus Co, Ltd.	Leicester-Sileby Loughborough-Sileby (Thursdays only)	122 ?	None	£2 150 £100	30
23rd Mar 1938	R Vallance, Stanley Common.	Stanley Common-Mapperley Colliery	?	None	£325	
12th May 1938 (wef 1st May)	Heanor & District Omnibus Co, Ltd.	Ripley-Ilkeston, via Kilburn, Horsley Woodhouse, Smalley and Smalley Common Horsley Woodhouse-Mapperley Colliery, via Smalley and Smalley Common	165 ?	None	£2 583	31
14th May 1938 (wef July 1938)	J H Haywood, Sileby.	Loughborough-Sileby, via Walton and Seagrave. Excursions from Seagrave	127/28	None	£525	32
??? Sept, 1938	Birmingham & Midland Motor Omnibus Co, Ltd.	Excursions & Tours from Barrow on Soar.		None	?	33
28th Jan 1939	Mrs Hilda Swinn, Bulwell.	Cinderhill-Gedling Colliery (Express). Bulwell-Gedling Colliery (Express). Plus goodwill of contract carriage business.	? ?	None	£1 700	
21st Mar 1939	F Harris, Barrow on Soar.	Barrow on Soar-Leicester (Express for football only) Excursions from Barrow on Soar	?	None	£475	
11th Nov 1940	W E Wells, Wells' Service, Aston on Trent.	Derby-Weston on Trent, via Aston and Thulston	40	None	£3 000	34
19th Mar 1946	Barton Transport, Ltd.	Castle Donnington-Derby service, temporarily suspended, but previously operated by E & H Frakes	inc into 34?	None	£150	35
5th Oct 1945	T A Lewis Ltd, East Bridgford.	East Bridgford-Nottingham, via Newton or Shelford and Radcliffe on Trent. East Bridgford-Newark Excursions from East Bridgford	68 81	5	£11 000	36

Additional Notes referred to in the table on pages 156-158.

Note	Remarks
1	**Dawkins & Ballard, Alfreton.** The goodwill of Dawkins and Ballards' service was purchased for £200. Their Thornycroft vehicle was bought for £950 and sold on to Barnsley & District for the same price. Subsequently, from July, 1916, Trent leased a garage from Dawkins and Ballard, following expiry of the lease on their existing premises.
2	**Loughborough Road Car Co, Ltd.** The one vehicle taken over from this Company was sold on and not operated.
3	**G J Hawksworth, Tutbury.** No vehicle changed hands, and no record has been found of any payment to Hawksworth, who was taken on by Trent as a driver. The services were modified and incorporated into the existing Trent services.
4	**Retford Motor Services.** This takeover involved East Midland and Lincolnshire. The Doncaster service was taken over jointly with East Midland, and operated on a pool basis in proportion to the mileage operated by each Company. Other services operated were Retford-Mansfield, which was taken by East Midland, and Retford Town Services, Retford-Newark, Retford-Gainsborough, Retford-Nottingham and Retford-Laxton, which were all taken by Lincolnshire, who later cut the Nottingham service back to Ollerton.
5	**J Wade, The Bean Bus Service, Nottingham.** The sum of £145 was paid to Wade in return for agreement to stop operating in the Company's area.The services shown are those for which Wade had been licensed by Nottingham Corporation, but it seems unlikely that all were being operated at the time of Trent's take over.
6	**Hubert de Tracey Wilkinson, Britannia Omnibus Service, Nottingham.** This service was operated from J Wade's garage, de Tracey Wilkinson having taken the service over in a business split around 1928/9, probably when Wade sold to Trent..
7	**Barton Transport Ltd.** This service had just been acquired by Barton from J Turner's Eagle Motor Services at approximately the same time that Turner had sold his Derby-Mickleover service to Trent. However, it was clearly on Trent territory, and Barton were immediately prevailed upon to sell it on to Trent.
8	**J Turner, Eagle Motor Services, Derby.** Turner was the original user of the name "Eagle Motor Services. However, part of the business was taken over by S O Stevenson, who sold out the remaining parts of the business, and others which he operated under the Eagle name, to Trent in stages.
9	**L H Dutton, Dutton's Motor Service, Radcliffe on Trent.** This was a separate business from Dutton's Unity Service, Ltd of Nottingham, although there was a family relationship.
10	**E Bramley, Prince of Wales Service, Cotmanhay.** This operator was taken over jointly with Midland General and its two operating subsidiaries, Dawson's Enterprise Omnibus Co, Ltd, and Williamson's Garage, Ltd, which it had recently acquired. There were nine vehicles involved, but only three passed into Trent ownership. The remaining six passed to the Midland General companies, although only one was used. Half of the purchase price was paid by Trent, and half by Williamson's, but the service was operated on the basis of two Williamson's or Dawson's Enterprise buses to one Trent, with total receipts pooled and divided two thirds to Williamson's, and one third to Trent. Williamson's and Dawson's Enterprise were absorbed by Midland General in 1931.
11	**Reynolds Brothers, Bulwell.** This operator was taken over jointly with Nottingham Corporation. There were ten vehicles involved, five Leylands, which passed to Trent, and five Gilfords which passed to the Corporation and were sold on.
12	**Arthur Farnsworth, Blue Bird Service, Huthwaite.** Arthur Farnsworth's principal business was that of vehicle bodybuilder. However, when his customers found themselves in financial difficulties, he took them over. Such was the case with Blue Bird at the time of the sale to Trent, and Farnsworth had taken this business over from Johnson, of Sutton in Ashfield, running the service on a short term licence from 4th November, 1931, for just 20 days! There was also a financial interest in the Pinxton Bus Company, which was later taken over by Midland General. The five vehicles which Trent acquired with the business of Blue Bird were sold on without being used.
13	**P & J W Poundall, Belper.** This operator continued to run a Belper-Shottle service, which was later sold to H S North Transport. North later sold the service to Trent in 1955. Poundall also continued to run a Belper-Heanor, via Kilburn and Smalley service.
14	**J Clews, Spondon Ex-Servicemen's, Spondon, and W Liewsley, Liewsley's Bus Service, Spondon.** These two operators ran a combined service, and were both taken over by Trent at the same time.
15	**E G Buxton, Vincent's Reliance, Ockbrook, F H Rolstone, Vincent's Devonian, Ockbrook, and H O Oxenham, Orange Coaches, Borrowash.** These three operators ran a combined service and were all taken over by Trent at the same time.
16	**J W Harwood, Costock.** This operator was taken over jointly with R E Horspool of Loughborough. The two operators paid half each.

Note	Remarks
17	**J C & W Severn, Severn Bros, Swanwick. G Shaw, G Shaw & Sons, Ironville. W E Topham, Leabrooks. R Fearn, Alfreton.** The Alfreton Bus Association continued to operate an Alfreton-Heanor service, in which J C & W Severn, and R Fearn had an interest. Also, a Ripley-Pinxton service, in which G Shaw and W E Topham had an interest. Both of the other services passed later to Midland General.
18	**J Henshaw & F Upton, Henshaw's Bus Service, or White Lion Service, Jacksdale.** This service had originally been owned solely by Henshaw, but Upton, an Insurance Broker, of Ripley, had bought the goodwill, whilst Henshaw retained the licence and continued to operate the service on Upton's behalf.
19	**J W Taylor, Maroon Services, Whatstandwell.** This takeover was effected in conjunction with Alfreton Motor Transport Co, Ltd (AMT). AMT had agreed with J W Taylor to take over his services, and applied for the necessary licences. Trent also applied for the licences, as a result of which AMT agreed not to proceed, and Trent agreed with Taylor to take over his business instead. The two larger operators agreed to use their best endeavours to obtain the licences for Taylor's services which had been assigned to them by agreement, and each not to accept licences unless the other party obtained theirs. In addition to the services shown in the table, which passed to Trent, there was also a Whatstandwell-Ripley, via Pentrich service, which was abandoned, a Lea Mills-Crich service and Whatstandwell-Crich via Lea Mills service, both of which passed to AMT. Trent also made a payment of £117-10s (£117-50) to AMT.
20	**Midland General Omnibus Co, Ltd.** Midland General acquired the business of J H Booth of Westhouses on 4th July, 1934. The Excursions from Alfreton were based in Trent territory and therefore were sold on to them.
21	**Retford Coachways, Ltd.** This company had been bought by East Midland for £18 500, and consisted of 8 buses, two leasehold properties at Retford and stage carriage services Retford-Dunham, Retford-Nottingham, via Tuxford and Ollerton, and Retford-Nottingham, via Ordsall and Ollerton. The business was divided between East Midland, Lincolnshire and Trent, with the buses split three ways and paid for at valuation, the Retford-Dunham service taken over by Lincolnshire, and the two Nottingham services taken over by Trent and East Midland. The service via Ordsall was abandoned, and that via Tuxford run jointly by the two companies. The cost of the goodwill was paid by each company in proportion to the mileage of the services taken over and added to the cost of the vehicles. The total sums paid were: Lincolnshire £2424 7s 10d (£2424-39p), East Midland £10071 13s 9d £10071-69p) and Trent £6003 18s 5d (£ 6003-92).
22	**S O Stevenson, Eagle Services, Little Eaton.** The service to Sunnyhill had been taken over from J Turner, and that to Stenson had been taken over from Blue Bus Services (Derby) Ltd.
23	**Kingfisher Services, Ltd, Derby.** This operator was owned by E J Knight, of Derby, who also owned most of the shares in H S North, Ltd, by the time of the takeover.
24	**H S North, Ltd, Derby.** By the time the business was taken over by Trent, the share capital, was owned by Kingfisher Services, Ltd, Derby, (see above) or their nominees. The sale of H S North, Ltd, and Kingfisher Services, Ltd to Trent took place concurrently. It is said that this business was at one time managed by S O Stevenson (see above and below), on behalf of his employer, Sir George Kenning, the motor dealer, who ran in the business at a time when it was in financial difficulty, owing a debt to Kennings until the sale to Trent. Also, that Stevenson brought the business back into order and subsequently returned the garage to North and his business partner J E Bird, at the same time paying North £1 000. North subsequently re-started in business. As part of the sale of the business to Kingfisher, a covenant by H S North was included, and this was to be guaranteed by Sir George Kenning.
25	**S O Stevenson, Eagle Services, Little Eaton.** The new Traffic Commissioners granted a licence for these two services as a single service on 31st July, 1931. It had been taken over by S O Stevenson from J Turner, the original operator of Eagle.
26	**Dutton's Unity Service, Ltd, Nottingham.** This was a separate business from Dutton's Motor Service, Radcliffe on Trent, although there was a family relationship.
27	**R E Horspool, Loughborough.** The Loughborough-Nanpantan and Loughborough (Brush Works) services had been operated jointly with Allen's Motor Service, Mountsorrell who continued to operate them jointly with Trent, after the takeover.
28	**S O Stevenson, Eagle Services, Little Eaton.** This was a further collection of services which Stevenson had acquired from a variety of operators, as follows:- Belper-Ripley from H E Bell, Bargate. Heage-Spondon from A Eaton, Heage. Derby-Spondon from T C Cox, Derby. Derby-Sutton from J Turner. Derby-Longford, and Derby-Trusley from an unconfirmed operator, possibly J Turner, again, although Sutton is also a possibility. Derby-Hollington and Derby-Longford were services which Stevenson was acquiring from Mrs M Yeomans of Rodsley, the Longford service having been operated by her to Rodsley, via Longford, but curtailed as a result of an agreement between Stevenson and Mrs Frost of Yeavely, to run only to Longford. Derby-Lane Ends was a new service which had been licensed from 6th November, 1934.
29	**Heanor & District Omnibus Co, Ltd.** The reminder of this business was taken over in 1938, see below.

Note	Remarks
30	**Birmingham & Midland Motor Omnibus Co, Ltd.** The Loughorough-Sileby service had been acquired by BMMO from J Squires of Barrow on Soar, but transferred to Trent as it was clearly in their operating area. The goodwill of the existing Thursdays only service was added in to the agreement for similar reasons.
31	**Heanor & District Omnibus Co, Ltd.** This agreement provided for sharing the business of the Heanor & District Omnibus Co, Ltd between Trent, Barton and Midland General, as a result of Midland General having acquired the business. It was agreed that the H&D vehicles should be sold for the best price possible and the proceeds divided between the three parties in the same proportion as already agreed for the purchase of the business, i.e. 55.74% to Midland General, 24.6% to Trent and 19,66% to Barton. It was agreed that Trent would deal with the sale of the vehicles, but that the other two would be advised before the sale was confirmed. In the event, Midland General decided that they needed to use four of the vehicles, pending the delivery of new ones, and so the sale of the whole 18 H&D vehicles could not be completed until June, 1938. The services taken over by Midland General were:- Ripley-Spondon, via Codnor, Loscoe, Heanor and Smalley, Brinsley-Spondon, via Hill Top, Eastwood, Langley Mill, Heanor and Smalley. The services taken over by Barton were:- Smalley-Spondon, via Stanley Common and Stanley, and Stanley Common-Spondon, via Mapperley and West Hallam.
32	**J H Haywood, Sileby.** This operator was related to W Haywood of Ilkeston, who owned Boxall's Service when that business was sold to Trent, and W Haywood had had an interest in that business, also.
33	**Birmingham & Midland Motor Omnibus Co, Ltd.** This item is listed because it appeared as a licence transfer in the Traffic Commissioners' "Notices & Proceedings" dated 16th September, 1938. However, no confirmation of the takeover has been found in Trent official records.
34	**W E Wells, Wells' Service, Aston on Trent.** In addition to the purchase price of £3 000, there was a premium of 25% of the amount by which the first twelve months takings exceeded £3 000.
35	**Barton Transport, Ltd.** The agreement held by Trent for this takeover is dated 1946, but Barton records state 1945. It is not known which is correct.
36	**T A Lewis Ltd, East Bridgford.** Five vehicles were acquired in this takeover. However, they were sold on to Robin Hood Transport, and not operated by Trent.

The information given above has been assembled almost entirely from Company and other official records. The dates given are usually those of the takeover agreement, but the dates of taking effect have also been given, where these are known. The allocated route numbers are taken from the official timetable, but route numbers were not used before early 1922. In some cases, the competitor duplicated the route already followed by Trent, in which case the legend given "inc into xx" means that the service taken over was incorporated into the existing Trent service numbered as shown. Works services were not included in the Company's published timetables, so in most cases it has not been possible to determine the number allocated. Works services may not have been allocated service numbers originally, although by the fifties they were numbered into a 2XX series.

Early Service History, to publication of first timetable book in November, 1917.

a) Commercial Car Hirers, Limited. 1909 to October, 1913.

Date of Event	Route and Event Details	Date of Event	Route and Event Details
14th September, 1909	**N** Ashbourne-Derby, via Kirk Langley and Brailsford.	23rd March, 1912	**N** Derby Melbourne. Saturday evenings only.
27th October, 1909	**N** Alfreton-Derby, via Ripley.	6th February, 1913	**W** Alfreton-Mansfield.
28th October, 1909	**N** Ripley-Nottingham, via Aldercar. Thursday only.	??? May, 1913	**I** Derby Melbourne. Increased to all day Saturday.
16th December, 1909	**W** Ripley-Nottingham, via Aldercar.	??? September, 1913	**N** Derby-Uttoxeter.
20th December, 1909	**N** Ripley-Nottingham, via Heanor, and Eastwood.	3rd November, 1913	Ashbourne-Derby, Alfreton-Derby, Alfreton-Chesterfield, Derby-Melbourne and Derby-Uttoxeter services handed over to Trent.
January/February, 1910	**W** Ripley-Nottingham.		
6th February, 1910	**N** Alfreton-Chesterfield, via Clay Cross.		
6th March, 1912	**N** Alfreton-Mansfield.		

b) Trent Motor Traction Co, Ltd. From November, 1913.

Date of Event	Route and Event Details	Date of Event	Route and Event Details
8th November, 1913	**N** Derby-Stapleford, via Spondon and Borowash.	September, 1914	Services reduced to Alfreton-Derby, Belper-Derby, Ashbourne-Derby and Burton-Derby.
6th March, 1914	**R** Above service reduced to Derby-Spondon		
1st May, 1914	**N** Derby-Ambergate, via Duffield. To Matlock on Sundays.	October, 1914	**W** Derby-Belper.
By June, 1914	**N** Mansfield-Bulwell, via Sutton in Ashfield and Annesley.	October, 1914	**W** Derby-Burton on Trent.
??? June, 1914	**N** Chesterfield-Brimington.	??? May, 1915	Derby-Alfreton. Reinstated.
" " "	**N** Chesterfield-Staveley.	??? September, 1915	Derby-Burton on Trent. Reinstated.
" " "	**N** Chesterfield-Clowne.	??? September, 1915	Derby-Spondon. Reinstated.
By August, 1914	**N** Derby-Burton on Trent.	??? September, 1915	Derby-Belper. Reinstated.
??? August, 1914	**N** Derby-Belper.	??? September, 1915	Derby-Melbourne. Reinstated.
??? August, 1914	**N** Belper-Bakewell.	??? September, 1915	**N** Derby-Wirksworth.
??? August, 1914	**N** Mansfield-Nottingham, via Sutton in Ashfield and Hucknall. Replacement for Mansfield-Bulwell service.	After April, 1916	**N** Nottingham-Ilkeston, via Stapleford.
		After April, 1916	**N** Alfreton-Ilkeston, via Heanor.

Key:-

N - New Service
W - Service Withdrawn
R - Service Reduced
I - Service Increased

List of Major Route Number Changes. From published timetables, dated as shown at top of columns.

Jan 1922	Jun 1923	Jan 1924	Dec 1934	Terminal and Intermediate Points
1	1	1	1	Derby-Alfreton, via Ripley
4	2	2	2	Derby-Belper, via Allestree and Duffield.
	11	2A	Rev	Derby-Matlock, via Duffield, Belper, Ambergate and Cromford.
		2B	4	Derby-Buxton, via Belper, Ambergate, Cromford and Matlock.
5	5	5	5	Derby-Burton, via Repton.
		5A	6	Derby-Burton, Direct
9	7	7	7	Derby-Heanor, via Morely and Smalley.
7	20	21	W/d	Derby-Mansfield, via Alfreton.
7A	21	20	W/d	Derby-Clay Cross, via Alfreton.
		6A	Rev	Derby-Etwall, via Mickleover.
8	6	6B	W/d	Derby-Hatton, via Mickleover.
12	8	8	8	Derby-Nottingham, via Sandiacre.
		9	9	Derby-Spondon Village, via Spondon Lane.
		9	10	Derby-Spondon Village, via Church Street and Chapel Street.
		9	11	Derby-Spondon Village, via Willowcroft Road.
		9	12	Derby-Spondon Village, via Langley Lane.
		9A	13	Derby-Ockbrook
6	9	9B	14	Derby-Borrowash
	6	6	15	Derby-Mickleover, via Western Road.
		6A	16	Derby-Mickleover LNER Station.
		6	17	Derby-Mickleover Mental Hospital.
		6B	18	Derby-Tutbury, via Hatton.
11	3	3	19	Derby-Melbourne.
		3A	20	Derby-Chellaston and Swarkestone.
		3A	21	Derby-Ashby.
		3B	22	Derby-Swadlincote.
		3C	23	Derby-Barrow and Twyford. Circular.
10	10	10	24	Derby-Ilkeston, via Chaddesden, Stanley and West Hallam.
		10B	25	Derby-Ilkeston, via Breadsall Windmill, Morley and Smalley.
		10C	26	Derby-Cotmanhay, via Breadsall Windmill, Morley and Smalley.
		10A	27	Derby-Ilkeston, via Breadsall Village, Morley and Smalley.
		22	29	Derby-Horsley.
2	4	4	31	Derby-Ashbourne, via Brailsford.
3	14	11	32	Derby-Ashbourne, via Cross o' th' Hands.
	26/15	14	W/d	Derby-Uttoxeter, via Hatton.
		14A	W/d	Hatton-Uttoxeter.
		4B	33	Derby (LMS Station)-Uttoxeter, via Ashbourne.
41		41		Loughborough-Coalville, via Shepshed.
		42	120	Loughborough-Markfield Sanatorium
18	40	40	121	Loughborough-Leicester, via Sileby.

Jan 1922	Jun 1923	Jan 1924	Dec 1934	Terminal and Intermediate Points
18A	40A	40A	122	Loughborough-Leicester, via Mountsorrell.
	12	12	34	Derby-Castle Donington, via Alvaston and Shardlow.
		12A	36	Derby-Loughborough.
		20	37	Derby-Wirksworth.
		20A	38	Derby-Blackbrook.
		9D	39	Derby-Dale Abbey.
			40	Derby-Ingleby
		6B	41	Derby-Church Broughton.
		19	42	Ashbourne-Leek, via Main Road.
		19	43	Ashbourne-Leek, via Cauldon Lowe.
		19	44	Ashbourne-Leek, via Waterfall.
		19	45	Ashbourne-Leek, via Stanton?
	25	13	47	Hatton-Burton.
		13A	48	Rolleston-Burton.
15	32	32	W/d	Nottingham-Heanor, via Stapleford and Ilkeston.
	33	32A	67	Nottingham-Heanor, via Wollaton and Ilkeston.
		30	60	Nottingham-Hucknall, via Bulwell.
14	30	30	61	Nottingham-Mansfield, via Hucknall.
		37	62	Nottingham-Mansfield, Direct via Harlow Wood.
		12A	63	Nottingham-Chesterfield.
		36	64	Nottingham-Doncaster.
		31	65	Nottingham-Wilford Hill Cemetery
17	31	31	66	Nottingham-Loughborough, via Bunny and Ruddington.
		32	67	Nottingham-Ilkeston, via Wollaton and Trowell.
		32	68	Nottingham-Cotmanhay, via Wollaton and Trowell.
		34	69	Nottingham-Netherfield, via Colwick.
	35	34	70	Nottingham-Gedling, via Netherfield.
		34A	71	Nottingham-Burton Joyce.
		34B	72	Nottingham-Lowdham.
		34C	72	Nottingham-Gunthorpe.
		33A 33C	73	Nottingham-E Bridgford, Radcliffe Circular.
		34D	74	Nottingham-Southwell.
		34E	76	Nottingham-Burton Joyce.
16	34	33	77	Nottingham-Radcliffe.
		33 33A	78	Nottingham-Bingham, via Radcliffe.
		33C	79	Nottingham-Grantham
		35	35	Nottingham-Skegness. (Previously Un-numbered.)
		11	90	Derby-Belper, via Holbrook.
		U/N	X1	Derby-Manchester.
		U/N	X2	Nottingham-Manchester.

Lists of Timetabled Services at Significant Dates.

Services listed in the first timetable book, published in November, 1917.

Derby-Melbourne	Derby - Burton
Derby - Alfreton	Ilkeston - Nottingham (not Thursday or Friday)
Derby - Ashbourne	Alfreton - Ilkeston via Heanor (not Thursday or Friday)
Derby - Duffield and Belper	Nottingham - Mansfield (not Tuesday or Friday)
Derby - Spondon and Borrowash	Ripley - Alfreton (Saturday only)

Services listed in timetable book for Jan-Feb 1930, a year or so before the 1930 Road Traffic Act took effect.

Route No	Service Details
1	Derby-Alfreton, via Little Eaton, Denby and Leabrooks
2	Derby-Belper, via Allestree, Duffield and Milford
2A	Derby-Matlock, as 2, then via Whatstandwell and Cromford
3	Derby-Melbourne, via Allenton, Chellaston and Swarkstone
3A	Derby-Ashby, as 3, then via Wilson, Breedon and Lount
3B	Derby-Swadlincote, as 3, then Ticknall and Woodville
4	Derby-Ashbourne, via Kirk Langley and Brailsford
5	Derby-Burton, via Littleover, Findern and Repton
5A	Derby-Burton, DIRECT, via Clay Mills
6	Derby-Mickleover, via Western Road
6A/B	Derby-Tutbury, via Chain Lane, Mickleover, Etwall, Hilton and Hatton
7	Derby-Heanor, via Breadsall (Windmill), Broomfield, and Smalley
8	Derby- Nottingham, via Borrowash, Risley, Sandiacre and Stapleford
9	Derby-Borrowash, via Spondon Village and Ockbrook
10	Derby-Ilkeston, via Chaddesden, Stanley and West Hallam
10A	Derby-Breadsall Village, via Breadsall (Windmill)
11	Derby-Belper, via Little Eaton, Holbrook, and Openwood Gate
12	Derby-Castle Donington, via Alvaston and Shardlow
12A	Derby-Loughborough', as 12, then via Lockington, Kegworth and Hathern
13	Hatton-Burton, via Tutbury, Rolleston, Clay Mills and Stretton
14/14A	Derby-Uttoxeter, via Mickleover, Burnaston, and Sudbury, Wed/Fri only
15	Belper-Ripley, via Ambergate, Bull Bridge and Lower Hartshay
16	Belper-Ripley, via Far Lawn and Heage
17	Belper-Ripley, via Openwoodgate and Heage
21	Alfreton-Mansfield, via South Normanton, Fulwood and Sutton in Ashfield
30	Nottingham-Mansfield, via Bulwell, Hucknall, Newstead, Annesley, Kirkby in Ashfield and Sutton in Ashfield

Route No	Service Details
31	Nottingham-Loughborough', via Ruddington, Rempstone and Cotes
32	Nottingham-Cotmanhay, via Wollaton, Trowell and Ilkeston. Joint with Williamson's and Dawson's Enterprise
33	Nottingham-Radcliffe on Trent, via Gamston and Bassingfield
33A/33B	Nottingham-Gunthorpe (Circular), via Lowdham, Gunthorpe, East Bridgford and Bingham, or reverse
33C	Nottingham-Grantham, via Radcliffe, Bingham and Bottesford and Barrowby. Joint with Lincolnshire
34	Nottingham-Gedling, via Colwick and Netherfield
34A	Nottingham-Burton Joyce, via Colwick and Netherfield
34B	Nottingham-Gunthorpe (Circular), via Radcliffe on Trent
34C	Nottingham-Gunthorpe (Circular), via Burton Joyce and Lowdham
34D	Nottingham-Southwell, via Lowdham, Hoveringham and Bleasby
34E	Nottingham-Burton Joyce DIRECT, via Carlton Hill
36	Nottingham-Doncaster, via Redhill, Bilsthorpe, Ollerton, Edwinstowe, Worksop, Langold, Tickworth and Wadworth. Joint with East Midland 80
37	Nottingham-Mansfield, via Redhill, Newstead and Harlow Wood
38	Nottingham-Granby, via Gamston, Tollerton, Cotgrave, Cropwell Bishop and Langar
40A	Loughborough-Leicester, via Quorn, Mountsorrell, Rothley and Birstall. Joint with Midland Red
40	Loughborough-Leicester, via Quorn, Barrow, Sileby, Cossington and Syston. Joint with Midland Red
-	Derby-Manchester, via Ashbourne, Leek, Macclesfield and Stockport
-	Nottingham-Manchester, via Ilkeston, Matlock, Buxton and Stockport

Services listed in timetable book for 3rd Dec, 1939 - 6th Jan 1940, following consolidation after the 1930 Road Traffic Act took effect, and just after the start of the war.			
Route No	**Service Details**	**Route No**	**Service Details**
1	Derby-Alfreton, via Little Eaton, Denby Swanwick and Leabrooks.	47	Hatton-Burton, via Tutbury and Rolleston.
2	Derby-Belper, via Allestree, Duffield and Milford.	48	Burton-Rolleston, via Horninglow and Anslow Cross Roads.
4	Derby-Buxton. **SUSPENDED.**	49	Derby-Cavendish, via Littleover, Blagreaves Lane End and Sunnyhill.
5	Derby-Burton, via Littleover, Findern and Repton.	50	Derby-Stenson. **SUSPENDED.**
6	Derby-Burton, DIRECT, via Clay Mills.	51	Derby-Uttoxeter (DIRECT), via Denstone.
7	Derby-Heanor, via Breadsall (Windmill), Broomfield, and Smalley.	52	Ashbourne-Mayfield.
8	Derby- Nottingham, via Borrowash, Risley, Sandiacre and Stapleford.	53	Rocester-Uttoxeter. **SUSPENDED.**
9	Derby-Spondon Village via Spondon Lane.	54	Wootton, Rocester-Uttoxeter. **SUSPENDED.**
10	Derby-Spondon Village via Church Street and Chapel Street.	55	Derby-Heanor, via Kilburn Toll Bar.
11	Derby-Spondon Village via Willowcroft Road.	56	Derby-Allestree (Circular), via Kedleston Road.
12	Derby-Spondon Village via Langley Lane.	57	Derby-Allestree (Circular), via Duffield Rd, Darley Abbey and Kedleston Rd.
13	Derby-Ockbrook, via Main Road and Borrowash.	58	Derby-Quarndon (Church).
14	Derby-Borrowash, via Spondon Village.	59	Derby-Park Nook. **SUSPENDED.**
15	Derby-Mickleover, via Western Road.	60	Nottingham-Hucknall, via Basford and Bulwell.
16	Derby-Mickleover, LNER Station.	61	Nottingham-Mansfiled, via Hucknall and Newstead Abbey.
17	Derby-Mickleover, Mental Hospital.	62	Nottingham-Mansfield, via Redhill, Newstead and Harlow Wood.
18	Derby-Tutbury, via Chain Lane, Mickleover, Etwall, Hilton and Hatton.	63	Nottingham-Chesterfield. **SUSPENDED.**
19	Derby-Melbourne, via Allenton, Chellaston and Swarkstone.	65	Nottingham-Wilford Hill Cemetery.
20	Derby-Swarkestone, via Allenton and Chellaston.	66	Nottingham-Loughborough.
21	Derby-Ashby, as 20, then via Wilson, Breedon and Lount.	67	Nottingham-Ilkeston, via Wollaton and Trowell.
22	Derby-Swadlincote, as 20, then Ticknall and Woodville.	68	Nottingham-Cotmanhay, via Wollaton and Trowell.
23	Derby-Barrow and Twyford. **SUSPENDED.**	70	Nottingham-Gedling, via Colwick and Netherfield
24	Derby-Ilkeston, via Chaddesden, Stanley and West Hallam.	71	Nottingham-Burton Joyce, via Netherfield and Gedling.
25	Derby-Ilkeston, via Breadsall (Windmill) Broomfield, Morley and W. Hallam.	72	Nottingham-Gunthorpe, via Burton Joyce.
26	Derby-Breadsall Windmill. **SUSPENDED.**	73	Nottingham-Gunthorpe-Nottingham. **SUSPENDED.**
27	Derby-Ilkeston, via Breadsall Village, Broomfield, Morley and W. Hallam.	74	Nottingham-Southwell, via Netherfield, Gedling, Lowdham and Thurgaton.
28	Derby-Horsley Woodhouse, via Smalley Mill. **SUSPENDED.**	75	Nottingham-Fiskerton. **SUSPENDED.**
29	Derby-Ilkeston, via Breadsall Village, Morley Moor and W. Hallam.	76	Nottingham-Burton Joyce, via Carlton. **SUSPENDED.**
31	Derby-Ashbourne, via Cross o' th' Hands.	77	Nottingham-Radcliffe on Trent.
32	Derby-Ashbourne, via Kirk Langley and Brailsford.	78	Nottingham-Bingham.
33	Derby-Uttoxeter (DIRECT), via Brailsford, Ashbourne, and Rocester.	79	Nottingham-Grantham, via Bottesford. Joint with Lincolnshire 33C.
34	Derby-Castle Donington, via Alvaston and Shardlow.	80	Nottingham-Retford, via Ollerton. Joint with East Midland 37.
35	Derby-Donington Park. **SUSPENDED.**	81	Annesley-Sutton in Ashfield. **SUSPENDED.**
36	Derby-Loughborough. **SUSPENDED.**	82	Nottingham-Burton Joyce, via Carlton and Stoke Bardolph. **SUSPENDED.**
36	Nottingham-Doncaster, via Redhill, Bilsthorpe, Ollerton, Edwinstowe, Worksop, Langold, Tickworth and Wadworth. Joint with East Midland 80.	83	Nottingham-Burton Joyce, via Netherfield Gedling and Stoke Bardolph.
		84	Nottingham-Sutton in Ashfield (DIRECT).
37	Derby-Wirksworth, via Allestree, Duffield and Idridgehay.	85	Nottingham-Sutton in Ashfield, via Annesley Woodhouse.
38	Derby-Blackbrook, via Duffield, Hazelwood and Farnah Green. (Friday only).	86	Nottingham-Sutton in Ashfield, via Summit Pit.
39	Derby-Shottle via Turnditch and Windley. (Friday only).	87	Nottingham-Chesterfield. **SUSPENDED.**
40	Derby-Ingleby. **SUSPENDED.**	88	Nottingham-Stoke Bardolph, via Netherfield and Gedling.
42	Ashbourne-Leek, via Main Road.	89	Nottingham-Balloon Houses. **SUSPENDED.**
43	Ashbourne-Leek, via Cauldon Lowe.	90	Derby-Belper, via Little Eaton and Holbrook.
44	Ashbourne-Leek, via Waterfall. **SUSPENDED.**	91	Belper-Ripley, via Kilburn Toll Bar.
45	Ashbourne-Leek, via Stanton and Cauldon Low.	92	Belper-Ripley, via Kilburn Toll Bar and Street Lane. **SUSPENDED.**

Services listed in timetable book for 3rd Dec, 1939 - 6th Jan 1940, continued from previous page.

Route No	Service Details
93	Belper-Ripley, via Openwood Gate.
94	Belper-Ripley, via Far Lawn.
95	Belper-Ripley, via Ambergate.
96	Crich-Ripley, via Bull bridge.
97	Whatstandwell-Ripley. **SUSPENDED.**
98	Belper-Ripley, via Horsley Woodhouse and Smalley.
99	Belper-Ripley, via Holbrook Moor. **SUSPENDED.**
100	Alfreton-Mansfield, via Fulwood and Sutton in Ashfield.
101	Alfreton-Ripley, via Swanwick and Butterley.
104	Alfreton-Belper, via Somercotes, Leabrooks, Pentrich and Ambergate.
120	Loughborough-Markfield Sanatorium, via Nanpantan and Copt Oak.
121	Loughborough-Leicester, via Mountsorrell. Joint with Midland Red.
122	Loughborough-Leicester, via Sileby. Joint with Midland Red.
123	Loughborough-Nanpantan. Joint with Allen's.
124	Loughborough-Willoughby. **SUSPENDED.**
125	Loughborough-Wysall. **SUSPENDED.**
126	Loughborough-Markfield Sanatorium, via Qourn, Mountsorrell and Rothley.
127	Loughborough-Seagrave via Quorn and Barrow.
128	Loughborough-Walton on the Wolds. **SUSPENDED.**

Route No	Service Details
129	Loughborough-Barrow on Soar, via Catsick Lane. **SUSPENDED.**
150	Derby-Ashbourne, via Quarndon and Kedleston.
151	Derby-Heanor, via Horsley. **SUSPENDED.**
152	Derby-Sutton on the Hill. **SUSPENDED.**
153	Derby-Longford District, via Osliston. **SUSPENDED.**
154	Derby-Longford District, via Dalbury Lees and Thurvaston.
155	Derby-Trussley, via Church Broughton.
156	Derby-Hollington (Circular).
157	Crich-Belper. **SUSPENDED.**
159	Belper-Ripley, via Kilburn Toll Bar.
160	Belper-Ripley, via Denby and Loscoe.
161	Belper-Heage, via Ambergate and North Heage.
163	Belper-Belper (Isolation Hospital). **SUSPENDED.**
164	Ripley-Belper (Isolation Hospital).
165	Ripley-Ilkeston, via Denby, Kilburn, Horsley Woodhouse and Smalley.
181	Nottingham-Ruddington. **SUSPENDED.**
X1	Derby-Manchester. **SUSPENDED.**
X2	Nottingham-Manchester. **SUSPENDED.**

Note: - Those services shown "**SUSPENDED**" were listed in the timetable as "suspended until further notice". This was the result of the mileage savings implemented at the outbreak of war, in which those services with low useage, or paralleled by other nearby services were withdrawn.

BIBLIOGRAPHY

The following documents were used as original sources for my research:-

Records of the Trent Motor Traction Co, Ltd:-

- Board Minute books.
- Rolling Stock Register.
- Ledgers.
- Trent Bulletin
- Timetable Collection.
- Fleet records.
- Photographs.

Local Authority Minute Books at:-

- Birmingham
- Chesterfield
- Derby
- Doncaster
- Ilkeston
- Leicester
- Loughborough
- Luton
- Mansfield
- Nottingham
- Sheffield
- St Albans

Government Records at:

The Public Records Office, Kew, London.
Companies House, London Branch.
The British Library, Newspaper Library, Colindale, London.

Museums and Photographic Collections:

- Dennis, Guildford
- Reeve Burgess
- National Motor Museum, Beaulieu
- Science Museum, London

Principal Newspapers and Journals

- Alfreton and Belper Journal
- Derby Evening Telegraph
- Ilkeston Advertiser
- Nottingham Evening Post
- Commercial Motor
- Derbyshire Advertiser
- Heanor Observer
- Loughborough Echo
- Buses/Buses Illustrated
- Motor Traction/Transport

In addition, Midland Red Part 1, by Gray, Keely and Seale, published in 1978 by TPC, Glossop, provided an excellent exposition of the development of SOS vehicles.

ACKNOWLEDGMENTS

This book would not have been possible without all the help and encouragement that I received with my research. I will try to record all my helpers, but if anyone feels forgotten, then I apologise and assure them that their help was no less appreciated.

Firstly, I must record my thanks to the Chief Officials Team at Trent at the time that the project started, for generously agreeing to allow me free access to Company records. These were Dion Wilson, General Manager, Ray Day, Company Secretary, Bill Gunning, Traffic Manager, and Trevor Yeo, Chief Engineer. Subsequently, Dion Wilson left for a post at NBC Headquarters, and Brian King, who took his place, kindly allowed my work to continue, and I am also grateful to him for writing the Foreword to this volume in his present capacity of Managing Director. Trevor Yeo also gave special help, as did his Secretary, Kath Gent.

Other Trent staff who gave assistance were Ian Frances, Malcolm Hitchin MBE, John Skidmore, and all the staff of the mid eighties Secretarial Department, who gave friendly tolerance of my company and help with locating records and information on a long series of research visits.

Former Trent staff were W F Bull, the late Des Gilbert, John Megson, John Palmer, Ellen Paradise, Eric Tuxford, E A Yeomans, J C Clymo and former Midland General staff were the late W L Screen, MBE and the late K H Wellman.

Fellow enthusiasts were always helpful, and these included Geoff Atkins, John Bennett, John Clarke, the late Stan Denton, Neville Evans, Philip Groves, Roy Marshall, David Stanier, Les Tuxford, Reg Westgate, R T Wilson and, of course, my publisher, Alan Oxley. The Omnibus Society and PSV Circle have provided me with a great deal of information over the years, and I commend membership of these two bodies for those with a deeper interest in the subject.

Geoff Atkins, Roy Marshall and Alan Mills kindly read the manuscript, and made a number of helpful suggestions, as did Alan Oxley. However, the responsibility for all interpretation, and any errors, rests entirely on my shoulders. My good friend, Dave McDonald, gave much help and support with the project over the years, and also produced the superb cover illustration.

Finally, it would not be right to close without recording my thanks to the unsung staffs of the various libraries, museums and records offices which I visited throughout the country during the course of my research, all of whom patiently brought out records and information for me to consult.

PHOTOCREDITS

G H F Atkins 40, 45, 51, 61, 83 (upper), 88(upper), 89 (upper), 90 (lower), 92 (lower), 93 (upper, and lower left), 94 (lower), 96 (upper left), 97 (lower), 100 (upper), 107, 111 (lower), 113, 114 (lower), 115 (upper right), 123 (lower).
D J Bean Collection 12, 14, 16, 24, 27, 29, 32, 34, 36, 43, 44, 47, 49, 50, 53, 65, 67, 76, 79 (upper), 80, 84, 85, 86, 87, 92 (upper), 96 (lower left), 99, 127 (upper), 128 (upper), 130, 132 (lower), 133 (lower), 134, 135 (centre and lower), 138 (upper), 139 (upper).
M D Bean This page.
Derby Local Studies Library 135 (upper).
J P Bennett Collection 75 (upper right).
A Bower Collection 6, 78.
J Clarke Collection 54, 129 (upper) 136, 137, 138 (lower).
J D Deakin 19.
Duple 119.
W J Haynes 48, 57, 60, 120 (upper).
R Marshall 55, 70, 71, 98 (lower), 101 (upper), 114 (upper), 115 (lower), 116, 117 (upper), 120 (lower), 121, 122, 123 (upper), 124 (lower), 125 (lower).
R Marshall Collection 30, 88 (lower).
Motor Transport 74, 77 (right).
A F Oxley Collection 37, 129 (lower).
RHG Simpson 124 (upper).
Omnibus Society 63, 64, 69, 73, 97 (upper).
D J Stanier Collection 77 (left).
Reeve Burgess (Plaxton) 139 (lower).
Trent 8, 10, 20, 26, 58, 62, 66, 68, 75 (left and lower right), 78, 79 (lower), 81, 82, 83(lower), 89 (lower), 90 (upper), 93 (lower right), 96 (upper right), 100 (lower), 101 (lower), 102, 103, 104, 105, 106, 108 (upper right), 109, 110, 111 (upper), 112, 115 (upper left), 118, 125 (upper), 127 (lower), 128 (lower), 132 (upper), 133 (upper).
R T Wilson 23, 56, 59, 98 (upper), 107, (upper), 108 (upper left, and lower), 117 (lower).
W W Winter 46, 91, 94, 95(upper), 126 131.

THE AUTHOR

David Bean was born in Derby in 1948, and lived in Allestree until 1959. During this time, the buses of the Trent Motor Traction Co, Ltd kindled his interest in transport matters, and this led to a lifelong interest. Despite moving away from Derby, first to Croydon and later to Hertfordshire, where he still lives, he has maintained his interest in Trent throughout, with frequent visits to the Company's operating area.

A Chartered Engineer by profession, he is employed as Director of Technical Services by St Albans City and District Council. Other interests are Do it Yourself, Photography, Walking and "struggling to keep fit!" He has two teenage children.